Signature Tastes of SEATTLE

To my editor, Nicole, who resisted most of my assaults on the English language, grammer rules, and accepted style sheets. Thank you, MP.

To the restaurants, for making these incredible recipes available, and constantly improving them so that we can do a second edition.

Welcome to Seattle: The Emerald City photography from Washington State University archives, and the Seattle Museum of History and Industry.

Welcome to Seattle: The Emerald City from www.Seattle.com.

To others unnamed, because my memory is as short as my hair.

You can find us at www.signaturetastes.com and on Facebook: Signature Tastes of Seattle

Layout by Steven W. Siler

Photography by Rosalie Freudes and team, except where noted

Library of Congress Control Number: 2010914234

Siler, Steven W.

Signature Tastes of Seattle: Favorite Recipes from our Local Kitchens

ISBN 978-0-9867155-8-7

1. Restaurants Washington-Seattle-Guidebooks. 2. Cookery-Washington-Seattle

Printed in the United States of America

This book is dedicated to the emergency responders…

From the first frantic call to 9-1-1
To the comforting hands at Harborside
You give your time...

away from spouses,
away from friends,
away from children,
And yes, even from meals…

To assure all of us:

"Tonight, I will make it better for you
no matter what,
I will watch over you…"

TO
PEDESTRIANS
Pike St 1400
Pike Pl
Pike St
Hillclimb

I have always wondered if anyone really reads the Table of Contents. Now since this is a cookbook, I should have organized everything under its proper heading, like soups, pasta, desserts and the like. This is not just a cookbook as much as a Culinary Postcard; a celebration of the city itself...about the eateries, fine dining, casual dining, bars, drive -ins, and of course, the people.

The Eateries...

"We have examined the valley of the Duwamish river and find it a fine country. There is plenty of room for one thousand settlers. Come at once."

David Denny's note to Arthur Denny
ca. September 28, 1851

Seattle, the great capital of the Pacific Northwest, has had a tumultuous past, often by placing itself on the road to ruin by relying on a single industry and then rebounding gracefully with a typical Seattle resilience.

In the fall of 1851, two intrepid brothers, Arthur and David Denny, (and a handful of others who had migrated west during the Gold Rush), landed at Alki Point on the western edge of Elliot Bay. After spending a miserable winter they migrated to the eastern shores where

David Denny outside his cabin. And yes, he does have coffee with him.

they established the small settlement that would become Seattle – a name derived from the joint Chief of the two native tribes that inhabited the region.

The first major industry to grace the emerald shores of Elliot Bay was logging. From the time of the first colonial activities in 1851, the timber trade proved to be the primary source of growth in this small northwestern town. The combination of the safe bay and the proximity of lush and dense millennia-old coniferous forests made Seattle the perfect location and in 1852 Henry Yesler began construction on the first steam-powered mill in the Pacific Northwest. Seattle quickly boomed, driven by the timber demands of an emerging shipbuilding industry in the area and massive San Francisco building projects kept money flowing into the town.

Some of the old growth trees
harvested from the area.

Traditionally it was believed that the strip of land that Yesler was given by the settlers (and which is now occupied by Yesler Way) was the first "Skid Row" in America, named for the logs that were dragged down the hill to Yesler's mill. The abundance of alcohol, gambling and prostitution located around this center of the logging industry gave "Skid Row" its modern connotation. True or not, the tale as been part of Seattle myth for nearly a century.

The abundance of timber, however, would prove disastrous for the fledgling town. On June 6th, 1889 a Seattle fire broke out. Since nearly every building was constructed of affordable, but flammable timber, the fire quickly spread, engulfing nearly the entire downtown including most of the wharves and crippling the port. While the fire was catastrophic, Seattle weathered the disaster and emerged stronger than before. The city was rebuilt in brick and stone and the massive rebuilding effort stimulated the economy providing thousands of new jobs and ensuring that the economic downturn which had affected much of the country in the last decade of the 19th century would not be felt as strongly in the Emerald City.

Newspaper print of the Seattle Fire.

In August of 1896, gold was discovered in the Klondike region of Canada and the following year the steamship Portland docked in Seattle's reconstructed harbor with a famed "ton of gold" in its cargo hold. Seattle's temperate climate and location made it the obvious transportation and supply center for those heading to the frozen north in search of fortune. While the cold climate and harsh conditions of the Klondike and Alaska ensured migrations were not nearly as extensive as they were to Oregon and California during its 1849 counterpart, the Klondike Gold Rush brought thousands of people to Seattle and flooded Seattle with reconstruction money.

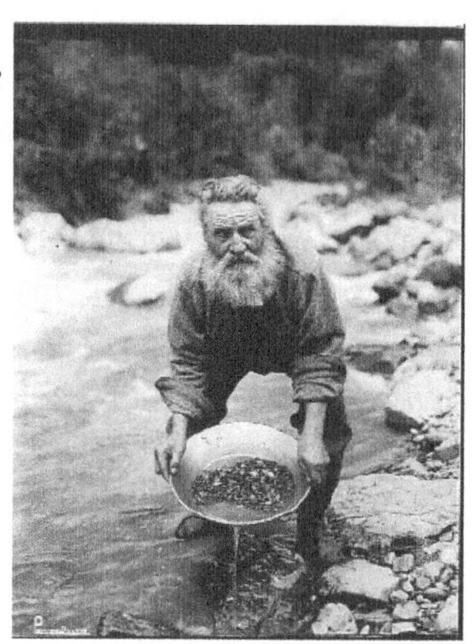

Boeing, the largest aircraft manufacturer in the world, and the biggest exporter in the United States, had its humble beginnings on the shores of Elliot Bay. William Boeing, the company's founder, had his start in the timber industry that had previously dominated this new capital of the great Northwest. Boeing's knowledge of wood allowed him to begin designing planes and he founded his own airline manufacturing company in 1916.

William Boeing, circa 1918.

By 1938, the Boeing company had become a world leader in aircraft design and manufacturing. During World War II Boeing was responsible for the design of the B-17 and the B-29, the Allies' most important bombers. Seattle's biggest employer, Boeing churned out nearly 350 planes each month at the height of the war. All this activity brought tremendous amounts of capital and labor to Seattle.

The end of World War II, however, was disastrous for the adolescent city as nearly 70,000 people lost their jobs overnight when the government cancelled all its pending contracts. While the end of the war proved temporarily catastrophic, the technology developed during the global conflict, namely the jet engine, ensured Boeing's and consequently Seattle's healthy survival, as would the escalation of military spending during the Cold War.

Above: A Boeing B17.

Left: Nose of a Boeing B29.

To combat the decline of downtown Seattle in the wake of the postwar economic downturn and the nationwide flight to the suburbs, the city hosted the Century 21 Exposition and the World's Fair in 1962. The futuristic theme of the fair provided Seattle with many of its signature structures including the iconic Space Needle, the Monorail and the rest of the Seattle Center. While the project proved to be a success, revitalizing Seattle's civic center, it had the unforeseen effect of creating a Seattle transportation nightmare as people began to return to the city – a problem that exists to this day.

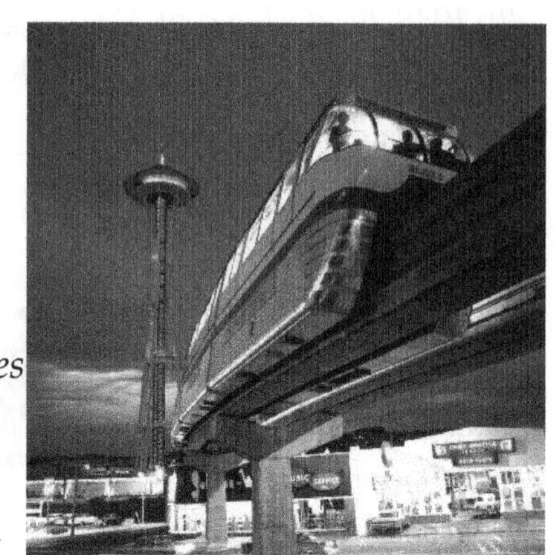

Bill Gates and Paul Allen, the co-founders of Microsoft, were both raised in the Seattle metropolitan area. While not originally founded in Washington State, Microsoft quickly relocated to its founders' home following its initial successes in the computer industry. By 1995, Microsoft had become the world's most profitable company bringing in billions of dollars in revenue and creating new millionaires in the Seattle area almost overnight. The result was the creation of over 40,000 new jobs and thousands of new investors who often created their own companies. Within a few years, Seattle had gone from being Boeing's burg to a thriving center of information technology and research, rivaling California's Silicon Valley and diversifying Seattle's economy, ensuring that the economic setbacks of the 1970s would not be repeated.

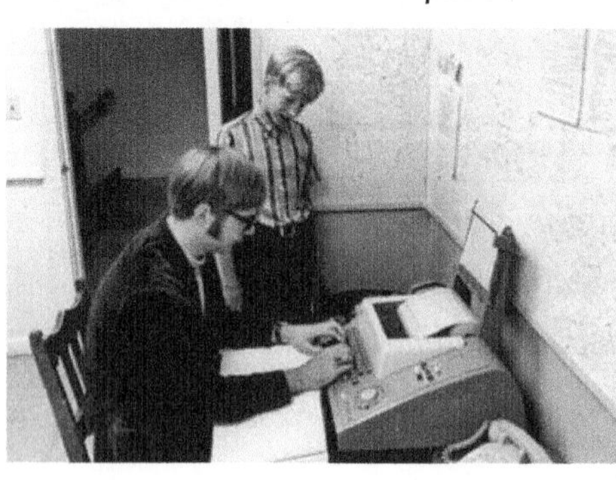

Seattle in the closing decades of the 20th century became the caffeine capital of the world producing three of the country's largest coffee chains and spawning the anti-corporate globalization movement's greatest nightmare – Starbucks. Founded in 1971, the company made a fortune selling warm specialty coffee drinks to its weary, cold and parched patrons in an inviting café atmosphere. The result was a worldwide phenomenon as the small café branched out from its humble home in Pike Place Market, opening its doors to similar customers around the world and spawning dozens of imitators. The grand Starbucks Center is now Seattle's largest building by volume, an indication of its economic and social prominence within the city.

Seattle, throughout its history, has proven to be one of America's most resilient cities – constantly weathering disasters, economic and natural, from its Pacific perch. In less than two centuries it has come to stand tall as one of the great cities of the American West. In recent years it has become the home of several biotechnology companies and research institutes in addition to remaining one of the capitals of aerospace and computing and is without a doubt a city looking toward the future (although a future quite different from the one imagined in 1962). It is certain that great things are to be expected in the 21st century from the emerald of the Pacific Northwest.

Pike Place vendors, circa 1940's.

PIKE PLACE FISH MARKET
FRESH
MEDIUM
KING
VISA

Recipes & Restaurants

5
SPOT
DRIVE IN

Val Verde Scramble

The 5 Spot on Queen Anne explores the breadth of American regional foods, while Endolyne Joe's menus wander the Americas from the frigid Klondike to the southernmost reaches of South America. If you're in the mood for seasonal Northwest dishes, try the Hi-Life, which spotlights the in-house wood-fired grill and oven. With this menu program, we effectively open a new restaurant every three months so our neighborhood residents have a brand new set of menu selections to choose from. Labeled by local press as "boredom-defying menus," we strive to keep it fresh for our customers and staff alike.

Savory Corn Cake:
2 tbsp diced roasted red peppers
2 tbsp sliced green onions
¼ C. diced green chiles
1 ear corn on the cob, kernels removed
1 egg
¼ C. grated jack cheese
1 C. buttermilk
4 tbsp melted butter, divided
1 C. cornmeal
1 C. corn flour
1½ tsp salt

Scramble:
3 whole eggs
1 tbsp roasted red peppers
1 tbsp chopped scallions
2 tbsp grated jack cheese
¼ avocado, small dice

griddled chorizo sausage, for serving

Savory Corn Cake:

1. In a bowl mix together the roasted red peppers, green onions, green chiles, corn kernels, egg, jack cheese, buttermilk and 2 tablespoons of the melted butter.

2. In another bowl, mix together the cornmeal, corn flour, and salt, then slowly stir the dry ingredients into the wet, do not over mix.

3. Heat a cast iron skillet over medium heat and brush with the remaining 2 tablespoons melted butter.

4. Scoop ¼ cup mounds of the mixture into the skillet leaving ½-inch of space between the cakes. When they are nice and golden on the bottom turn them over and cook for about 2 more minutes.

Scramble:

1. Heat a non-stick pan, add the eggs and scramble lightly. When the eggs are almost done, add the remaining ingredients.

2. To serve, place the corn cakes on a platter, place the eggs alongside and serve with griddled chorizo sausage.

5 Spot
1502 Queen Anne Avenue North

"A man can live and be healthy without killing animals for food; therefore, if he eats meat, he participates in taking animal life merely for the sake of his appetite."
Leo Tolstoy

Twenty-Four Hour Dining

Cheesecake

The "13 Coins" name is of Peruvian origin. The story is about a poor young man who loved and wished to marry a wealthy girl. Her father asked what he had to offer for his daughter's hand in marriage. The young man reached into his pocket. He had only 13 coins, but assured the father he could pledge undying love, care and concern. The father was so touched, he gave his daughter's hand and "13 Coins" has come to symbolize undying love, care and concern.

Crust:
- *2 C. graham crackers, crushed (approx. 2 packs)*
- *¼ C. confectioners' sugar*
- *8 tbsp butter, melted*
- *1 tbsp cinnamon*

Filling:
- *16 oz. cream cheese*
- *1¼ C. sugar*
- *½ tsp almond extract*
- *2 tsp vanilla extract*
- *3 whole eggs*
- *24 oz. sour cream*
- *¼ tsp salt*
- *2 small or 1 large can pineapple, drained (optional)*
- *1 can of cherry pie filling (optional)*

Crust:
1. Mix ingredients for the crust thoroughly (a fork or hands work well), then pack into a large spring form pan or a 13x9-inch flat cake pan.
2. Refrigerate the crust for a ½ hour, or at the very least while you make the filling.

Filling:
1. In a large bowl, use a mixer to cream the cream cheese thoroughly with the sugar until it is light and fluffy.
2. Add the almond extract and vanilla and mix well.
3. Add the eggs, one at a time, mixing well after each addition.
4. Add the sour cream and mix again.
5. Spread the pineapple over the chilled crust (optional). Cheesecake purists may wish to skip this step, but it does make the cake very moist.
6. Pour the cream cheese mixture into the crust. You can save some of the crust and sprinkle it over the top in an artistic pattern.

Bake:
1. Preheat oven to 350°F.
2. Bake cheesecake for 35-40 minutes. Test cake in the center using a toothpick. Take the cheesecake out when the toothpick comes out with a little cake on it (do not over bake). The cake will continue to cook after removing from the oven. Cool.
3. When the cheesecake is cool, refrigerate for 1 day.
4. If using, spread the cherry pie filling over the top and serve.

13 Coins
125 Boren Avenue North

"Food can become such a point of anxiety—not because it's food, but just because you have anxiety. That's how eating disorders develop."
Vanessa Carlton

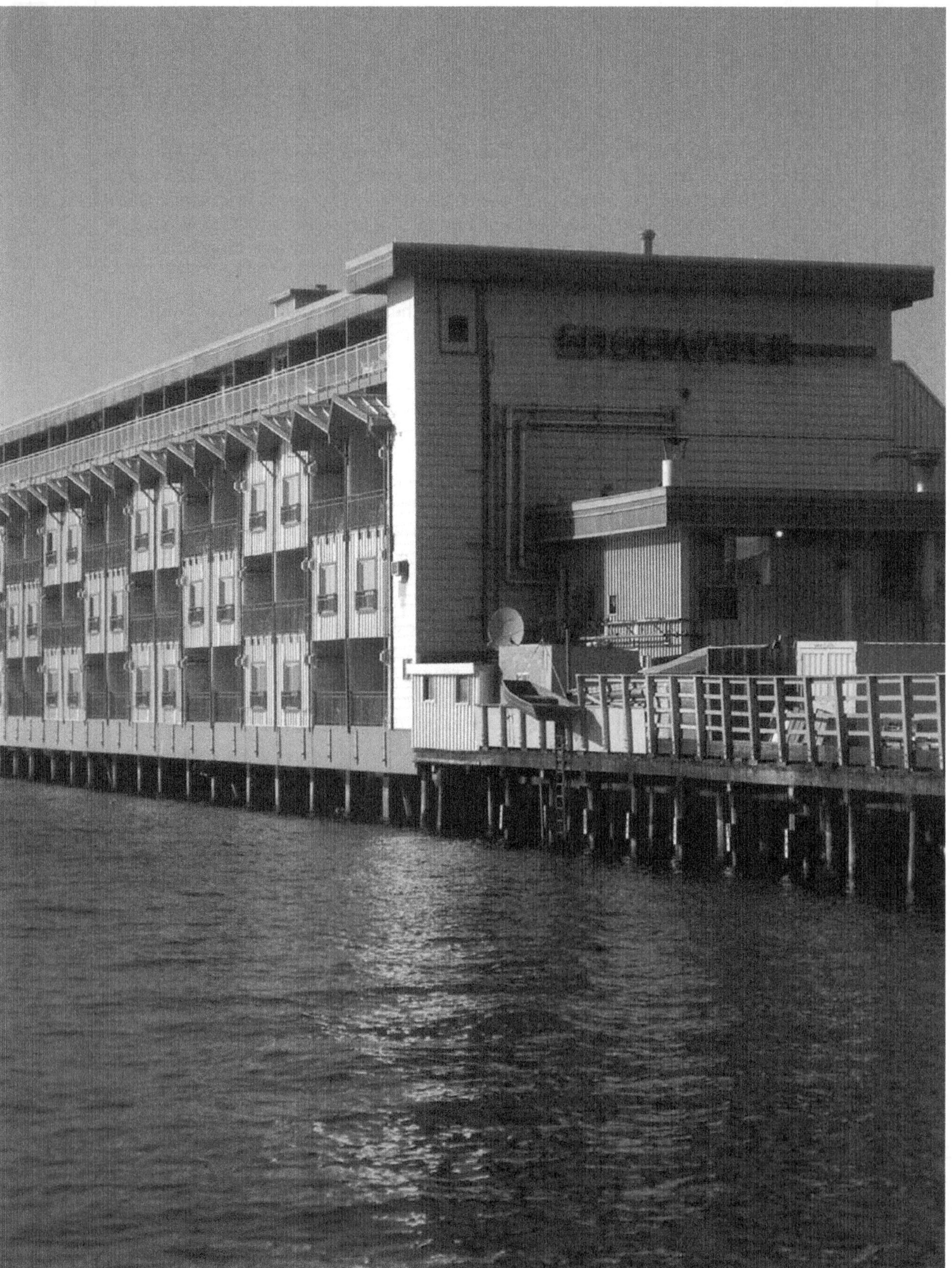

Brown-Butter Glazed Sea Scallops with Cauliflower Mousse and Vanilla-Carrot Fondue

All the makings of a breathtaking Seattle holiday await you at The Edgewater. Nestled on Seattle's waterfront at Pier 67, the hotel is surrounded by beauty: admire the majestic Olympic Mountains, the sparkling waters of Elliott Bay, and the velvety-pink sunsets of the northwest sky. The hotel is in the heart of Seattle city center, so you'll be within walking distance to the city's favorite sites. But you just might decide to relax right in the hotel, soaking up the view beside a river-rock fireplace.

Vanilla-Carrot Fondue:
2 lb. carrots, juiced
½ vanilla bean, scraped
2 tbsp unsalted butter
Kosher salt
lemon juice

Cauliflower Mousse:
1 head cauliflower, florets removed, finely chopped
2 C. half and half
2 tbsp unsalted butter

Scallops:
24 U-10 sea scallops
8 tbsp unsalted butter

2 bunches of spicy greens
olive oil
cracked pepper

Vanilla-Carrot Fondue:

1. Add the carrot juice, vanilla bean, and scraped seeds to a small sauce pan and cook over low heat; reduce until the consistency of maple syrup.
2. Slowly stir in 2 tbsp of butter to create a light and buttery sauce.
3. Remove vanilla bean pod, season sauce with a little lemon juice and Kosher salt.
4. Keep warm until ready to plate.

Cauliflower Mousse:

1. In a small sauce pan, combine chopped florets with half and half and simmer until cauliflower is tender.
2. Add mixture to a blender and puree on high speed until very smooth and creamy.
3. Stir in 2 tbsp of butter and season with Kosher salt.
4. Keep warm until ready to plate.

Scallops:

1. Add 8 tbsp of butter to a large skillet and heat until very hot.
2. Add scallops in batches and sear while basting with butter until cooked to desired level of doneness.
3. Meanwhile, lightly wilt the greens in a small amount of olive oil and season with salt and cracked pepper.

To Serve:

1. Place scallops and greens on a plate, spoon cauliflower mousse around the scallops, and drizzle the carrot-vanilla fondue over top.

67 at The Edgewater Hotel

2411 Alaskan Way, Pier 67

"We are indeed much more than what we eat, but what we eat can nevertheless help us to be much more than what we are."
Adelle Davis

611 Supreme
Crêperie
Café

Poached Eggs with Sauce of Mushrooms, Shallots and Pancetta

Owner & chef Margaret Edwins opened 611 Supreme in 1997 as a crêperie serving traditional to Breton buckwheat crêpes "crêpes de sarrasin". Since then the restaurant has doubled its size and expanded the menu to include a variety of bistro fare while still serving traditional crêpes. The housemade pâté, salade niçoise and brined pork rack are some of the regular favorites. From the beginning a fairly-priced yet unique wine list focusing on small, French producers has been available. In 2002 the 611 Supreme lounge opened in the adjacent building and created both additional seating for the restaurant and a hip, nightlife destination with plenty of atmosphere to spare. Saturday and Sunday mornings the restaurant & lounge are transformed into a bustling brunch where you can enjoy a French press coffee, wine and cocktails, and a large selection of breakfast crêpes.

Shallot Sauce:
olive oil, as needed
1 lb., 14 oz. shallots, cut into 1/8-inch slices
1½ C. thinly sliced garlic
12 sprigs thyme
6 bay leaves
3 tbsp black peppercorns
3 tbsp fennel seeds
12 oz. pancetta, julienned
1½ C. balsamic vinegar
3 C. red wine
1½ C. cooking sherry
6 C. chicken stock
1½ oz. dried shiitake mushrooms
salt and pepper, to taste
Mushroom Sauce:
1½ lb. cremini mushrooms, quartered
1½ lb. shiitake mushrooms, sliced
1½ lb. portabella mushrooms, ½-in. cubes
6 oz. shallots, minced
6 garlic cloves, minced
6 sprigs thyme
6 sprigs rosemary
3 C. olive oil
1½ C. white wine
¾ C. lemon juice
salt and pepper, to taste
To Serve with Quanity of Sauce:
48 large eggs
48 thick slices baguette

Shallot Sauce:

1. In a large pot, sweat shallots, garlic, thyme, bay leaves, peppercorns, and fennel seeds in oil until golden and soft.
2. Add pancetta, sauté on low heat until shallots are caramelized.
3. Add vinegar and reduce by three-fourths.
4. Add red wine and sherry, reduce by three-fourths.
5. Heat chicken stock with the dried shiitake mushrooms and remove the mushrooms once they rehydrate (reserve for mushroom sauce).
6. Add the heated stock to the sauce and reduce until sauce coats the back of a spoon.
7. Remove thyme sprigs and bay leaves; season to taste. (Makes about 6 cups.)

Mushroom Sauce:

1. Slice the rehydrated shiitake dried mushrooms and mix them together with fresh mushrooms, minced shallots, garlic, thyme, rosemary, olive oil, white wine, lemon juice, and salt and pepper to taste.
2. In a large pan, sauté on medium to low heat until mushrooms release their juices and are tender. (Makes about 6 cups.)

To Serve:

1. Poach 2 eggs.
2. Toast and butter 2 slices of baguette.
3. Reheat ¼ cup shallot sauce with ¼ cup sautéed mushrooms.
4. Plate eggs on toast and gently pour sauces over top.

611 Supreme
611 E Pine Street

"It may be hard for an egg to turn into a bird: it would be a jolly sight harder for it to learn to fly while remaining an egg. We are like eggs at present. And you cannot go on indefinitely being just an ordinary, decent egg. We must be hatched or go bad."
C.S. Lewis

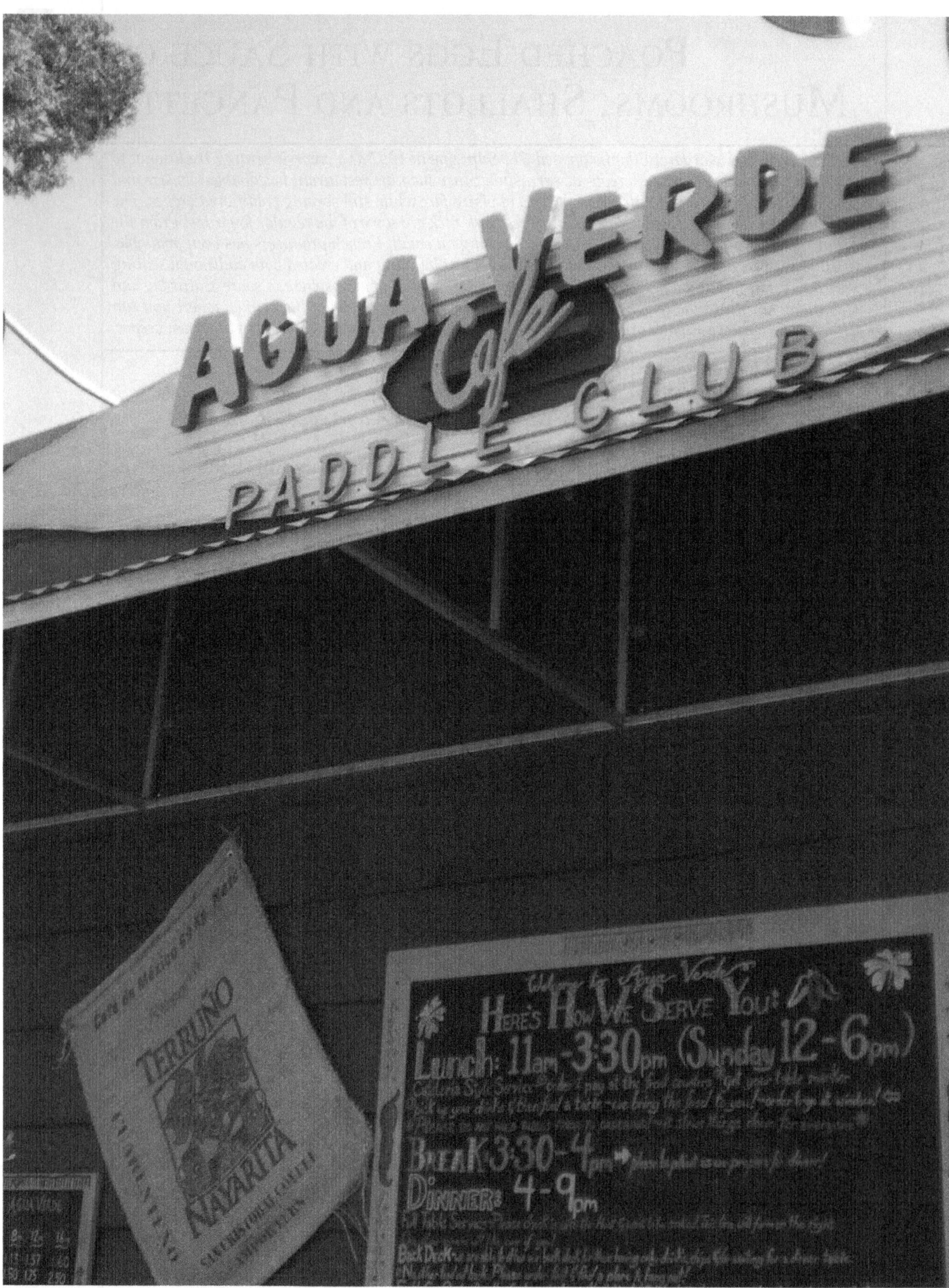
AGUA VERDE
Café
PADDLE CLUB
TERRUÑO
NAYARITA
Here's How We Serve You:
Lunch: 11am-3:30pm (Sunday 12-6pm)
Break 3:30-4pm
Dinner: 4-9pm

Tacos de Mero (Halibut Tacos)

Agua Verde Café and Paddle Club takes its name from a beautiful bay in the Sea of Cortez, Baja California Sur, Mexico. We offer casual waterfront dining at reasonable prices, and our food is prepared fresh, from scratch daily. We incorporate organic, local and sustainable foods into our menu, creating daily lunch and dinner specials. Remember, we also rent kayaks for a memorable Seattle experience.

1 lb. halibut fillets
lemon pepper seasoning
12 (6-in.) corn tortillas
1 C. chopped cabbage
½ cup creamy avocado sauce

Creamy Avocado Sauce:
1 avocado
2 green onions, chopped
1 to 2 cloves garlic, chopped
1 C. sour cream
2 C. mayonnaise
1 tsp green habanero sauce
1 tsp apple cider vinegar
1 tsp lemon pepper seasoning

1. Spray a grill or charcoal broiler with non-stick coating.

2. Season the fillets with lemon pepper and cook for approximately 15 minutes, turning once. Fillets should be white throughout and flaky; do not over cook.

3. Place ¼ pound of the halibut over 3 heated tortillas.

4. Add ¼ cup cabbage and top with 2 ounces of creamy avocado sauce.

5. Repeat the process for remainding ingredients.

Creamy Avocado Sauce:
1. Mix all of the ingredients together in a medium sized bowl.

Agua Verde Café
1303 NE Boat Street

"If more of us valued food and cheer and song above hoarded gold, it would be a merrier world."
J.R.R. Tolkien

ANDALUCA
RESTAURANT

COMPLIMENTARY
VALET
PARKING

Pumpkin Risotto

From Andaluca's front door it is just a short walk to the 5th Avenue Theatre, Paramount Theater and the Convention Center. Catch the monorail, connected next door to Andaluca, and you are 3 minutes away from McCaw Hall. Andaluca is an independently, family owned restaurant that prides itself on pintxos, great paella and impeccable service. Complimentary valet parking is always provided, even for dinner and a show! We look forward to serving you!

Arborio Rice:
1 tbsp unsalted butter
½ C. onions, diced
2 C. Arborio rice
2¼ C. chicken broth

Pumpkin Puree:
29 oz. can pumpkin puree
3 C. water
3 oz. brown sugar
⅛ C. sherry vinegar

Vegetable Stock:
1 oz. olive oil
1 lb. mushrooms, sliced
2 gal. water
3 bunches leeks, washed
1 bunch celery, chopped
1½ lb. carrots, chopped
1 lb. yellow onion, chopped
½ oz. thyme, sprigs
1 bay leaf
3 whole black peppercorns

Spice Mix:
¼ C. cumin, ground
1 tsp cayenne
¼ C. paprika, Spanish
1 tbsp ginger, ground
1½ tsp cinnamon, ground
2 tbsp salt (mix 3:1)

Pumpkin Risotto:
2 tbsp olive oil
4 oz. onion, diced
2 tsp garlic, minced
2 chilies, sliced thin
1½ C. pre-roasted pumpkin
3 tbsp spice mix
4 C. Arborio rice base
12 oz. pumpkin puree
4 C. vegetable stock, heated
5 oz. Swiss chard
4 oz. butter
4 roasted mini pumpkins
¾ C. spiced walnuts
12 chive sprigs
walnut oil

Arborio Rice:
1. In a large pot, melt the butter over medium heat.
2. Add onions and sauté, stirring constantly until translucent.
3. Add Arborio rice and sauté, stirring constantly until slightly translucent. Do not brown!
4. Add chicken broth, ½ cup at a time, and simmer, stirring constantly, until no liquid releases when you scrape a spoon on the bottom of the pan, about 20 minutes.
5. Spread rice on a sheet pan and refrigerate until cold (shelf life 5 days).

Pumpkin Puree:
1. Combine all ingredients and mix until smooth.

Vegetable Stock:
1. In a stock pot, heat oil and sauté vegetables until golden brown.
2. Add herbs and water; simmer for 1 hour.
3. Strain through a fine mesh sieve. Cool.

Pumpkin Risotto:
1. In a sauté pan, sauté onions in the olive oil over medium heat until translucent.
2. Add the garlic and chilies and sauté about 1 minute.
3. Add the roasted pumpkin, spice mix, Arborio rice, pumpkin puree, and hot vegetable stock.
4. Cook until rice is creamy, stirring occasionally.
5. Toss in the Swiss chard and finish with butter.
6. Serve risotto in the roasted mini pumpkins, garnish with spiced walnuts and chives. Drizzle with walnut oil.

ANDALUCA
407 OLIVE WAY

"The only man who is really free is the one who can turn down an invitation to dinner without giving an excuse."
Jules Renard

EXIT
EXIT

KUMQUAT-GLAZED DUCK BREAST

ART provides exquisite views of Elliott Bay through floor to ceiling windows from the main dining room--the perfect spot for a business lunch or dinner with friends. ART Lounge is the city's hottest spot for happy hour and inventive cocktails, the private dining room is an intimate dining experience--The Communal Table is a stunning13-foot Douglas Fir table set in front of the 12-foot wine wall.

12 kumquats, sliced, seeds removed
2 bottles kumquat-flavored dry soda
1 garlic clove
4 pieces star anise
1 Thai chili, chopped
¼ C. chopped onion
salt and freshly ground pepper
4 (6-oz.) boneless duck breasts
½ C. grapeseed (or canola) oil

Marinade:
1. A day before serving, mix half of the kumquat slices, soda, garlic, 2 pieces star anise, chili, onion, and a pinch of salt and pepper in a sealable container.
2. Trim excess fat from duck and score skin with a sharp knife to form a grid pattern. Add duck to marinade and refrigerate overnight.
3. The next day, remove duck from liquid, pat dry, and place on a baking sheet fitted with a wire rack.
4. Leave to dry in the back of the refrigerator near the fan for 3 hours.
5. Strain marinade and save both liquids and solids.

Kumquat-Glazed Duck Breast:
1. Preheat oven to 375°F.
2. Heat ¼ cup of oil in a large skillet over high heat. When hot, add reserved marinade solids, and sauté for 5 minutes, or until soft.
3. Add liquid and bring to a boil. Lower heat, and simmer until reduced by ⅔, about 10 more minutes. Set aside.
4. Heat a heavy oven-proof skillet over medium-high heat with the remaining ¼ cup of oil and 2 remaining pieces of star anise.
5. When hot, place duck skin-side down in oil and cook for a few minutes until golden brown.
6. Decrease heat to medium, turn breast over, and cook for about 1 minute.
7. Transfer pan to oven and roast 5 minutes.
8. Transfer the duck to a plate, cover, and set aside.
9. Meanwhile, blend the reduced marinade. Drain fat from duck pan and remove star anise.
10. Strain the blended marinade back into the pan and bring to a boil.
11. Add the remaining kumquat slices, salt, and pepper, reduce heat, and simmer until kumquats are soft and sauce is thick, about 5 minutes. Spoon onto individual plates, and serve duck on top.

ART RESTAURANT AND LOUNGE
99 UNION STREET

"Without question, the greatest invention in the history of mankind is beer. Oh, I grant you that the wheel was also a fine invention, but the wheel does not go nearly as well with pizza."
Dave Barry

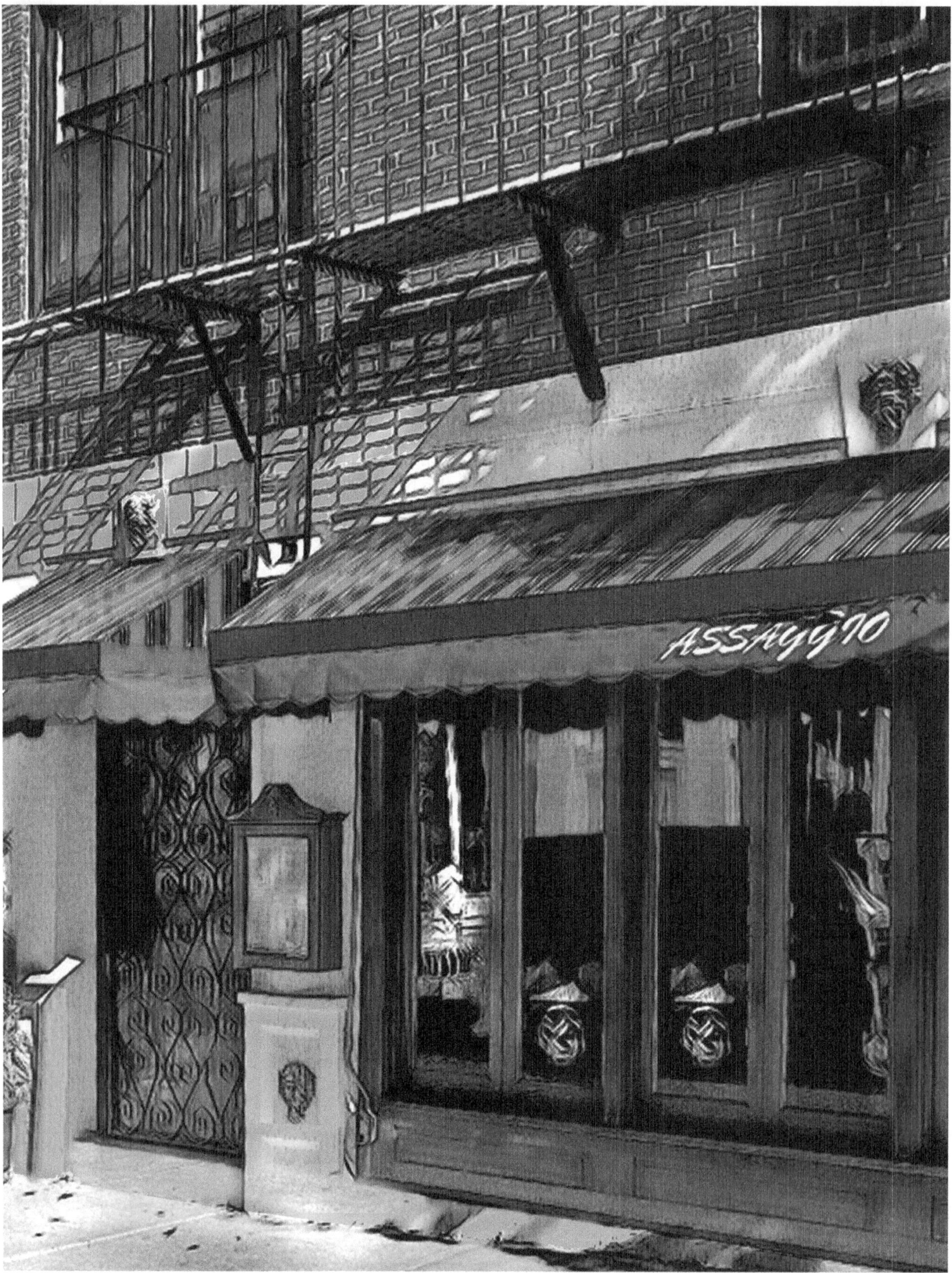
ASSAGGIO

Mauro Golmarvi's Insalata di Panzanella

From the moment you enter, the atmosphere is welcoming – the walls are painted with Michelangelo-inspired art and the place buzzes with convivial chatter. You'll find Mauro there with a smile, traveling from table to table to ensure each diner's comfort and satisfaction. Of course, the best reason to come to Assaggio is the food. A carefully composed menu of bold, robust central and northern Italian cuisine has received accolades since Assaggio first opened its doors in 1993.

½ lb. Tuscan-style dark bread, lightly grilled or toasted, cut into ½ to ¾ in. cubes
6 Roma tomatoes, cut into ½ to ¾-in. cubes
1 lb. fresh mozzarella, cut into ½ to ¾ in. cubes
½ C. red onion
2 garlic cloves, minced
⅓ C. thinly sliced fresh basil
1 tbsp finely chopped fresh Italian parsley
¼ C. extra-virgin olive oil
3 tbsp cold water
½ tsp salt
½ tsp freshly ground black pepper

1. In a large non-reactive bowl, combine bread, tomatoes, mozzarella, onion, garlic, basil, and parsley.

2. Stir in olive oil, water, salt, and pepper.

3. Mix ingredients well with your hands.

4. Let stand for 20 minutes before serving.

"My dream was so vivid and detailed, I could never forget it. Even 20 years later I remember the color of the walls, the shape of the doorways, the feel of the kitchen. I didn't know how or when, but I always knew that someday I would own this restaurant."
Mauro Golmarvi

Assaggio Ristorante
2010 4th Avenue

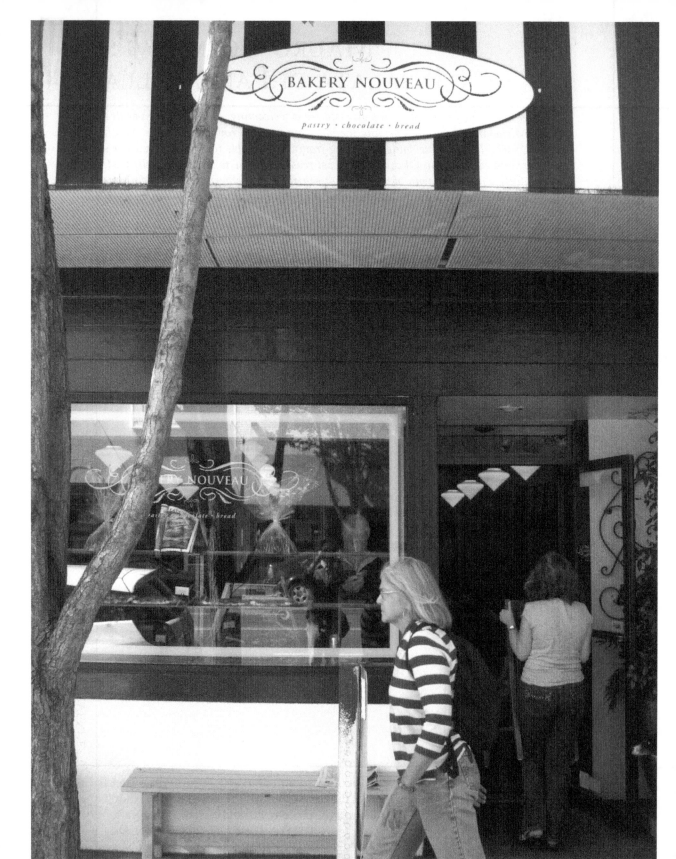

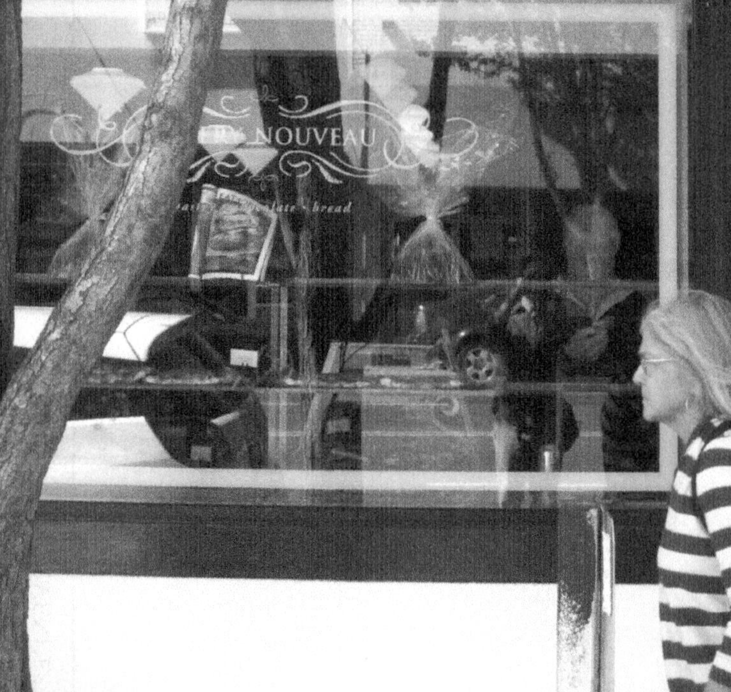
BAKERY NOUVEAU
pastry · chocolate · bread
NOUVEAU

Shaker Style Rosemary & Walnut Bread

Located in West Seattle where the historic Blake's Bakery once stood, William and Heather Leaman continue to make history daily with one-of-a-kind creations. With over 20 years experience in pastry, bread and chocolate, and as the captain of the 2005 Bread Bakers Guild Team USA, where he led his team to victory at the Coupe du Monde de Boulangerie (World Cup of Baking), William is quickly making Bakery Nouveau a Seattle icon.

2¼ C. very warm whole milk (120°F)
3 tbsp sugar
2 tbsp unsalted butter, cut into ½-inch pieces, softened
2 tsp salt
¼ C. warm water (110°F to 115°F)
2 envelopes active dry yeast
1 large egg, beaten
6½ C. all-purpose flour
1 C. coarsely chopped walnuts
2 tsp chopped fresh rosemary
vegetable oil
1 large egg yolk, beaten with 1 tbsp whole milk (for glaze)

1. Preheat oven to 375°F and position a rack in the bottom third of the oven.
2. Pour the milk into a large bowl. Mix in sugar, butter, and salt; cool to lukewarm.
3. Place ¼ cup warm water in a small bowl; mix in yeast. Let stand for 6 minutes.
4. Stir yeast mixture and 1 egg into lukewarm milk mixture, then mix in 4 cups flour and beat with a wooden spoon until mixture is smooth.
5. Cover the bowl with plastic wrap and let the sponge stand until bubbles appear at edge, about 15 minutes.
6. Mix nuts and rosemary into the sponge. Mix in flour, ⅓ cup at a time, until soft, slightly sticky dough forms (you may not need all the flour).
7. Turn dough out onto a floured surface and knead until smooth and no longer sticky, sprinkling with flour as needed, about 10 minutes.
8. Brush a clean large bowl with oil. Add dough; turn to coat. Cover bowl with plastic wrap. Let the dough rise in a warm draft-free area until doubled in volume, about 1 hour.
9. Brush two 8½×4½×2½-inch non-stick loaf pans with oil.
10. Punch dough down and turn out onto work surface; shape into two 8-inch-long loaves. Place in pans. Let rise, uncovered, until almost doubled in volume, about 45 minutes.
11. Using a serrated knife, make a shallow cut down the center of each loaf. Brush loaves with glaze and bake until golden and crusty, about 35 minutes.
12. Turn breads out of pans. Cool on racks.

Bakery Nouveau
4737 California Avenue Southwest

"Food is your body's fuel. Without fuel, your body wants to shut down."
Ken Hill

Apple and Pear Galettes

Barbara moved to Seattle in 2002 and fell in love with the Pacific Northwest. She has been baking pies for St. Clouds Restaurant in Madrona since 2007. Many hundreds of pies later, she decided she could "spread the gospel" and teach people the joy of creating their own delicious and beautiful pies! Barbara practiced medicine in California for 18 years as an obstetrician-gynecologist before moving to Seattle. She lives with her husband and their cat, Sasha, who always wants to know what kind of pie is in the works!

Pastry Crust:
1¼ C. all-purpose flour
½ tsp sugar
½ tsp salt
½ C. unsalted butter, cubed, cold
¼ C. ice water

Filling:
1 large tart apple (such as Granny Smith) peeled and cored
1 large pear (any variety), slightly under-ripe, peeled and cored
1 tsp lemon juice
¼ C. sugar
¼ tsp cinnamon
pinch of ground nutmeg
pinch of salt
1 tbsp flour
2 tbsp dried cranberries (optional)
1 egg white
1 tsp sugar

Pastry Crust:

1. Prepare crust by adding the flour, sugar, and salt in a food processor and pulse a few times to mix.
2. Add butter to flour mixture and pulse 5 times until butter is in pea-size lumps. Do not over mix!
3. Pulse in ice water a little at a time and mix together only until the mixture looks moistened throughout.
4. Cover bowl of food processor with plastic wrap and invert contents onto plastic wrap, remove the processor blade. Gather edges of plastic wrap and press dough together to form a ball, then flatten into a disc. Rest in the refrigerator, covered, for 30 minutes to 1 hour (or as long as 24-48 hours).
5. After the crust has rested, roll out on parchment paper into an 11-inch round, ⅛-inch thick, then place in refrigerator while mixing the filling.

Filling:

1. Preheat oven to 425°F.
2. Slice the apple and pear into ¼-inch slices, then dice. Sprinkle with lemon juice.
3. Mix sugar, spices, salt, flour, and cranberries, if using. Stir mixture into the apples and pears.
4. Transfer crust along with the parchment paper to a sheet pan and spoon filling into the center of the crust and spread out, leaving a 2-inch border free. Fold edges over the filling in overlapping fashion, leaving a small center of the filling uncovered. Brush the edge of the pastry with egg white then sprinkle with 1 tsp sugar.
5. Bake at 425°F for 10 minutes, turn oven to 375°F and bake for 20-25 minutes more, or until the crust is browned and the filling bubbles. Serve warm.

Barbara Schwartz

Baked Pies for St. Clouds, 1129 34th Avenue

"Don't get fancy. Have you cooked an apple pie? You don't know what you did wrong? Do this: Take two or three apples. Put them on a table. Study them."
Paul Prudhomme

THE
barKING
FROG

Smoked Lobster Bisque

The Barking Frog restaurant is truly a destination all its own. One of the most highly regarded restaurants in the Northwest, Barking Frog excels in American regional cuisine with Pacific Northwest influences with dishes like pan roasted sea scallops with confit chicken hash–need we say more! Or try the truffled macaroni & cheese...the first bite is an eye-closer.

5 lobster heads
2 tbsp unsalted butter
extra-virgin olive oil
½ large carrot
½ small onion
½ celery stalk
¼ bulb fennel
1 Roma tomato, chopped
½ tsp tomato paste
½ oz. cognac
1 qt. chicken stock
1 oz. Arborio rice
4 sprigs thyme
12 parsley stems
½ tsp fennel seed
½ tsp coriander seed
½ tsp red chili flake
½ tsp black peppercorn
¾ C. heavy cream
salt and pepper, to taste

1. Clean lobster heads by scraping out gills and cutting off faces.

2. Place cleaned heads into a smoker with desired smoke flavored chip and smoke heavy for 5 minutes.

3. In a large stock pot, mix lobster heads and butter with a little extra-virgin olive oil and roast until shells are red. Remove heads from pot and discard.

4. Add vegetables, tomato, and tomato paste and cook until vegetables are tender.

5. Deglaze pot with cognac; add stock and rice.

6. Place all the herbs in a cheesecloth sachet and tie with twine and add to the pot.

7. Cook on low heat for 15 to 20 minutes. Remove the spice sachet.

8. Add the heavy cream then blend with a hand blender until smooth. Strain the bisque twice and season to taste with salt and pepper.

Barking Frog
14580 Northeast 145th Street

"Sharing food with another human being is an intimate act that should not be indulged in lightly."
M.F.K. Fisher

Wild Boar Scallopine with Truffles

It's where tradition and innovation merge in modern comfort; Italian ancestry and family spirit, encased in a warm and inviting setting surrounded by wax-dripping candelabras, Italian glass chandeliers, a 20-seat communal table, comfortable booths to watch the action in the room or a cozy table for two to catch a private moment.

1 lb. wild boar tenderloin
¼ C. butter
flour (enough to dredge meat)
salt and pepper, to taste
1 tbsp black truffle, shaved
5 oz. Pinot Grigio (or other dry white wine)
3 oz. stock or water
1 lemon, juiced
1 tsp white-truffle oil
1 tbsp chopped Italian parsley

1. Slice the boar and pound thin with a meat mallet. Dredge the meat in flour and shake off excess.

2. In a frying pan, melt the butter over medium heat.

3. Place the boar in the pan and brown lightly, then turn over.

4. Add salt and pepper, to taste and then add the shaved black truffle.

5. Deglaze the pan with wine, add the stock, simmer for two minutes.

6. Remove from heat and finish with lemon juice, white-truffle oil, and chopped parsley. Serve with your favorite vegetables.

Barolo Ristorante
1940 Westlake Avenue

"I love food and feel that it is something that should be enjoyed. I eat whatever I want. I just don't overeat."
Tyra Banks

Barrio Podensac Smash

Barrio is a restaurant that combines Mexican cuisine with innovative craft cocktails in an energetic urban environment. Our menu takes a modern approach to Mexican cuisine, with an emphasis on fresh, seasonal ingredients. To deliver the highest possible quality, we make most of our ingredients on-site, from our fresh tomato salsas to our handmade tortillas to our slow-smoked pork.

10 fresh mint leaves, plus more for garnish
dash of Fee Brothers peach bitters
2½ oz. Lillet Blanc
½ oz. freshly squeezed lemon juice
simple syrup, to taste

1. Muddle the mint leaves with the peach bitters in a double old-fashioned glass.

2. Combine the Lillet Blanc and lemon juice in a shaker filled with ice and shake, then strain into the old-fashioned glass.

3. Fill the glass with crushed ice and stir.

4. Clap a mint leaf between your palms to release the aroma and place in the drink to garnish.

5. If desired, add simple syrup to taste.

Barrio Mexican Kitchen & Bar

1420 12th Avenue

"I love food and I love everything involved with food. I love the fun of it. I love restaurants. I love cooking, although I don't cook very much. I love kitchens."
Alma Guillermoprieto

BEECHER'S HANDMADE CHEESE

World's Best Mac and Cheese

At the Beecher's Handmade Cheese shops in Seattle's historic Pike Place Market and New York's Flatiron District, visitors press their noses against the windows to witness a vat of creamy white milk transformed by the expert hands of the cheesemaker. Although he is aided in the process by simple machinery, the cheesemaker is crafting cheese using the same techniques that have been used for 5,000 years.

6 oz. penne pasta
2 C. Beecher's Flagship sauce (recipe follows)
1 oz. cheddar, grated (¼ cup)
1 oz. Gruyere cheese, grated (¼ cup)
¼ to ½ tsp chipotle chili powder

Flagship Cheese Sauce:
¼ C. unsalted butter
⅓ C. all-purpose flour
3 C. milk
14 oz. semi-hard cheese, such as Beecher's Flagship, grated (about 3½ C.)
2 oz. grated semi-soft cheese, such as Beecher's Just Jack
½ tsp Kosher salt
¼ to ½ tsp chipotle chili powder
⅛ tsp garlic powder

1. Preheat oven to 350°F.
2. Oil or butter a deep 8-inch round baking dish.
3. Cook the penne pasta 2 minutes less than package directions. (It will finish cooking in the oven.) Rinse pasta in cold water and set aside.
4. Combine cooked pasta and Flagship Cheese Sauce in a medium bowl and mix carefully but thoroughly.
5. Scrape the pasta into the prepared baking dish. Sprinkle the top with the cheeses and then the chili powder.
6. Bake, uncovered, for 20 minutes. Let sit for 5 minutes before serving.

NOTE: If you double the recipe to make a main dish, bake in a 9x13-inch pan for 30 minutes.

Flagship Cheese Sauce:
1. Melt the butter in a heavy-bottom saucepan over medium heat and whisk in the flour. Continue whisking and cooking for 2 minutes.
2. Slowly add the milk, whisking constantly. Cook until the sauce thickens, about 10 minutes, stirring frequently.
3. Remove from heat. Add the cheeses, salt, chili powder and garlic powder and stir until the cheese is melted and all ingredients are incorporated, about 3 minutes. Use immediately or refrigerate for up to three days.

NOTE: A single batch of sauce makes enough for a double recipe of macaroni and cheese.

Beecher's Handmade Cheese
1600 Pike Place

"The clever cat eats cheese and breathes down rat holes with baited breath."
W. C. Fields

BICK'S

Broadv Gri

Neighborhood
Dining!

"Eat the Heat"

Rib Eye Steak Topped with Gorgonzola-Mushroom Butter

Expect legions of professionals looking for a little down time amidst sleek halogen lamps juxtaposed with natural woods and high-backed booths. Servers offer suggestions and bustle around, but the real talent comes out in keeping kids happy while their parents relax. The flavors can be summed up in a single word: bold. The menu offers selections under the headings "Eat Light" and "Eat Hearty." Flavors are all over the map: everything from a Tuscan-inspired risotto to fusion-style rock-shrimp spring rolls. The "house" burger consists of ground chuck, caramelized onions, avocados, roasted poblano and bell peppers, fresh salsa and jack cheese on a kaiser roll. A cornmeal-crusted oyster club sandwich also scored high marks. The kitchen also works well with local seafood, including Penn Cove mussels in a coconut/red curry broth and chipotle-rubbed salmon steak served atop a succulent mound of mashers.

1 tbsp olive oil
1 tbs. butter
2 oz. white mushrooms, sliced
pinch of minced fresh sage
pinch of minced fresh thyme
2 oz. Oloroso sherry
2 oz. Gorgonzola cheese
1 tbsp sour cream
pinch of salt and pepper
1 (10-oz.) boneless rib eye steak
Gorgonzola cheese, for garnish

1. In a sauté pan, heat olive oil and butter over medium heat. Add mushrooms, sage and thyme to the pan. Sauté mushrooms until soft.

2. Add sherry, Gorgonzola, sour cream and salt and pepper to mushroom mixture. Stir slightly until warm.

3. Meanwhile, grill steak to desired doneness. Let rest 5 minutes.

4. Pour mushroom sauce over top of the steak.

5. Crumble extra Gorgonzola cheese over the steak and serve.

Bick's Broadview Grill

10555 Greenwood Avenue North

"The history of government regulation of food safety is one of government watchdogs chasing the horse after it's out of the barn."
David A. Kessler

Specials

Gnocchi Cavolfiore

Bizzarro has been a Seattle favorite since it opened in 1986 by original owner, chef and visual artist David Nast. He converted the building which was originally an auto workshop into his dream restaurant on a shoestring budget with a lot of hardwork, ingenuity, artistic inspiration, and love.

5 medium Yukon gold potatoes
4 large eggs
12 oz. all-purpose flour
1 large bulb of garlic
1 medium head of cauliflower, cut into small pieces
olive oil
salt and pepper
1 C. heavy cream
½ C. grated parmesan

1. Fill a large pot with cold water and bring potatoes to a gentle boil. Slowly cook until tender when pierced with a knife. It is important to use a large volume of water and cook the potatoes as slowly as possible. This "lazy boil" takes approximately one hour.
2. Peel the potatoes with a spoon while they are still hot. Run potatoes through a ricer onto a sheet pan to cool and dry the potatoes.
3. Crack 4 eggs into mixing bowl and mix thoroughly with potatoes, add the flour, and hand mix.
4. Take a handful of mixture and rub palm to palm creating a cohesive softball-sized sphere. Place on lightly floured surface and roll into a long cylinder just under 1-inch in diameter. Cut into 1-inch long gnocchi, then lightly sprinkle with flour to keep them from sticking.
5. Repeat process with the remaining mixture.
6. Drop gnocchi into salted boiling water and cook for two minutes. Drain in a colander and let cool.

Cavolfiore:
1. Preheat oven to 350°F.
2. Cut the top off of a large bulb of garlic and place the garlic bulb in a small oven-safe dish and pour a ½ cup of olive oil over bulb. Roast until soft and caramelized, about 30 minutes. Remove garlic bulb from oil and set aside to cool and reserve oil.
3. In a large skillet, sauté cauliflower in the reserved oil from the roasted garlic until the cauliflower starts to brown. Add salt and pepper to taste. Add ¼ cup of water and remove from heat.
4. Squeeze garlic bulb, removing the tender meat and add directly to skillet. Add gnocchi, heavy cream, and parmesan. Mix gently.
5. Bring back up to heat. Stir until the sauce is hot and the cheese has completely melted.

Bizzarro Italian Café
1307 N 46th St

"The thought of two thousand people crunching celery at the same time horrified me."
George Bernard Shaw

BLACK BOTTLE
gastro-tavern

Roasted Broccoli with Garlic and Red Pepper

Black Bottle is a casual tavern committed to great eating and drinking at fair prices. Every dish is made fresh-to-order using local and sustainable ingredients whenever possible. We have a full bar and hard-working wines. The atmosphere is convivial and uncluttered; a modern design in a century old building. Our service standard is efficient and informal. Come with a large group or for an intimate evening for two. Cheers!

1¼ lb. broccoli crowns, cut into florets (about 8 C.)
3½ tbsp olive oil, divided
2 garlic cloves, minced
large pinch of dried red pepper flakes

1.Preheat oven to 450°F.

2. Toss broccoli and 3 tablespoons of the oil in large bowl to coat. Sprinkle with salt and pepper. Transfer to a rimmed baking sheet and roast for 15 minutes.

3. Stir remaining ½ tablespoon oil, minced garlic, and red pepper flakes in small bowl and drizzle garlic mixture over broccoli; tossing to coat. Roast until broccoli begins to brown, about 8 minutes longer.

4. Season to taste with salt and pepper. Serve immediately.

Black Bottle
2600 1st Ave

"My philosophy from day one is that I can sleep better at night if I can improve an individual's knowledge about food and wine, and do it on a daily basis."
Emeril Lagasse

blueacre

Smoked King Salmon Collars

If there is one thing that Seattleites know, it's seafood. And finally, we have the quintessential American seafood restaurant, Blueacre Seafood. Chef Kevin and Terresa Davis, owners of Steelhead Diner, are passionate seafood lovers themselves and having secured the opulent Oceanaire property on 7th and Olive, the Davis duo has transformed the space into a fresher, more approachable seafood destination. "This used to be a place where expense accounts reigned and champagne flowed. People came to celebrate and spend big. We want everyone to be able to visit us, whenever they want, without having to take out a second mortgage," smiles Davis.

12 salmon collars

Brine:
2 C. brown sugar
1 C. Kosher salt
1 gal. water
2 bay leaves
12 peppercorns
2 serrano chilies

Garlic Red-Chile Glaze:
2 C. honey
1 C. brown sugar
½ C. sambal
6 tbsp chopped garlic
salt and pepper, to taste

Hot Smoking:
*any wood chips you like: hickory, apple, mesquite, alder**
heavy-duty aluminum foil
charcoal grill with lid
charcoal or charcoal briquettes

**They should be soaked for at least two hours or overnight.*

Brine:
1. Bring all ingredients to a boil, then cool.
2. Place salmon collars in brine and remove after one hour. Drain on a baking rack until dry and slightly tacky (this coating is called a pellicle, it's what the smoke sticks to).

Garlic Red-Chile Glaze:
1. Preheat broiler.
2. Mix all ingredients together and bring to a boil. Cool then glaze salmon collars liberally.
3. Broil salmon collars until glaze is bubbly and brown.

Hot Smoking:
Warning: Do not attempt with a gas grill!
1. Make a shallow pan a couple inches deep out of the heavy-duty foil. You can also use a foil pie tin.
2. Place salmon collars on the foil pan. Season with salt and pepper to taste.
3. This technique works best with white, dying coals. The coals need to be hot enough to smoke the wood, but you don't want them so hot that the collars are cooked before a nice smokiness is imparted. Remove the grill grates and spread the white ashy coals evenly around the grill and up the sides. There should be no coals in the center of the grill.
4. Take about a cup of wet wood chips and sprinkle evenly on top of hot coals. It will take about five minutes for the chips to start to smoke enough to begin smoking the salmon.
5. Once the chips are smoking, replace the grill grates and slide the foil pan with the salmon collars into the center of the grill. Cover the grill and make sure the vents on the lid are closed to keep in all the smoke.
6. Smoke the collars for an hour and a half, adding more chips if needed during the smoking process.

Blueacre Seafood
1700 7th Avenue

"There are some achievements which are never done in the presence of those who hear of them. Catching salmon is one, and working all night is another."
Anthony Trollope

704
the
blue
glass

Caramelized Bacon with Maple-Bourbon Goat Cheese

Casual and cozy neighborhood restaurant featuring global comfort food 7 days a week. Full bar offering craft cocktails, local microbrews and an approachable wine list.

1 lb. Hempler's thick sliced bacon
1 C. dark brown sugar
½ C. goat cheese
2 oz. grade B maple syrup
2 oz. Bulleit Bourbon
1 Granny Smith apple, cored and sliced ¼-inch thick

1. Preheat oven to 500°F.

2. Line a baking sheet with parchment paper or aluminum foil (sprayed).

3. Lay out bacon slices on baking sheet and cover generously with the brown sugar.

4. Bake at 500°F for 20 minutes, until sugar is caramelized, bubbly and crispy.

5. Meanwhile, blend the goat cheese, maple syrup, and Bourbon with a whisk in a small bowl. Refrigerate until bacon is cooked.

6. Serve bacon with apple slices and maple-Bourbon goat cheese.

The Blue Glass

704 Northwest 65th Street

"Thy food is such As hath been belched on by infected lungs."
William Shakespeare

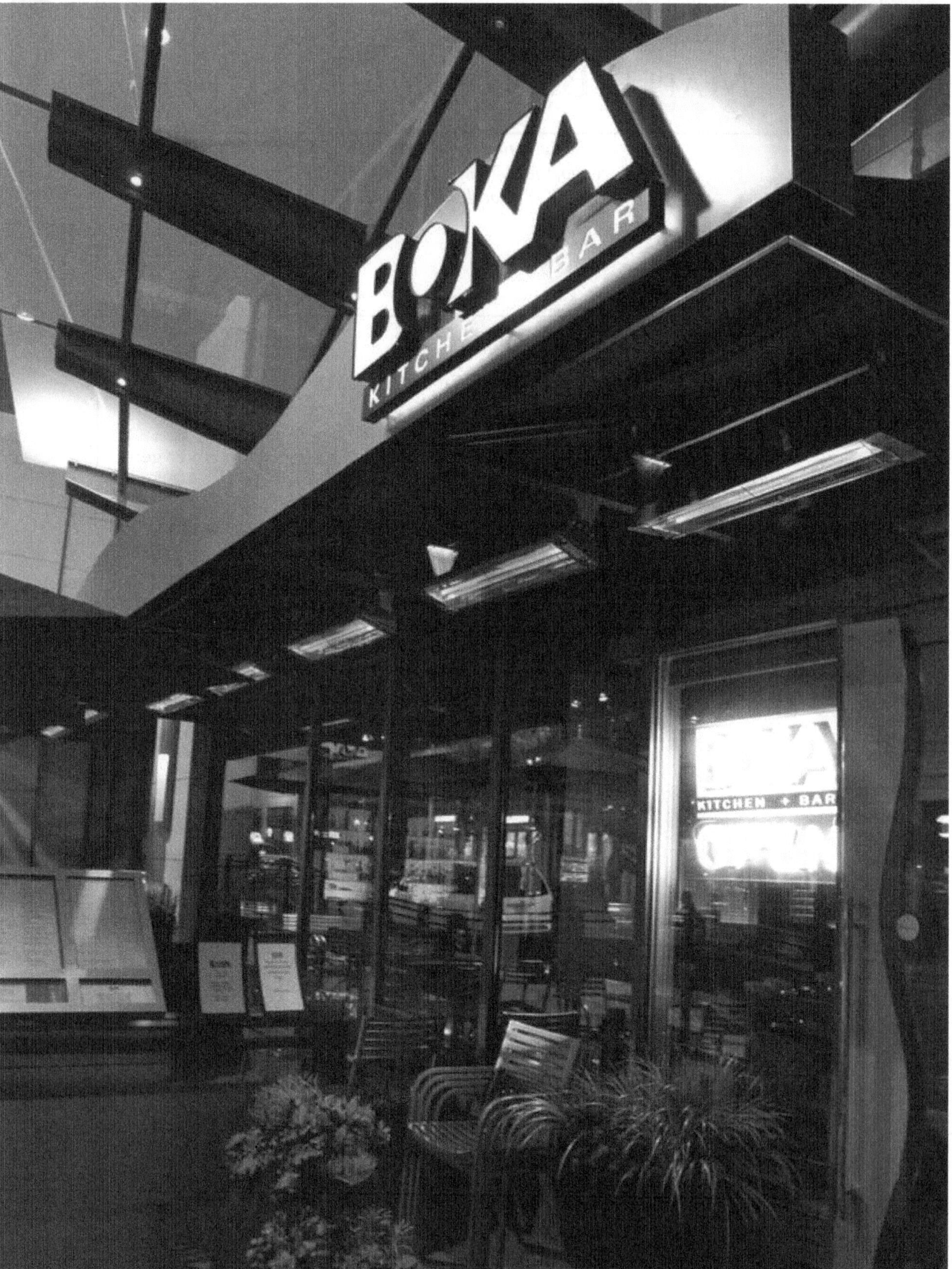
BOKA
KITCHEN + BAR

Seared Sea Scallops with Sesame-Avocado Salad

BOKA is a vibrant, communal blend of lounge, bar and restaurant. Sleek, contemporary design is infused with a menu of urban American food, handcrafted cocktails, and a wine list reflecting a heavy Northwest influence. Meal services include breakfast, lunch, cocktail hour, dinner, late night, weekend brunch, and seasonal patio dining.

Scallops:
1 lb. of fresh U-10 dry pack sea scallops
salt and pepper
canola, vegetable or grapeseed oil for searing
butter
2-3 cloves of garlic, smashed

3 sprigs of thyme

Sesame-Avocado Salad:
4 semi-firm avocados (small to medium dice)
1 tbsp sesame oil
1 tbsp black sesame seeds
3 tbsp sugar
2 tsp Kosher salt
2 tsp red chili flakes
2 tbsp unseasoned rice wine vinegar

1 whole grapefruit segmented
1 whole navel orange segmented

Scallops:

1. Heat approximately 1 tablespoon of oil until just below smoke point; the oil is hot enough when it moves easily across the pan.

2. Season the scallops with salt and black pepper on both sides.

3. Working in batches if necessary, add the scallops to the hot pan and sear until golden brown before flipping. Flip them and brown on the other side. When the scallops are slightly firm on the outside and a little soft in the center add 1 tablespoon of butter to the pan along with the smashed garlic cloves and thyme sprigs. The butter will begin to bubble slightly, turn brown and froth. Spoon the hot butter over the scallops, basting them until they are golden brown and glazed.

4. Remove the scallops from the pan, place on a paper towel to absorb excess oil and set aside.

Sesame-Avocado Salad:

1. Toss all ingredients together and allow to marinate.

2. Taste and adjust the seasonings if necessary.

To Serve:

1. Place a large spoonful of Sesame-Avocado Salad on each plate with 2-4 scallops and garnish with citrus segments.

Boka Kitchen & Bar

1010 1st Avenue

"The disparity between a restaurant's price and food quality rises in direct proportion to the size of the pepper mill."
Bryan Miller

RESTAURANT
BOMBAY
GRILL
INDIAN CUISINE
NHS
সরবরাহ
INDIAN CUISINE
BOMBAY GRILL
TEL: 020 7247 6707

Halibut Masala

Bombay Grill is an exclusive Indian restaurant in Seattle downtown University District, that serves authentic Indian cuisine in a sophisticated, romantic, and traditional Indian environment.

½ tsp carom/ajwain seeds (available in Asian food stores)
½ tsp onion seeds
4 tbsp olive oil
1 tsp finely chopped fresh ginger root
1 tsp finely chopped fresh garlic
2 medium onions, thinly sliced
½ green pepper, julienned
½ red pepper, julienned
1 tsp dry mango powder/ amchoor (available in Asian food stores)
½ tsp turmeric
½ tsp ground coriander
½ tsp ground cumin
½ tsp ground red pepper
½ tsp salt
2 tomatoes, finely chopped
1 lb. fresh halibut, cut into 1–1½ inch cubes
1 C. water
3 tbsp fresh lemon juice
2 tbsp chopped cilantro, for garnish

1. Lightly spray a large skillet with a squirt or two of olive oil, and bring to medium heat. Sprinkle the carom and onion seeds over the bottom of the skillet, and lightly toast until fragrant. Stir constantly for about 30 seconds. Do not scorch. If this happens, discard and begin again.

2. Pour 4 tablespoons olive oil onto the seeds in the skillet, and add the garlic and ginger. Cook until golden, stirring often. Add onions and bell peppers, and cook slowly until golden brown.

3. Mix the ground spices together and add to the pan, stirring well to combine evenly with the onion mixture.

4. Finally add the chopped tomatoes and cook, stirring until heated through.

5. Just before serving, add the halibut pieces, water and lemon juice, and cook until the mixture begins to bubble, approximately 3 minutes.

6. Serve with basmati rice and garnish with chopped cilantro.

Bombay Grill
4737 Roosevelt Way NE

"The most remarkable thing about my mother is that for thirty years she served the family nothing but leftovers. The original meal has never been found."
Calvin Trillin

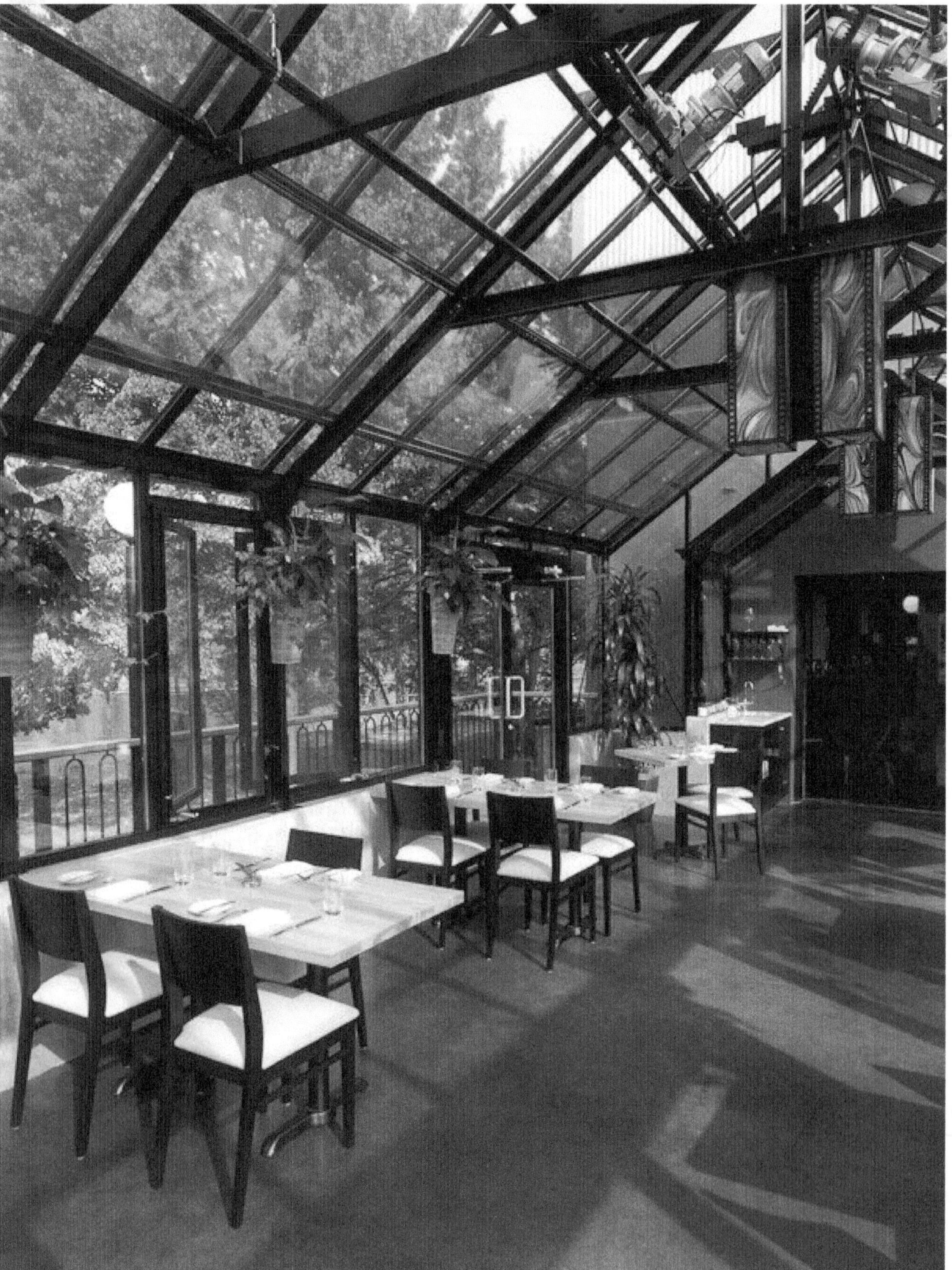

Avocado and Crab Soup

The Book Bindery sits on the southern bank of the Ship Canal in a space that once served as a book bindery. The main dining room resembles a luxurious reading room that is book-ended by views of the waterway on one side and, on the other, the winery next door. Our comfortable bar offers diners a more casual perch from which to enjoy the surroundings, while the light-filled greenhouse offers guests the expansive experience of dining al fresco all year round, regardless of the weather.

½ C. lump crabmeat
1 celery stalk, diced
½ tbsp chervil, chopped
1 tsp finely grated lemon zest
2 avocados
1 C. vegetable stock
2 tbsp crème fraîche
1 tbsp fresh lime juice
1¼ C. water
¾ tsp Kosher salt
fresh ground pepper

1. Mix crabmeat, celery, chervil, and lemon zest in a bowl. Cover and chill.

2. Halve and pit avocados; scoop flesh into a blender. Add vegetable stock, crème fraîche, lime juice, Kosher salt, and 1¼ cups water. Puree until smooth. Season soup to taste with salt and pepper; chill.

3. Divide soup among 4 bowls. Spoon crab salad into center of each bowl.

Book Bindery

198 Nickerson Street

"I recollected the thoughtless saying of a great princess, who, on being informed that the country people had no bread, replied, 'Then let them eat pastry!'"

Jean Jacques Rousseau

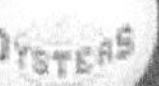
OYSTERS

Brooklyn Horseradish Mashers

Join us for the freshest ideas in Northwest cuisine! Enjoy fresh seafood delivered daily, the largest rotating selection of fresh oysters in the city, 28-day aged beef and a delicious selection signature desserts. Dine with us and celebrate 20 years of award-winning food and service. The Brooklyn is centrally-located in downtown Seattle, directly across the street from the Seattle Symphony at Benaroya Hall and the Seattle Art Museum. We are within easy walking distance of Pike Place Market and Seattle Waterfront.

5 lb. Washington russet potatoes
6 oz. parmesan cheese, shredded
3 oz. prepared horseradish
3 oz. sour cream
2 C. heavy cream
salt and freshly ground white pepper

1. Peel and cut potatoes into 3-inch pieces. Place in a stock pot and cover with cold water. Bring to a boil, reduce heat, and simmer until potatoes are fork tender.

2. Drain potatoes and transfer to a large mixing bowl. Break up pieces with wire whisk. Add parmesan cheese, horseradish, and sour cream; gently whip mixture. Add heavy cream and season to taste with salt and pepper; whip only until mixed.

NOTE: Do not over whip or starches in the potatoes will make the mashed potatoes gummy or shiny.

THE BROOKLYN
1212 2ND AVENUE

"There is no sincerer love than the love of food."
George Bernard Shaw

Le Monde

Campagne Confit Tomatoes

"I could close my eyes and imagine I was in any café in Paris," Jeremiah Tower, the renowned chef, is quoted to have said on his first visit to Café Campagne. "Endearing," "charming," "quaint," "bohemian," are just a few of the words critics have used to describe Campagne's younger sibling. Café Campagne embraces many moods, many tastes, many budgets. The Café has received rave reviews from its inception. Named as one of the top ten restaurants in its opening year by the Seattle Times and as one of the best restaurants in America by The Wine Spectator, Café Campagne has received the designation as Seattle's top French Café/Bistro consistently by Zagat Survey. Discover Café Campagne for yourself, and fall in love with your own petite slice of France.

Roma Tomatoes:
15 to 20 Roma tomatoes (depending on their size)

Light Syrup:
3 sprigs fresh thyme
1 tsp mustard seeds
2 tsp broken star anise
1 tsp anise seeds
1 tsp coriander seeds
2 bay leaves
½ tsp black peppercorns
½ bulb garlic, crushed
1½ liters white wine
1 C. sugar

To Assemble and Serve:
2 tbsp poaching liquid
sea salt and freshly ground black pepper
butter

Roma Tomatoes:
1. To peel the tomatoes first score an "X" on bottom ends, remove the stem cores, and submerge into boiling water for 10 to 15 seconds.
2. Shock the tomatoes in an ice bath and remove at once when cool. Remove skins.
3. Working over a bowl, halve the tomatoes from the top to bottom and remove the seeds without damaging the ribs.
4. Strain the resulting tomato juice into a bowl and reserve.

Light Syrup:
1. Put the thyme, mustard, star anise, anise seeds, coriander seeds, bay leaves, peppercorns, and garlic in a sachet.
2. Put the wine, sugar, reserved tomato juice, and sachet in a pot and bring to a boil; simmer for 10 minutes.

To Assemble and Serve:
1. Transfer the tomato halves to a baking sheet and cover with the light syrup and sachet. Cover the pan with foil and poach for 1 hour on the slow part of the grill.
2. Remove foil and transfer the contents to a fresh pan to cool. Tomatoes should maintain their shape when finished.
3. Once cooled, place the tomatoes in a sauté pan with 2 tbsp poaching liquid. Season to taste with salt and pepper.
4. Heat the tomatoes through and reduce the liquid to a glaze, adding a small nub of butter to bind the glaze. Use the tomatoes as a component or garnish to a dish.

Café Campagne
1600 Post Alley

"Throughout history, the Poles have defended Europe. They would fight, and—between battles—they would eat and drink."
E. de Pomiand

Yakima Valley Polenta

Since opening its doors, Café Flora has been at the forefront of utilizing local, organic and sustainable produce and herbs and building strong and direct relationships with Washington farms. It's culinary team draws inspiration from international culinary traditions along with the availability of an abundance of locally grown produce to create imaginative and dynamic vegetarian, vegan, and gluten-free cuisine.

Cherry Reduction:
1 C. port cooking wine (recommended: Paul Mason)
½ C. balsamic vinegar
½ tbsp herbes de Provence
½ tsp Kosher salt
¼ tbsp ground black pepper
1 tsp light brown sugar
½ lb. organic Bing cherries, pitted

Polenta:
1½ jumbo organic yellow onions, diced
1 tbsp Kosher salt
½ C. white cooking wine (recommended: Farron Ridge)
3 qt. water
1 qt. polenta
2 tbsp herbes de Provence
cooking spray, for sheet pan
olive oil, for brushing polenta

Green Bean Sauté:
½ cup olive oil
12 oz. organic green beans
12 oz. organic grilled sweet onion
Kosher salt
ground black pepper
1½ teaspoons herbes de Provence
6 tbsp lemon juice (recommended: Rosella's)
1½ cups cherry reduction
6 oz. Cambazola cheese, cut into small bits, for garnish

Cherry Reduction:
1. Place all ingredients, except cherries, in a medium pot. Bring to a boil, lower the heat and cook until slightly viscous and reduction coats the back of a spoon.
2. Add the pitted cherries and heat briefly. Set aside.

Polenta:
1. In a medium sauté pan, add the onion, salt, and cooking wine and cook until liquid had reduced.
2. Bring water to a boil in a large stock pot. Slowly add polenta and herbes de Provence. Reduce the heat, add the onion mixture and continue to stir polenta until thickened, about 10 minutes.
3. Prepare a sheet pan with cooking spray and pour polenta onto sheet pan. When polenta has cooled completely, cut into portion size squares. Refrigerate until ready to use.
4. Preheat oven to 400°F or preheat grill over medium-high heat.
5. Brush polenta with olive oil and place on a baking sheet or grill and bake or grill until browned.

Green Bean Sauté:
1. In a sauté pan, heat olive oil, add green beans and onions, and cook until heated through. Add salt and pepper, to taste, and herbes de Provence. Sauté until herbs are fragrant and then add lemon juice. Remove from heat.

To Serve:
1. Reheat the cherry reduction.
2. Lay out portions of polenta on each plate. Place green bean sauté over polenta and pour cherries and juice on top.
3. Garnish with Cambazola cheese.

Cafe Flora
2901 East Madison Street

"What I've enjoyed most, though, is meeting people who have a real interest in food and sharing ideas with them. Good food is a global thing and I find that there is always something new and amazing to learn—I love it!"
Jamie Oliver

Venetian Livers with Caramelized Onion, Anchovy, and Currants

Café Juanita has been a labor of love, allowing Holly to express her passion for Northern Italian food and wine; a commitment to organics and sustainability and a holistic approach to the dining experience.

Onion Mixture:
1½ tbsp butter
1½ tbsp extra virgin olive oil
3 medium yellow onions, julienne
6 oil-packed anchovy fillets
1½ tbsp marjoram
2 tsp colatura (salted anchovy sauce)
2 tbsp dried currants

Livers:
9 rabbit livers, cleaned of sinew and connective tissue
6 rabbit kidneys, cleaned of membrane and sliced in half lengthwise
salt
black pepper
neutral oil, as needed

Sauce:
3 tbsp lime juice

Onion Mixture:
1. Sweat the onions in butter and oil over medium-low heat until nicely caramelized in a stainless steel sauté pan.
2. Move onions to one side of the pan and roast anchovy fillets until they are lightly browned and dissolved.
3. Add the marjoram, colatura, and currants to onion mixture and stir until combined. Keep warm.

Livers:
1. Heat a medium stainless steel sauté pan over high heat.
2. Season the smooth sides of livers and cut sides of kidneys with a light dusting of salt and pepper.
3. Add oil to the pan. When the oil begins to smoke add the livers and kidneys seasoned-sides down; sprinkle the other side with salt.
4. Immediately add butter to the pan and heat for 10 to 15 seconds or until the livers are cooked about halfway through.
5. Flip livers and kidneys and cook for 1 to 2 seconds. Transfer meat to a small plate.

Sauce:
1. Using the pan from cooking the liver, defat the pan and deglaze with lime juice.
2. Add the resting juices from the meat to the lime juice and stir to combine. Remove from heat.

To Assemble and Serve:
1. Spoon the onion mixture onto a warm plate and top with the livers and kidneys. Drizzle with sauce.

Café Juanita
9702 Northeast 120th Place

"When I eat with my friends, it is a moment of real pleasure, when I really enjoy my life."
Monica Bellucci

CAFE NOLA
CAFE NOLA

French Toast with Orange-Bourbon Butter

A short, relaxing ferry ride from downtown Seattle exists Café Nola – a European style cafe comprising innovative, eclectic cuisine in a bistro setting. Chef/owner Kevin Warren creates intelligent, artfully executed plates using seasonal ingredients at their most flavorful.

1 loaf challah bread
melted butter, to oil griddle
6 eggs
½ C. heavy cream
1 orange, zested and juiced
¼ tsp ground cinnamon
¼ tsp fresh ground nutmeg

Orange-Bourbon Butter:
1 lb. unsalted butter, softened
2 tbsp orange flavored liqueur (recommended: Cointreau)
2 tbsp Bourbon
3 tbsp orange zest

1. Cut challah bread into 1-inch thick slices. Allow to sit out for awhile to dry out.

2. Heat a griddle to 350°F.

3. Combine eggs, heavy cream, orange zest and juice, cinnamon, and ground nutmeg in a shallow wide dish.

4. Dip the slices of bread into the egg mixture allowing it to soak in on both sides.

5. Lightly brush preheated griddle with a butter-soaked piece of paper towel and transfer each piece of bread to the hot griddle and cook until golden brown on both sides, about 3 minutes per side. Try to flip only once.

6. Serve with orange-Bourbon butter.

Orange-Bourbon Butter:
1. Cream the butter in a mixer. Add the orange liqueur, Bourbon, and orange zest and mix well.

2. Leave at room temperature and serve with the French toast.

Café Nola
101 Winslow Way, Bainbridge Island

"You better cut the pizza in four pieces because I'm not hungry enough to eat six."
Yogi Berra

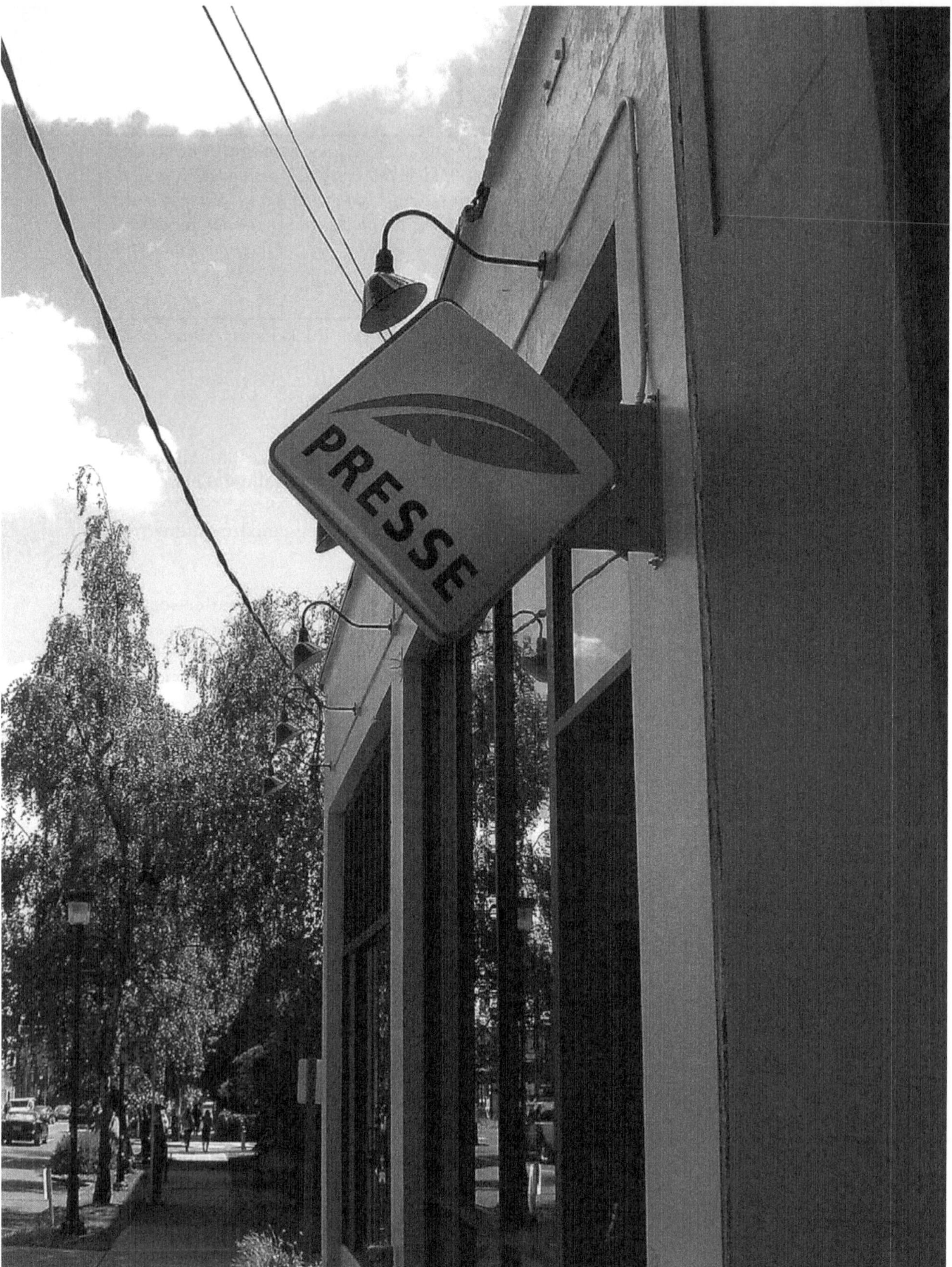
PRESSE

Gâteau de Riz

Café Presse is located on South Capitol Hill in the Seattle University neighborhood. The second collaboration of Le Pichet owners Joanne Herron and Jim Drohman offers full coffee service featuring Caffe Vita coffee and house-made pastries; affordable wines from the French countryside; a full bar open until 2am everyday; and a menu of casual Parisian café classics. The newsstand at Café Presse offers a wide selection of magazines and newspapers. Weekends at Café Presse mean soccer from America, Europe and around the globe in the bar. Café Presse is open everyday from 7am til 2am. "Café Presse, serving Capitol Hill since 2007."

7½ C. whole milk
2 vanilla beans (split and scraped) or 2 tsp vanilla extract
¾ C. rice
¾ C. sugar + 3 tbsp sugar
6 tbsp water
3 eggs
for serving, fresh cream, seasonal berries or stewed dry fruit

1. Preheat oven to 450°F.

2. In a medium sauce pan, add the milk and vanilla beans or extract and scald the milk over medium-high heat.

3. Add the rice, lower the heat and simmer, uncovered, for 40 minutes, stirring often. At the end of 40 minutes, the rice should be the consistency of a thick porridge. Remove from heat. Remove and discard the vanilla beans.

4. Meanwhile, in a small sauce pan, boil 3 tbsp of sugar and 3 tbps water until a dark caramel is achieved. Stop the cooking by adding the remaining 3 tbsp of water, stir, and pour caramel into the bottom of a 5x9-inch glass loaf pan. Set aside to cool.

5. In a small bowl, whisk together the eggs and remaining ¾ cup of sugar until the mixure turns light yellow (about 1 minute). Quickly stir the egg mixture into the rice and mix well.

6. Pour the rice custard into the loaf pan and bake on the bottom rack of a 450°F oven until the caramel starts to bubble up around the sides of the rice custard (about 10 minutes). Cool, uncovered, in the refrigerator.

7. When completely cool, run a small knife around the inside of the rice custard and then invert onto a serving platter. Serve with cold fresh cream and seasonal berries or stewed dry fruit.

Café Presse
1117 12th Avenue

"What children need most are the essentials that grandparents provide in abundance. They give unconditional love, kindness, patience, humor, comfort, lessons in life. And, most importantly, cookies."
Rudolph Giuliani

Caffe Ladro
ESPRESSO BAR & BAKERY
www.caffeladro.com

Espresso-Chip Poundcake

Celebrate green at Caffe Ladro, one of Seattle's most popular coffee bars in a city that takes its coffee seriously. Here, your fair trade-certified cup of joe translates into a fair wage for coffee farmers. Buying shade grown means you're supporting the naturally organic method of traditional, earth-friendly coffee bean cultivation. With ten Ladros, it's easy to bump into another if you miss the flagship Queen Anne location. Caffe Ladro Espresso Bar & Bakery serves the finest espresso drinks, baked goods and desserts to Seattle's discriminating coffee drinkers.

1 lb. butter
¾ C. sugar
2 C. brown sugar
5 eggs
1 tbsp vanilla extract
4 C. flour
1 tbsp baking powder
½ tbsp salt
⅛ C. sour cream
¾ C. buttermilk
1 C. espresso, liquid shots, not grounds
2 C. semisweet chocolate chips
confectioners' sugar, for garnish

1. Preheat oven to 275°F. Grease and flour a bundt pan.

2. Using a mixer, cream the butter and both sugars together; start on low speed to blend, then turn to high speed and beat until mixture is light and fluffy.

3. Add the eggs and vanilla to the mixture and mix on medium speed until the eggs are just incorporated. Do not over mix.

4. Sift the flour, baking powder, and salt together in a small bowl, then add to the mixture and mix until just combined.

5. Add the sour cream and buttermilk and mix until just combined.

6. Add the espresso and mix until just combined. If you are using hot espresso shots, pour them into the mixture slowly so that it does not cook the eggs.

7. Add the chocolate chips and stir until just combined.

8. Scoop the cake mixture into the prepared pan. Place the cake pan on a cookie sheet and bake for 1 hour and 45 minutes to 2 hours, or until a knife inserted in the center of the cake comes out clean.

9. Let the cake cool, then remove it from the pan upside down. Garnish with confectioners' sugar, if desired.

Caffe Ladro Espresso Bar & Bakery
2205 Queen Anne Avenue North

"Eat breakfast like a king, lunch like a prince, and dinner like a pauper."
Adelle Davis

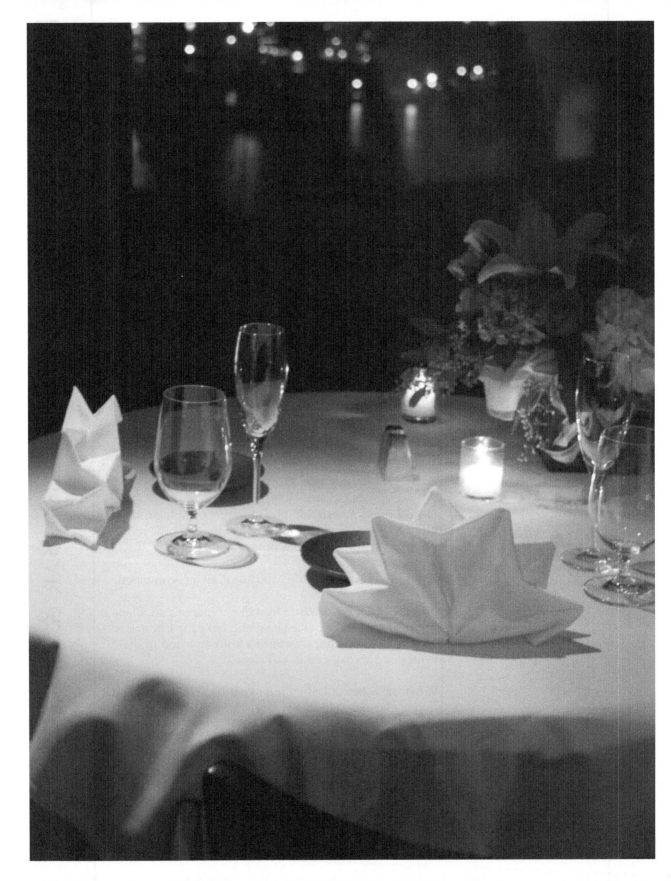

Canlis Salad

Our goal is to create the best dining experience possible – a vision, a shared commitment that has been passed down for three generations. Executing on this vision is the reason guests trust us with the most important moments of their lives. Newcomers may be surprised to learn that Canlis is our family name. To step into the restaurant is to be welcomed by our family and into our home.

Croutons:
3-4 slices country white bread, cubed
1 tsp dried thyme
1 tsp dried oregano
3 tbsp unsalted butter, melted
1 garlic clove, minced
salt and pepper, to taste

Dressing:
1 egg (in the shell), set in boiling water for 1 minute
¼ C. freshly squeezed lemon juice
¼ tsp minced garlic
½ C. olive oil
¼ tsp fresh ground tellicherry black pepper

Salad:
1 large head Romaine hearts, cut into 1" pieces
8 cherry tomatoes, halved
½ C. sliced green onion
¾ C. freshly grated Romano cheese
½ C. crisp-cooked bacon, chopped
½ C. thinly sliced fresh mint
1 tbsp thinly sliced oregano leaves
salt and pepper, to taste

Croutons:

1. Preheat oven to 350°F.

2. Toss bread, thyme, oregano, butter, salt, and pepper together and spread on a baking sheet.

3. Bake until croutons are golden, about 15-20 minutes, stirring halfway through.

Dressing:

1. Whisk together the egg, lemon juice, and garlic in a medium bowl.

2. Slowly drizzle in the oil, whisking constantly.

3. Season with pepper and set aside.

Salad:

1. Add the prepared Romaine hearts, sliced green onions, ½ cup Romano cheese, bacon, oregano, and mint to a large bowl. Pour dressing over salad and toss thoroughly. Season with salt and pepper, to taste.

2. Split the salad onto four chilled plates and divide croutons among the plates, sprinkle remaining ¼ cup of Romano cheese over the plates, and place 4 cherry tomato halves on each plate to finish the presentation.

Canlis
2576 Aurora Avenue North

"If the melting pot exists, the cheeseburger may well be its most palpable product; to take a bite of it is to take a bite of history..."
Elizabeth Rozin

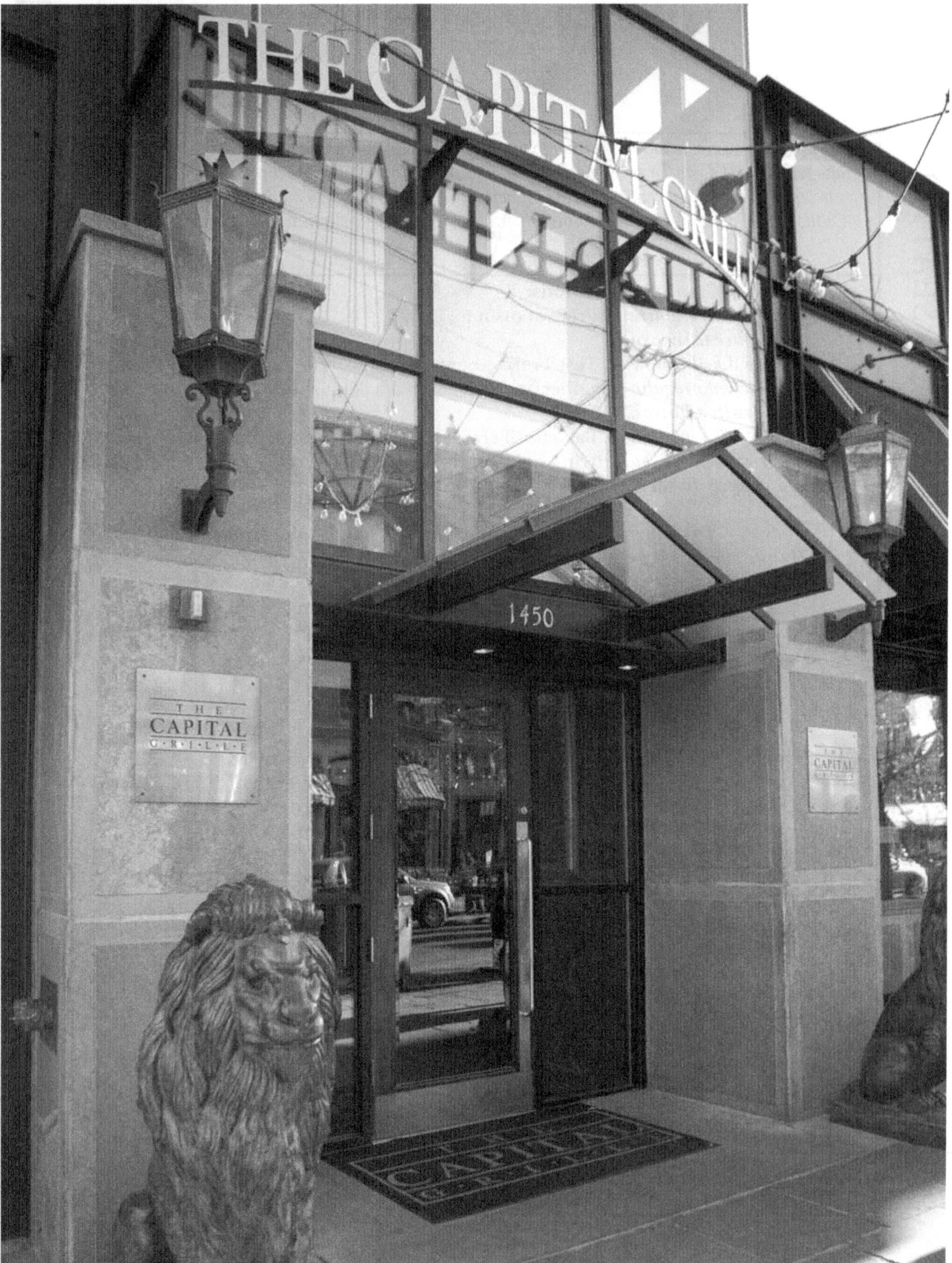
THE CAPITAL GRILLE
1450
THE
CAPITAL
G·R·I·L·L·E

Seared Halibut with Sweet and Sour Tomatoes

Whether you're seeking a relaxed setting for lunch, a gracious atmosphere for dinner, or a festive and elegant venue for your most special occasions, The Capital Grille will provide a dining experience you won't soon forget. Local, seasonal ingredients, the freshest seafood Seattle has to offer, and hand-cut, dry-aged steaks masterfully prepared, all served in the sophisticated environment of the historic Cobb Building.

4 (9½-oz.) halibut fillets
Kosher salt, to taste
freshly ground black pepper, to taste
2 oz. clarified butter
3 oz. white wine
3 oz. sweet & sour tomatoes (recipe below)
4 chervil sprigs
4 tsp sliced chives

Sweet & Sour Tomatoes:
4 shallots, minced (approx. ⅓ cup)
1½ tbsp granulated sugar
1½ tbsp brown sugar
⅓ C. aged sherry vinegar
⅓ C. champagne vinegar
3 medium tomatoes, peeled, seeded, diced (approx. 1½ cups)
½ tbsp freshly chopped chervil
pinch of Kosher salt
pinch of freshly ground black pepper

1. Preheat oven to 400°F.
2. Season halibut with Kosher salt and freshly ground black pepper.
3. Place the clarified butter in a preheated frying pan and heat until wisps of smoke appear.
4. Sear the flesh side of the fish for 5 minutes (the fish should be golden brown and very crisp). Flip the fish and cook it on the skin side for 3 minutes.
5. Place the fish in a baking pan, add the wine, and set pan in the oven to finish cooking. If the fish is thin (less than 1-inch thick) it will finish cooking in 2-3 minutes. A thicker piece may take 5-6 minutes. Do not over cook. The fish is done when you can insert a bamboo skewer or toothpick into the fish with little resistance.
6. Place the fish in the center of a serving plate. Top the fish with the tomatoes and allow some of the tomatoes to scatter around the fish. Garnish with chervil and sprinkle with chives.

Sweet & Sour Tomatoes:
1. Combine the shallots, sugars, and vinegars in a small sauce pan and simmer over low heat until the mixture has a consistency of syrup (about 45 minutes). Cool to room temperature.
2. Blend in the diced tomatoes, chervil, salt, and pepper. Serve at room temperature.

NOTE: Any leftover tomatoes can be refrigerated for a few days and served with grilled chicken, tossed with a green vegetable, or served with cheese and crackers. Consider doubling the recipe to have plenty to pair with other dishes.

Capital Grille
1301 4th Ave

"I've always relished wordplay and have a consuming interest in culinary puns. Sometimes I'll loaf around all day, devising bone mots just for the halibut."
Mark Morton

CHANDLER'S
CRABHOUSE

Hot Crab Dip

Reminiscent of a traditional fish house with expansive views of Lake Union, sailboats, and seaplanes from every table. Its main dining area features a high-domed ceiling with a live crab tank located next to the full-display kitchen. Chandler's Crabhouse menu highlights world-class seafood featuring a large selection of fresh crab, seafood, and shellfish.

½ C. grated parmesan cheese
1½ C. mayonnaise
6 oz. Dungeness crabmeat
4 oz. artichoke hearts, well drained, coarsely chopped
white pepper, to taste
2 green onions, minced (mostly green parts)
cayenne pepper, to taste

1. Preheat oven to 375°F. Lightly spray a small 1½-inch deep baking dish with non-stick coating.

2. In a bowl, combine the parmesan cheese, mayonnaise, crabmeat, chopped artichoke hearts, and white pepper. Stir ingredients together gently with a spoon.

3. Spoon into prepared baking dish. Sprinkle with extra parmesan, if desired, and bake for 10 minutes, or until brown and heated through.

4. Garnish hot dip with the minced green onion and cayenne pepper and serve with pita pieces or chips, baguette slices, mixed vegetables, tortilla chips, or sliced jicama.

Chandler's Crabhouse

901 Fairview Avenue North

"Eating is always a decision, nobody forces your hand to pick up food and put it into your mouth."
Albert Ellis, Michael Abrams, Lidia Dengelegi

COASTAL
KITCHEN

Cinnamon-Hazelnut Pancakes

Located in the culturally diverse Capitol Hill District, Coastal Kitchen is the quintessential neighborhood fish house. Its "fish forward" attitude is what drives its quarterly changing menu, focusing on the varied coastal regions of our beloved planet, with an emphasis on seafood. Recent menus have featured the cuisines of Tunisia, Jamaica, Peru, and Rome. No passport required!

1¼ C. hazelnuts (about 6 oz.)
1¾ C. all-purpose flour
¾ C. whole-wheat flour
2 tbsp sugar
2 tsp ground cinnamon
1½ tsp baking powder
½ tsp baking soda
½ tsp salt
2 large eggs
3 C. buttermilk
3 tbsp butter, melted
mild flovored oil

1. Preheat oven to 350°F.

2. Toast hazelnuts in a 10x15-inch baking pan in regular or convection oven until golden beneath skins, 7 to 10 minutes. Place nuts onto a clean linen towel to cool. When nuts are cool enough to handle, rub in towel to remove skins. Chop hazelnuts in a food processor or with a knife; you should have 1¼ cups. Reserve ¼ cup to sprinkle over cooked pancakes.

3. In a bowl, mix all-purpose flour, whole-wheat flour, sugar, cinnamon, baking powder, baking soda, and salt.

4. In a small bowl, whisk together the eggs, buttermilk, and melted butter until blended.

5. Stir egg mixture into flour mixture until evenly moistened, then gently stir in 1 cup of hazelnuts.

6. Set a non-stick griddle to 350°F. When hot, coat lightly with oil and adjust heat to maintain temperature.

7. Spoon batter onto griddle by ⅓-cup portions and cook until pancakes are browned on the bottom and edges begin to look dry, about 2 minutes; turn with a wide spatula and brown other side, 1½ to 2 minutes longer. Coat pan with more oil as necessary to cook remaining pancakes.

8. Serve pancakes as cooked or keep warm in a single layer on baking sheets in a 200°F oven for up to 15 minutes. Sprinkle with reserved hazelnuts.

"I no longer prep any food or drink with more than one ingredient."
Cyra McFadden

Cedarbrook Granola

Copperleaf Restaurant & Bar is the ideal venue to relish fresh farm-to-table local and regional bounty for lunch and dinner. The interior of the brand new 34-seat indoor dining room was designed by GGLO Seattle. The space is accented with 100% organic bamboo fabrics and hand-blown glass sculptures by renowned local artists. The focal point of the dining experience and what contributes predominantly to the room's unforgettable ambiance is the large stone fireplace. Large windows frame spectacular views of Cedarbrook's meticulously landscaped backyard and invite aromas from nearby cedar trees. Seasonal outdoor dining--late spring to early fall--on the 30-seat Copperleaf Terrace is extraordinary--made better only by the large wood-burning fireplace. Diners will appreciate their Seattle-Tacoma surroundings. In keeping with its quintessentially Northwest style, many food items are presented on artisanal hand-crafted serving pieces.

2 C. rolled oats
½ C. sunflower seeds
½ C. honey
½ C. vegetable oil or melted butter
¼ C. brown sugar
1 C. nuts (any variety)
1 C. mixed dried fruit (such as raisins, cherries, cranberries)
1 tbsp walnut or almond oil
½ tsp Kosher salt

1. Preheat oven to 375°F.

2. Mix oats, nuts, sunflower seeds, butter (or oil), sugar, and honey together in a mixing bowl.

3. Spread granola onto a baking sheet in an even, thin layer and bake until golden brown, approximately 7-12 minutes.

4. When granola is done, remove it from the tray and pour into a bowl and mix in the salt and flavored oil. Place granola back on the baking sheet and let cool to room temperature.

Copperleaf Restaurant

18525 36th Avenue

"Food is an important part of a balanced diet."
Fran Lebowitz

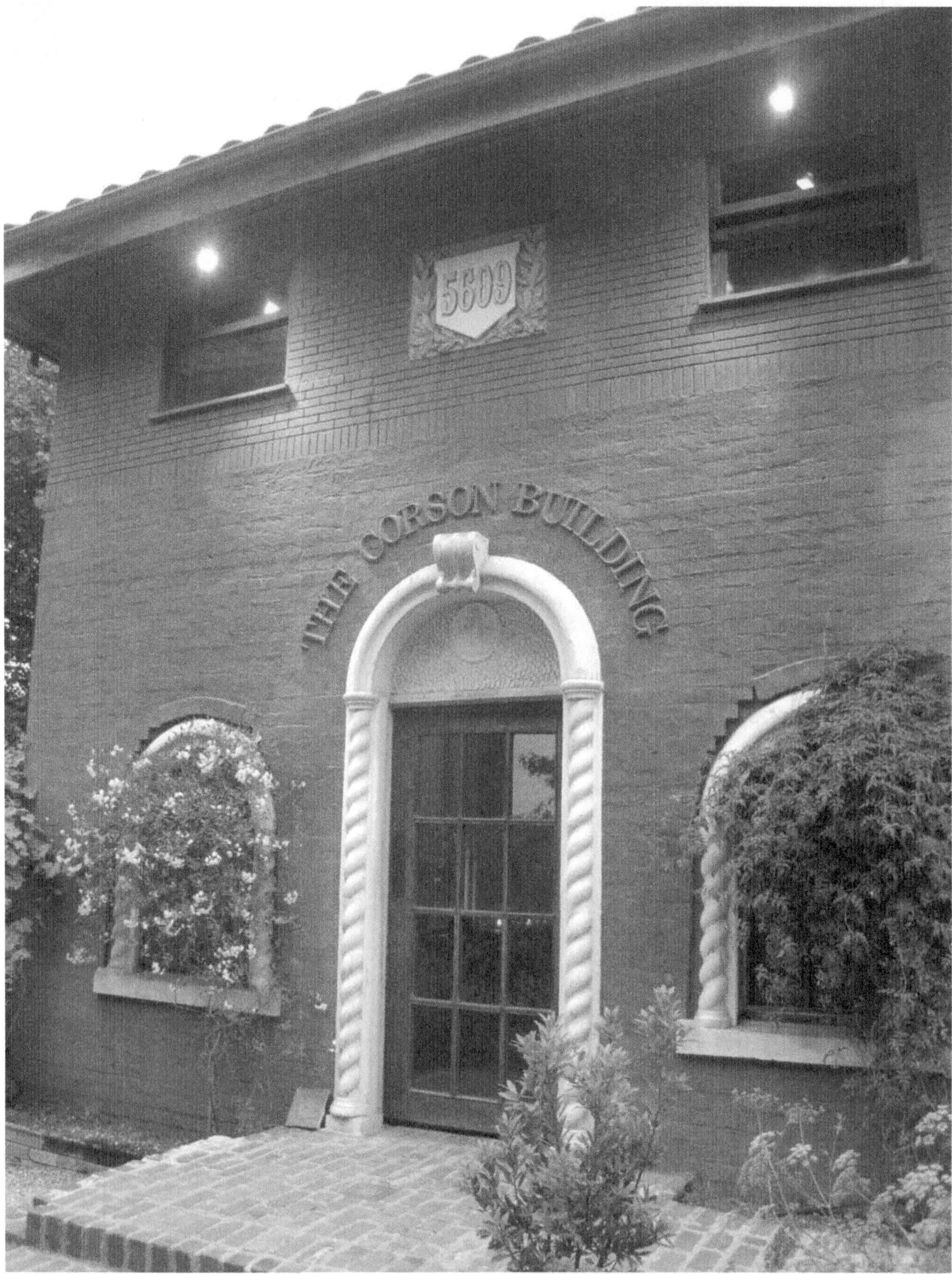
5609
THE CORSON BUILDING

Roasted Chicken with Hazelnut-Lemon Herb Butter

The Corson Building
5609 Corson Avenue

The Corson Building is a home, a restaurant, and a community. Dedicated to food and its direct connection to celebration, community, and culture. Providing one of the few human experiences we all have in common. Eating. Sharing at the table, we can open up our senses and our consciences to our place in the world, along with the place of our neighbors.

2 whole chickens (3½ lb. each), rinsed

Brine:
¾ C. sugar
¾ C. Kosher salt
6 qt. water
1 tsp black peppercorns
1 lemon, sliced
1 head garlic, halved

Herb Butter:
¾ lb. unsalted butter, softened
2 tsp minced garlic
2 tsp minced shallot
2 tbsp chopped thyme
2 tbsp chopped marjoram
grated zest of 1 lemon
Kosher salt and pepper
4 tbsp olive oil

Hazelnut-Lemon Butter:
¼ lb. unsalted butter
1 C. toasted, skinned hazelnuts, roughly chopped
juice of 1 lemon

4 ripe peaches, halved and pitted, each half cut into thirds
30 anise hyssop leaves

Brine:
1. Bring all the ingredients to a boil in an 8-quart pot to dissolve. Remove from heat; let cool entirely. Add the chickens to cooled brine and refrigerate overnight.

Herb Butter:
1. On a small plate, mash softened butter with garlic, shallot, thyme, marjoram, lemon zest, 1 teaspoon salt and ¼ teaspoon pepper; set aside.

Roast Chicken:
1. Preheat the oven to 400°F.
2. Rinse chickens inside and out and pat dry with paper towels. Beginning at the cavity, use your fingers to carefully loosen the skin all over the breast and legs. Stuff herb butter under the skin. Truss chickens with butcher twine. Transfer to a large roasting pan or sheet pan and use a pastry brush to brush all over with the olive oil. Sprinkle each with ½ teaspoon salt and ¼ teaspoon pepper.
3. Roast until an instant-read thermometer inserted into meat between the body and thigh reaches 170°F, 1 hour 20 minutes to 1½ hours. Remove from oven, cover with foil and let rest 15 to 20 minutes.
4. Meanwhile, in a sauté pan, cook butter over medium-low heat until it foams, smells nutty, and turns a nice tan color, 3 to 5 minutes. Remove from the heat. Add the hazelnuts, lemon juice, ¼ teaspoon pepper and any juices that have accumulated around the chickens.
5. Remove legs and cut thighs from drumsticks at joints. Remove breasts and cut each in half width-wise. Arrange chicken pieces on a platter and tuck in the peach wedges and hyssop leaves. Drizzle the warm hazelnut-lemon butter over top.

"We don't get fat because we overeat; we overeat because we're getting fat."
Gary Taubes

THE
COTERIE
ROOM

Sweet Onion Mac and Cheese

The Coterie Room is one snazzy place. The interior alone is enough reason to visit with the open, airy, European bistro-esque atmosphere and the beautiful chandelier. The fern display on the wall is interesting and adds a Northwest appeal to the upscale space.

4 C. orecchiette pasta
2 tbsp extra virgin olive oil
1 tbsp canola oil, plus more for frying
1 C. + 2 tbsp unsalted butter, divided
1 large sweet onion, coarsely chopped
Kosher salt & freshly ground black pepper
1 medium shallot, thinly sliced
¼ C. rice flour
1 C. all-purpose flour
5 C. whole milk
½ C. shredded Fontina cheese
3 tbsp freshly grated parmesan cheese
½ C. grated sharp white cheddar cheese
1 tsp chives, finely chopped
1 tsp flat-leaf parsley, finely chopped

1. Bring a stock pot full of salted water to a boil, add the orecchiette and cook until just al dente, about 10 minutes. Strain the pasta, toss with the olive oil and set aside.
2. In large sauce pan set over medium heat, add 1 tablespoon of canola oil, 2 tablespoons of the butter, and the onion. Cook until the onion is golden brown, about 10 minutes. Season with salt and freshly ground black pepper. Place the onions in a blender and purée until smooth. Set aside.
3. In a medium bowl, toss the shallot slices with the rice flour. Shake the excess rice flour out of the bowl.
4. In a medium sauce pan, add enough canola oil to come 2 inches up the side. Heat the oil to 320°F. Add the shallot slices to the oil and fry until they are light golden brown, about 1 to 2 minutes. Strain the shallots on a paper-towel-lined sheet pan and season with salt and pepper.
5. In a large sauce pan or Dutch oven set over medium heat, melt 1 cup of butter.
6. Add the all-purpose flour and cook, whisking constantly, until smooth and light brown in color, about 10 minutes.
7. Gradually whisk in the milk and continue whisking until the sauce is thickened, about 20 minutes.
8. Add the Fontina, parmesan, cheddar, and reserved onion purée. Whisk until cheeses melt. Season with salt and pepper.
9. Fold in the pasta, chives, and parsley and garnish with the fried shallots. Serve immediately.

The Coterie Room
2137 2nd Avenue

"All human history attests That happiness for man,—the hungry sinner!—Since Eve ate apples, much depends on dinner."
Lord Byron

3. Homemade soup &
homemade bread ½ sandwich
FAIR TRADE Organic Coffee
DRIP COFFEE
HOT CHOCOLATE
STEAMED MILK
STEAMED SOY MILK
CHAI
HOT OR ICED
Black ice tea
ICE TEA
BUNN
BUNN
nutella
nutella
nutella

CRUMPETS

The Crumpet Shop serves crumpets for breakfast, brunch, and lunch. You can get them simply buttered, or with nearly two dozen different toppings, including honey, Nutella, local jams, and pesto-colored eggs with ham. On the side, have a latte or a cup of imported tea.

¾ lb. all-purpose flour
½ tsp salt
1¾ C. milk (or butter-milk
1 tbsp dried yeast
pinch of sugar
butter

Special Equipment: crumpet ring molds

1. Sift the flour and salt together in a large bowl.

2. Heat the milk to 80-100°F. Pour ½ cup of the milk into a small bowl, stir in the yeast and sprinkle the sugar on top. After about 5-10 minutes, there should be a foamy head on the milk. (Reheat the rest of the milk to 80-100°F if it has dropped in temperature.)

3. Next, form a well in the center of the bowl of flour and salt. Fill the well with the milk and yeast mixutre, then add the rest of the milk. Fold ingredients together until a thick batter forms. Cover the bowl and set aside to rise for 45 minutes.

4. Grease a non-stick skillet with butter and set over medium heat. Grease the crumpet rings as well, and place them on the skillet. Make sure to heat the rings until they are the same temperature as the skillet, 3-4 minutes.

5. Just before adding the batter, raise the heat again slightly. Pour enough batter into the rings (about ½ cup per crumpet) so the ring isn't overflowing, but so the bottom is covered. The batter will be sticky, so be careful when adding it to the rings. Do not move the crumpet for 5-7 minutes, or until the surface looks dry and bubbles have formed holes throughout the top of the crumpet.

6. Carefully remove the ring, flip the crumpet, and cook the other side for 2-3 minutes more. Cool on a wire rack.

7. Serve immediately with butter and jam, use them as a base for an open-faced egg sandwich, or toast them the next day for breakfast.

THE CRUMPET SHOP
1503 1ST AVENUE

"It's important to begin a search on a full stomach."
Henry Bromel,

SLOW-BRAISED BEEF SHORT RIBS

Our vision is to bring to you an experience that speaks to our place and who we are. Between two great mountain ranges and at the center of the Puget Sound, in an urban setting with all the wild of the Northwest abounding around us. We deliver, through service, cuisine, and our warm ambiance, a dining experience that changes with the seasons, evokes emotion, and arouses the senses.

Marinade:
5 lb. (3-inch thick cut) bone-in beef short ribs
1 bunch each fresh thyme, rosemary, and sage leaves, chopped
2 tbsp each Kosher salt and freshly ground black pepper
2 (750-ml) bottles Cabernet Sauvignon

olive oil, for searing ribs
1 yellow onion, medium dice
2 carrots, peeled, medium dice
2 ribs celery, medium dice
3 cloves garlic
4 qt. veal stock
3 bay leaves
1 oz. dry porcini mushrooms

1. Season the ribs liberally with herbs and salt and pepper. Place in a large non-reactive bowl or deep container and cover with wine. Marinate for 12 hours in the refrigerator.

2. Preheat oven to 375°F.

3. Remove ribs from marinade, pour all the wine into a sauce pot, and reduce by half.

4. Meanwhile, heat a thin layer of olive oil in a large cast iron pan over medium-high heat. Sear ribs on all sides until well browned. Place browned ribs into a braising or deep-roasting pan.

5. Brown onion, carrots, celery, and garlic in the same cast iron pan, adding more oil as needed.

6. Scatter browned vegetables over the ribs. Add the reduced wine, veal stock, bay leaves, and mushrooms. Cover the pan with parchment paper and foil and place in the oven for 5 hours.

7. Remove pan from the oven and allow the ribs to rest for 1 hour before removing the bones. Skim any fat from the sauce. Remove vegetables from the pan and set aside.

8. While ribs are resting, strain sauce into a sauce pot and reduce for 1 hour. Pour hot sauce over ribs and vegetables and serve.

CRUSH RESTAURANT
2319 E. MADISON STREET

"Food is our common ground, a universal experience."
James Beard

Pan-seared Halibut with Lobster-Fennel Cream

Cutters Bayhouse is located next to historical Pike Place Market. The Bayroom offers exclusive private dining with an incredible view of Elliott Bay, Mt. Rainier, the Olympic Mountains and Port of Seattle. Our contemporary Northwest cuisine suits all tastes from the freshest local seafood to steaks, chicken, pasta, and sushi. Cutters legendary hospitality, engaging professional service, and genuine care for our guests has made us a local icon for more than 25 years. Whether you are entertaining clients, hosting a rehearsal dinner, business meeting, or a wedding brunch, Cutters is truly the Seattle experience.

4 (6-oz.) halibut fillets, block cut
Kosher salt and pepper, to taste
2 oz. canola oil
2 tsp olive oil
1 lb. baby spinach
roasted fingerling potatoes
12 oz. lobster-fennel cream
2 tsp. chives, 1/8-inch minced

Roasted Fingerling Potatoes:
1½ lb. fingerling potatoes cut in half lengthwise
1½ tbsp lemon juice
Kosher salt and pepper, to taste
1 tbsp extra virgin olive oil

Lobster-Fennel Cream:
4 tbsp unsalted butter
½ lb. fennel, fronds removed, chopped ½-inch
¼ lb. shallots, rough chopped ½-inch
2 oz. brandy
1 C. water
1 pt. heavy cream (36% fat)
2 tsp lobster base
pinch ground nutmeg
white pepper to taste
Kosher salt, to taste
1 bay leaf
1 tsp lemon juice

Roasted Fingerling Potatoes:
1. Preheat oven to 325°F.
2. Place potatoes in a large mixing bowl. Add lemon juice, salt, pepper, and toss to coat. Drizzle oil over potatoes and toss again. Place on sheet pan and roast for 20 minutes, or until tender.

Lobster-Fennel Cream:
1. Place butter in large, heavy sauce pan and melt over medium heat. Add fennel and shallots. Sweat the fennel mixture until the fennel becomes soft and tender. Deglaze the pan with the brandy and water. Simmer for 15 minutes. Add cream and remaining ingredients except for lemon juice and simmer for 30 minutes on low heat. Add the lemon juice and simmer an additional 5 minutes. Remove from heat and strain through a fine china cap.

To Serve:
1. Preheat oven to 400°F.
2. Dry fish with a paper towel. Season both sides of halibut with salt and pepper.
3. Heat a sauté pan over high heat and add 2 oz. of canola oil. Once oil begins to smoke, add the halibut and sear until golden brown on both sides. Remove fish from the pan and place halibut in the oven. Cook until internal temperature reaches 115-120°F.
4. While the halibut is cooking, heat another sauté pan and add the 2 tsp of olive oil. Once the oil is hot, add the spinach and season with salt and pepper. Sauté the spinach until tender.
5. Place the potatoes in the center of a bowl. Place two potatoes with the flat side down in the center of the bowl. In the opposite direction, place the other two potatoes on top of the first (creating a log cabin effect). Pour lobster fennel cream sauce around the potatoes and mound some spinach on top of the potatoes. Place the halibut on top the spinach. Garnish the sauce with the minced chives and serve.

Cutters Bayhouse
2001 Western Avenue

"Water is the most neglected nutrient in your diet but one of the most vital."
Kelly Barton

MENU
dahlia
lounge

Triple Coconut Cream Pies

From the smell of the wood burning grill, to the swirl of a silky Yakima Valley Cabernet in the glass, to the first bite of a gingery, pan-browned shrimp-scallion potsticker, Dahlia Lounge is the quintessential Seattle restaurant experience. For 20 years, we've been at the epicenter of Seattle's local, sustainable, and organic food movement.

Coconut Pastry Cream:
2 C. milk
2 C. sweetened finely shredded coconut
1 vanilla bean, split in half lengthwise
2 large eggs
½ C. + 2 tbsp granulated sugar
3 tbsp flour
4 tbsp unsalted butter, softened

Pies:
9 (3½-inch) pie shells, baked and cooled
2½ C. heavy whipping cream
⅓ C. sugar
1 tsp vanilla extract

Garnish:
1 (3-oz.) chunk white chocolate, at room temperature
1 C. unsweetened toasted coconut

Coconut Pastry Cream:
1. Put milk and coconut in a medium sauce pan over medium-high heat. Scrape seeds from vanilla bean and add both seeds and bean to sauce pan. Bring mixture to a gentle simmer, stirring occasionally.
2. In a medium bowl, whisk together eggs, sugar, and flour. While whisking, drizzle about ⅓ of the hot milk mixture into egg mixture, then slowly whisk egg-milk mixture back into sauce pan. Cook over medium-high heat, whisking, until pastry cream thickens and begins to bubble, 4-5 minutes. Remove from heat, stir in butter, and discard vanilla bean.
3. Spoon hot pastry cream into a bowl and set in a larger bowl of ice water, stirring occasionally, until cooled to room temperature. Cover with plastic wrap, pressing it directly onto surface (to prevent a skin from forming) and chill until cold, at least 3 hours.

Pies:
1. Carefully remove baked shells from brioche molds.
2. Spoon pastry cream into shells, filling each a little more than halfway.
3. With an electric mixer, whip cream with sugar and vanilla until it holds stiff peaks.
4. Fill a pastry bag fitted with a large star tip (no. 6) with whipped cream and pipe a double layer of cream onto each pie, or simply spoon it on top.

Garnish:
1. With a vegetable peeler, scrape wide curls or shavings from the chunk of white chocolate. Sprinkle curls or shavings over pies, dividing evenly, and top with toasted coconut. Serve immediately.

Dahlia Lounge
2001 4th Avenue

"Skillful and refined cookery has always been a feature of the most glorious epochs in history."
Lucien Tendret

delancey

Clam Pizza

One of the most popular specials at Delancey in Seattle is Brandon Pettit's clam pie, which was inspired not by New Haven's famous clam pizzas (he recently discovered he didn't care for them at all) but by the version prepared at Franny's in Brooklyn. This pie only appears on the Delancey menu on weekends, and it always sells out fast. Only fresh clams – delivered the same day the pizzas are made – are used. Canned clams just don't taste right. So Pettit and his cohorts Ryan Swanson and pastry chef Brandi Henderson are only able to make about 30 clam pizzas before they run out of the bivalves.

40 small Manila clams
2 oz. butter
2 C. white wine (preferably more dry than sweet)
2 shallots, sliced
¼ C. crème fraîche
¾ cup aged mozzarella
handful of fresh mozzarella, broken into chunks
1 or 2 preserved Meyer lemons (preferably organic), rinds sliced into thin strips
hot chile oil
fresh parsley
prepared Neapolitan-style pizza dough

1. Set a pizza stone in the bottom third of oven and preheat to 500°F for 1 hour.

2. In a large stock pot, melt the butter over medium-high heat. Add the shallots and saute for 1-2 minutes. Add the wine and bring to a boil. Add the clams and steam, covered, until shells open, about 8 minutes. Remove the cooked clams from the liquid and set aside to cool. Once cool, remove the meat, and discard the shells and any clams that did not open.

3. In a large sauce pan, reduce the wine and shallot liquid over high heat until only about 2 tablespoons remain, then strain over a bowl, discard shallots. Whisk in the crème fraîche, and stir for about 1 minute until incorporated.

4. Stretch pizza dough into a 10-12-inch circle. Top pizza with fresh and aged mozzarella, clams, drizzle the crème fraîche mixture over top, and place thin strips of preserved Meyer lemons peels around the pizza.

5. Bake until cheese is melted and crust is golden-browned and puffed, about 12-15 minutes (be careful not to over cook; the clams will get rubbery). Squirt some hot chile oil over the pizza and garnish with fresh chopped parsley.

Delancey
1415 Northwest 70th Street

"If I go down in for anything in history, I would like to be known as the person who convinced the American people that catfish is one of the finest eating fishes in the world."
Willard Scott

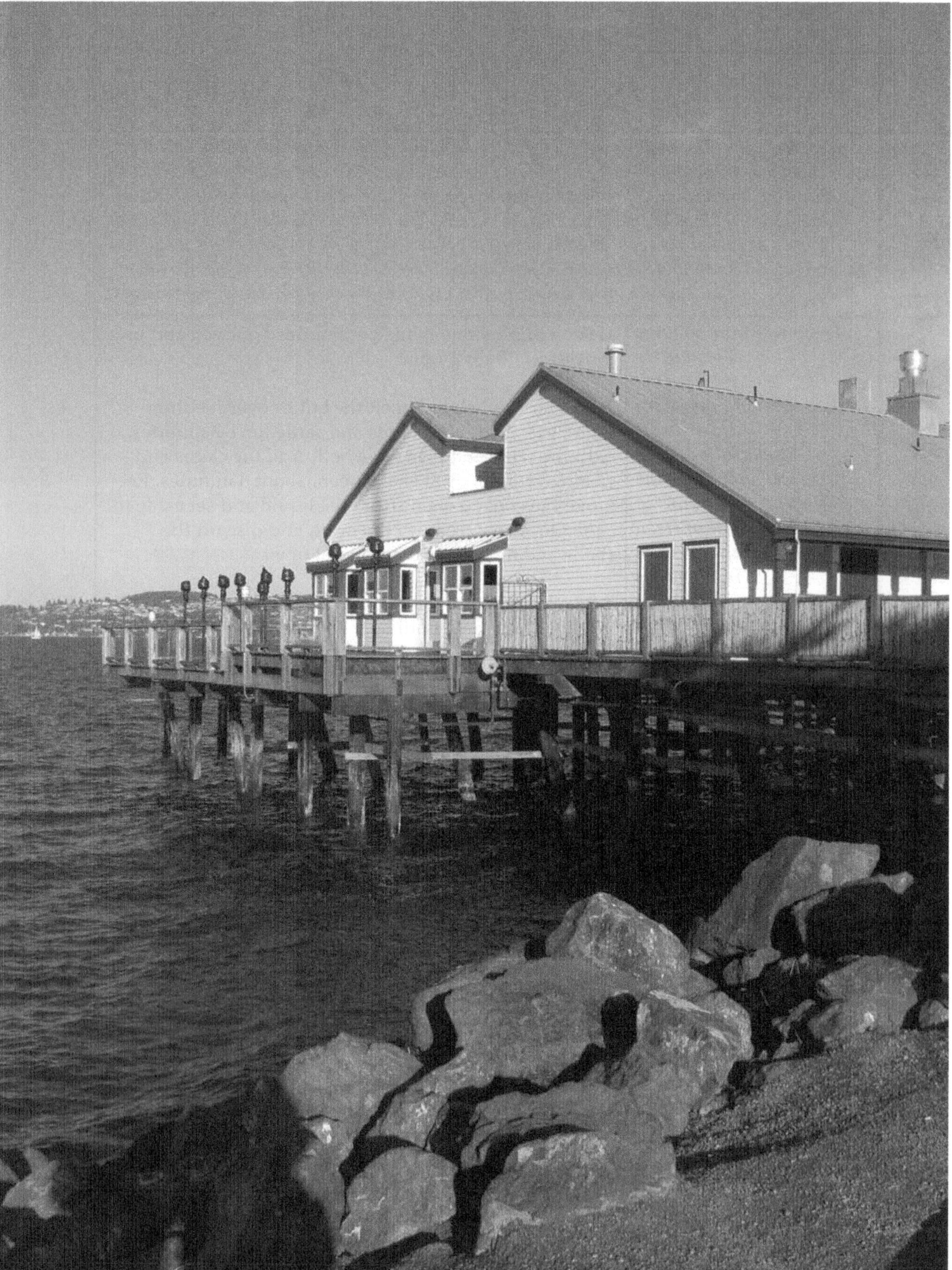

Wild Bill's Marinated BBQ Prawn Tower

Since Duke's first started our "Email Club", more than 250,000 people have taken advantage of our simple offer: Join Duke's Email Club, Receive Two Free Entrees. We started this way back in the late '90s because we knew that if you could just taste the flavor that we serve every day, you'd find a restaurant to come back to again and again and never have a bad experience.

32 Ocean Garden 16/20 prawns, peeled & deveined (tail attached)
8 (12-inch) bamboo skewers, soaked in 2 C. water and 1 C. olive oil

Marinade:
2 Meyer lemons, juiced
2 C. white wine
2 C. olive oil
6 garlic cloves, minced
½ bunch fresh tarragon
6 large leaves fresh basil
pinch of red pepper flakes
salt and pepper, to taste

1 cup prepared honey BBQ sauce
1 oz. minced garlic
4 oz. salted butter

2 Meyer lemons halved, for serving

1. Place 9 prawns on a cutting board in a vertical row so that they are level. Puncture each prawn with 2 skewers, one close to the head and one close to the tail. Repeat with remaining shrimp.

2. Mix marinade ingredients together. Pour over shrimp to cover and marinate for at least 4 hours in the refrigerator.

3. Heat 1 cup honey BBQ sauce in a small sauce pan. Add minced garlic and salted butter and stir to incorporate.

4. Remove shrimp skewers from marinade and grill or broil until shrimp is warmed through, flipping once.

5. Place Meyer lemons halves on a serving plate (rind-side up) and insert the grilled shrimp skewers directly into the middle of the lemon to form a tower. Serve with the BBQ sauce.

Duke's Chowder House
2516 Alki Avenue

"Fish is the only food that is considered spoiled once it smells like what it is."
P. J. O'Rourke

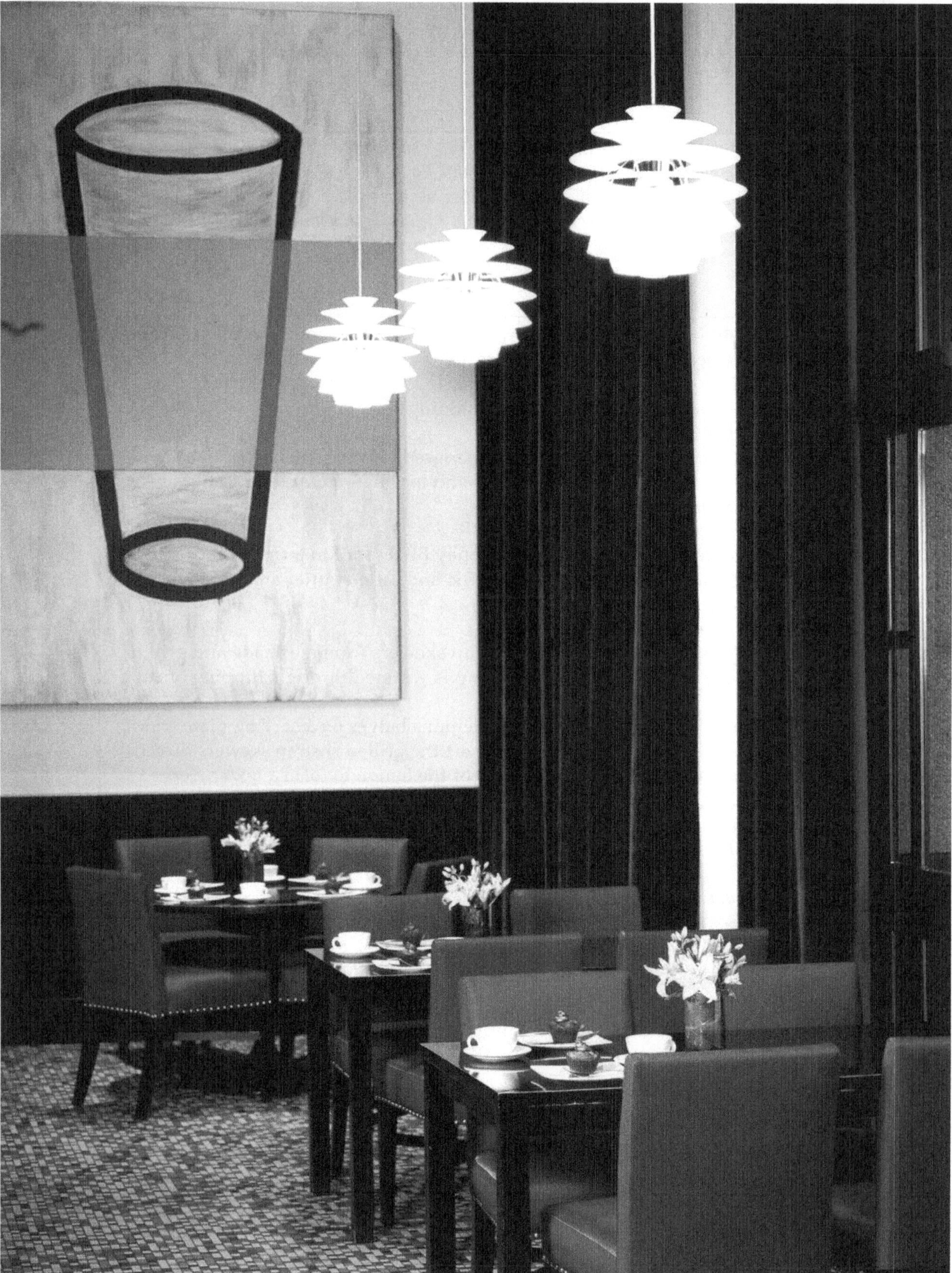

Mortadella

Executive Chef Adam Stevenson takes Earth & Ocean into a new era, offering a modern riff on American classics. His housemade charcuterie peppers dishes like Pancetta-Wrapped Hanger Steak with Gorgonzola Ravioli or Penn Cove Mussels with Fennel Sausage and Sambuca-Fennel Broth. Look for monthly winemaker dinners featuring 4-course menus with handpicked award-winning wines of the Pacific Northwest paired in perfect harmony to Chef Stevenson's beautifully presented dishes.

3½ lb. lean pork shoulder
2 lb. pork fat
68 grams salt
6 grams Insta Cure #1 curing salt
18 grams fresh garlic paste
30 grams dextrose
4 grams ground mace
2 grams ground coriander
2 grams ground cinnamon
2 grams ground cayenne
624 grams crushed ice
75 grams blanched pork jowl, pork fat or pancetta, diced into ⅜-inch cubes
61 grams unsalted, shelled pistachios
4 grams coarsely cracked peppercorns
1 beef bung casing

1. Chill the pork shoulder, pork fat, grinder parts, and food processor to 32°F or less.
2. Grind the pork shoulder meat through a small die into the chilled food processor bowl. Grind the fat into a separate chilled bowl and refrigerate.
3. Add the salt, curing salt, garlic paste, dextrose, mace, coriander, cinnamon, cayenne, and half of the ice to the shoulder meat.
4. Blend the meat in the food processor to a smooth paste with a temperature of 42-45°F. Push down the meat on the sides of bowl until fully incorporated and continue processing. Do not let the temperature of the mixture exceed 45°F.
5. Once the meat is smooth, add the remaining ice and the chilled ground fat to the processor bowl. Blend the fat into the meat until a smooth paste is formed, pushing down the sides from time to time.
6. Stop the machine when the paste reaches 58°F-62°F and transfer to a bowl and fold in the pork jowl, pistachios, and peppercorns.
7. Stuff the meat into a clean beef bung and pack tightly so that there are no air pockets. Secure the end with a strong knot and create a loop.
8. Place the mortadella in a large pot and cover with cold water. Lay a plate over the mortadella to keep it submerged while cooking.
9. Slowly heat the water to 160°F and hold it there for the duration of the cooking. Cook for 4 hours or until the mortadella reaches an internal temperature of 155°F. Check the temperature every 45 minutes.
10. When the mortadella reaches 155°F, immediately plunge into an ice bath. Transfer to a refrigerator and serve after 2 days.

Earth & Ocean
1112 4th Avenue

"Wine is the drink of the gods, milk the drink of babes, tea the drink of women, and water the drink of beasts."
John Stuart Blackie

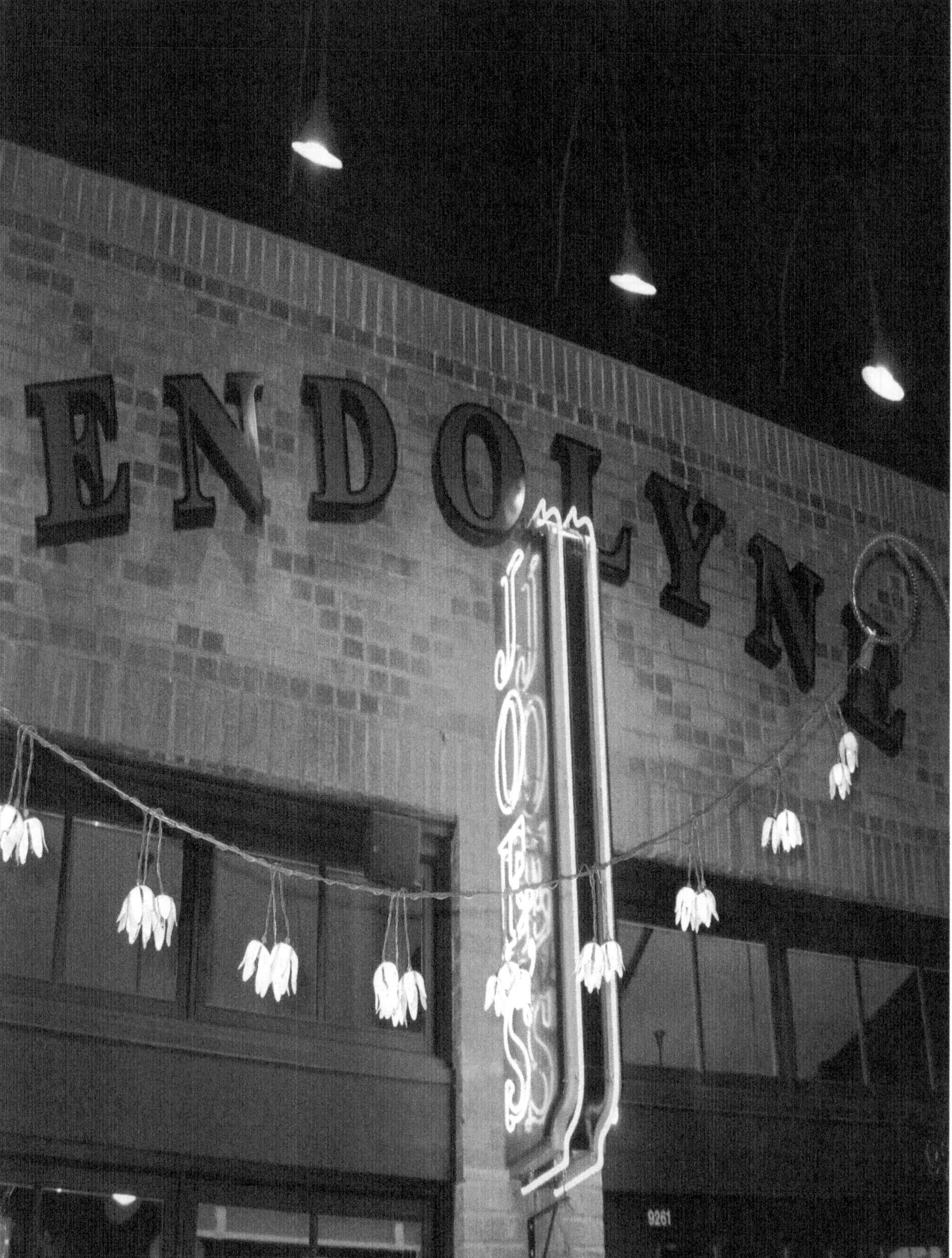
ENDOLYN
9261

Caribbean Steak Salad with Mango-Cider Dressing

Joe's jumps at breakfast, lunch, and dinner daily with a tasty menu of updated American classics. We keep things interesting by taking the rest of the menu for a spin through the Americas each quarter. While you might find yourself nestled in the bosom of Little Italy during the holidays, come spring you may be fey-do-doin' in the French Quarter of N'awl-ins. Summertime is island time at Joe's, where Mai Tais, Bonsai Pipelines, and Longboard Lager are the favored tropical libations, perfect on a lingering, sultry afternoon.

Steak:
2 ancho chiles, dried
1 oz. olive oil
3 tsp granulated garlic
½ tsp kosher salt
¼ tsp freshly ground black pepper

4 (8-oz.) flat iron steaks

Salad:
1 lb. plantains
oil for frying
4 oz. shredded coconut, sweetened
20 oz. mixed greens
3-4 oz. Mango-Cider Dressing (recipe follows)
salt and pepper, to taste
12 oz. red California seedless grapes, halved
2 oz. sliced green onions

Mango-Cider Dressing:
2 Champagne mangos
4 oz. vinegar
1 oz. clover honey
1 tsp kosher salt
½ tsp freshly ground black pepper
6 oz. olive oil

Steak:

1. Place whole dried ancho chiles in hot water until soft.

2. Blend the oil and spices together. Rub seasoning generously on steak and marinate overnight.

Salad:

1. Preheat oil to 350°F. Peel plantains and slice thinly using a mandoline. Deep-fry plantains for approximately 1 minute, or until golden brown and crispy. Set aside on paper towel to cool.

2. Toast coconut in a dry sauté pan until golden brown.

3. In large bowl, add mixed greens and dress with 3-4 oz. mango-cider dressing and a pinch of salt and pepper. Add halved grapes, green onions, and toasted coconut.

4. Grill flat iron steaks for 6-8 minutes. Slice on bias and place on top of salad. Garnish with fried plantains.

Mango-Cider Dressing:

1. Peel and chop mangos and place into a bowl. Add vinegar, honey, salt and pepper, then slowly incorporate oil while blending.

Endolyne Joe's
9261 45th Avenue

"A way to a man's heart is through his stomach, that is true as gold. You put some love in your food and a fool can taste it."
Raelle Tucker

UNION

Mac n' Cheese

At Ethan Stowell Restaurants we are about keeping it simple, using fresh ingredients and allowing the food to do the talking. Generous bowls of freshly made pasta, locally foraged mushrooms, delicately prepared fish, a T-bone for two and maybe a few animal innards, just a few of the things we like to highlight on our menus.

8 oz. Lagana pasta (Lumache shape, but any shape will work)
2 tbsp butter
2 tbsp flour
2 C. milk
salt and pepper, to taste
2 C. Fontina Val d'Aosta, shredded
2 balls fresh mozzarella, diced
½ C. Parmigiano-Reggiano, finely grated
½ C. bread crumbs

1. Preheat oven to 350°F.

2. Cook pasta until al dente and drain well.

3. In a sauce pan, melt butter over medium heat. Add flour and stir to remove lumps. Pour in milk and cook until thickened. Season with salt and pepper.

4. Add Fontina Val d'Aosta and stir until melted. Add pasta and stir. Add the fresh mozzarella and stir, just until combined (the fresh mozzarella should not be fully melted).

5. Pour mixture into 2 qt. casserole dish.

6. In a small bowl, combine the Parmigiano-Reggiano and the bread crumbs. Cover the top of the mac n' cheese with the bread-crumb mixture.

7. Bake for 20 minutes until bubbling and golden brown.

Ethan Stowell's Restaurant
2208 Queen Anne Ave N.

"Food is the most primitive form of comfort."
Sheila Graham

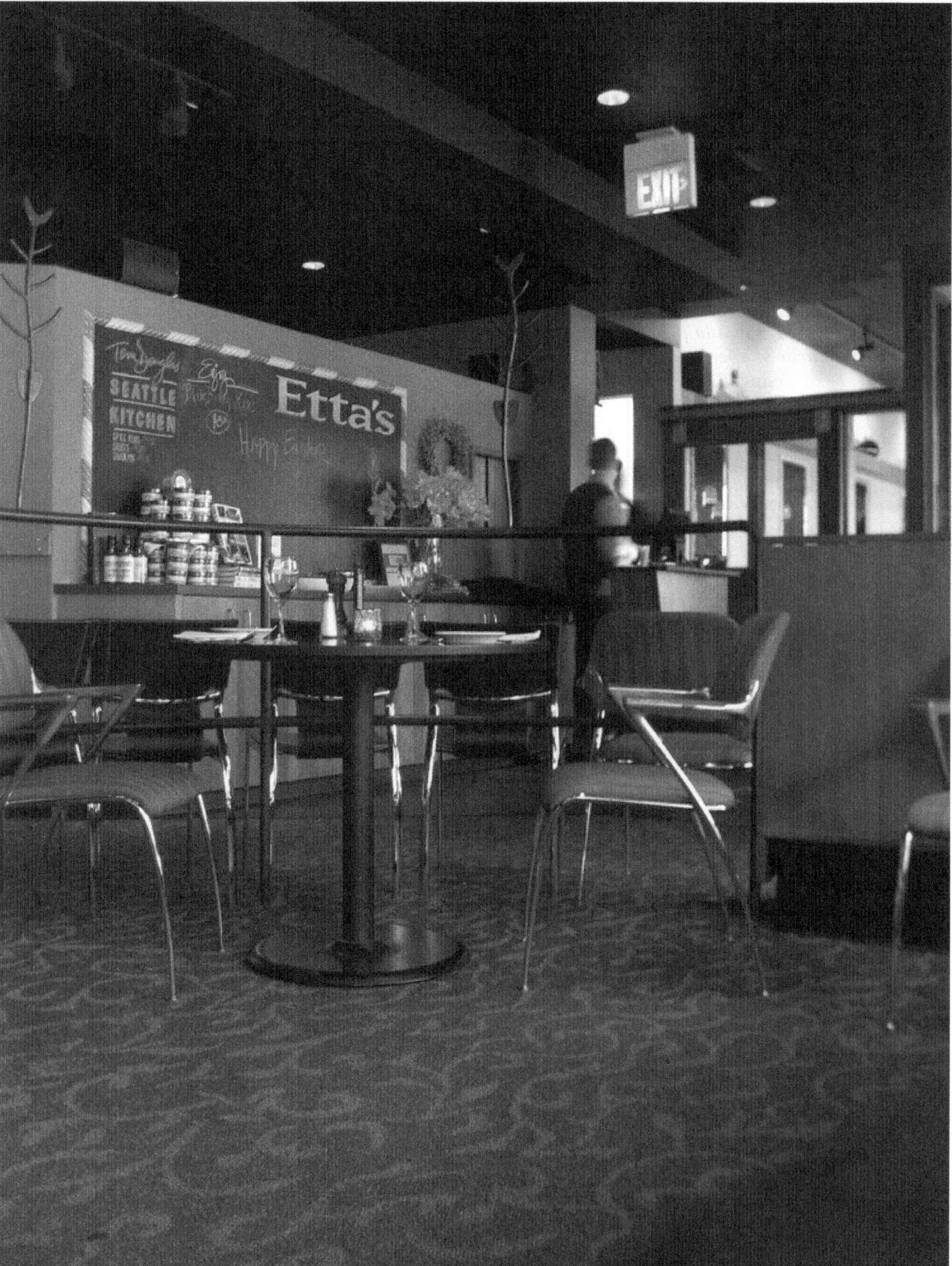
EXIT
SEATTLE
KITCHEN
Etta's

Crab Cakes

Etta's Seafood showcases the culinary flair of Chef Tom Douglas for every kind of seafood imaginable. From the classic fish & chips to live crab, pit-smoked salmon and Tom's famous crab cakes, Etta's extensive menu features superlative seafood. Situated near Seattle's famous Pike Place Market, Etta's Seafood offers both tourists and locals a rich experience of the best seafood in Seattle.

1 large egg yolk
1 tbsp cider vinegar
1 tbsp Dijon mustard
1 tbsp finely chopped red bell peppers
1 tbsp finely chopped onions
2 tsp chopped parsley
1 tsp Tabasco sauce
½ tsp paprika
½ tsp chopped fresh thyme
¼ tsp Kosher salt
¼ tsp fresh ground black pepper
¼ C. olive oil
¼ C. sour cream
1 lb. fresh Dungeness crabmeat, picked clean of shell and lightly squeezed if wet
4 C. fresh bread crumbs
3 tbsp chopped parsley
4 tbsp unsalted butter
lemon wedges, as garnish

1. In a food processor, combine egg yolk, vinegar, mustard, bell pepper, onion, parsley, Tabasco, paprika, thyme, salt, and pepper. Pulse to mince the vegetables and combine the ingredients.

2. With motor running, slowly add oil through the feed tube until the mixture emulsifies and forms a thin mayonnaise.

3. Transfer mayonnaise mixture to a large bowl and stir in sour cream, then carefully fold in crabmeat. Gently form into 8 crab cakes, about 3-inches across and ¾-inch thick.

4. Put the fresh bread crumbs in a shallow container and stir in parsley. Lightly dredge the crab cakes on both sides in the bread crumbs. Chill for at least 1 hour (preferably longer).

5. Put 2 large non-stick skillets over medium heat and add about 2 tablespoons butter to each pan.

6. When butter is melted, add 4 cakes to each pan. Gently fry until golden brown on both sides and hot through, turning once with a spatula, about 4 minutes on each side.

7. Serve 2 crab cakes per person, garnished with lemon wedges.

Etta's Seafood
2020 Western Avenue

"The sweetest honey is loathsome in his own deliciousness and in the taste confounds the appetite."
William Shakespeare

Ezell's
Famous Chicken
101

Spicy Southern Fried Chicken

Ezell's Famous Chicken has been bringing Seattle its best fried chicken for over 20 years. With a recipe right out of America's South and a genuine dedication to quality, we've won the chicken-hungry hearts of Seattleites and people the world over!

Marinade:
2½ lb. frying chicken
buttermilk
½ C. hot sauce (optional)

Spicy Egg Wash:
3 eggs
⅓ C. water
1 C. hot red pepper sauce (or to taste)

Breading Mix:
1 C. self-rising flour
½ C. corn meal
½ C. cracker meal
½ C. potato buds
Fried Chicken Seasoning, to taste (recipe below)
peanut or vegetable oil for frying

Fried Chicken Seasoning:
2 tbsp paprika
1 tbsp onion salt
1 tsp celery salt
1 tsp rubbed sage
1 tsp garlic powder
1 tsp ground allspice
1 tsp ground oregano
1 tsp chili powder
2 tsp black pepper
1 tsp basil leaves, crushed
1 tsp marjoram leaves, crushed finely
1 tsp thyme

Marinade:
1. Mix enough buttermilk with ½ cup of hot sauce (optional) to cover the chicken, and marinate the chicken overnight, preferably for 12 hours.

Spicy Egg Wash:
1. In a medium bowl, beat the eggs with the water. Add enough hot sauce so the egg mixture turns bright orange.

Breading Mix:
1. In a large bowl, combine the flour, corn meal, cracker meal, potato buds, and add some of the Fried Chicken Seasoning (to taste).

Fried Chicken Seasoning:
1. Combine all the ingredients together and mix well.

To Serve:
1. Season the buttermilk marinated chicken to taste with some of the Fried Chicken Seasoning.

2. Next, dip the chicken into the Breading Mix.

3. Then dip the chicken into the Spicy Egg Wash.

4. Dip the chicken a second time into the Breading Mix.

5. Heat the oil to 375°F in a deep pot, cast iron skillet, or fryer. Do not fill the pot or fryer more than ½ full with oil.

6. Fry the chicken in the oil until brown and crisp. For dark meat, about 13 to 14 minutes, white meat about 8 to 10 minutes. Fry the first couple of pieces, white and dark, one at a time, and sample to gauge cooking time.

Ezell's Chicken
11805 Renton Avenue South

"My dear boy, when curds are churned, the finest part rises upward and turns into butter. So too, dear boy, when food is eaten the choice parts rise upward and become mind."
Chandogya Upanishad

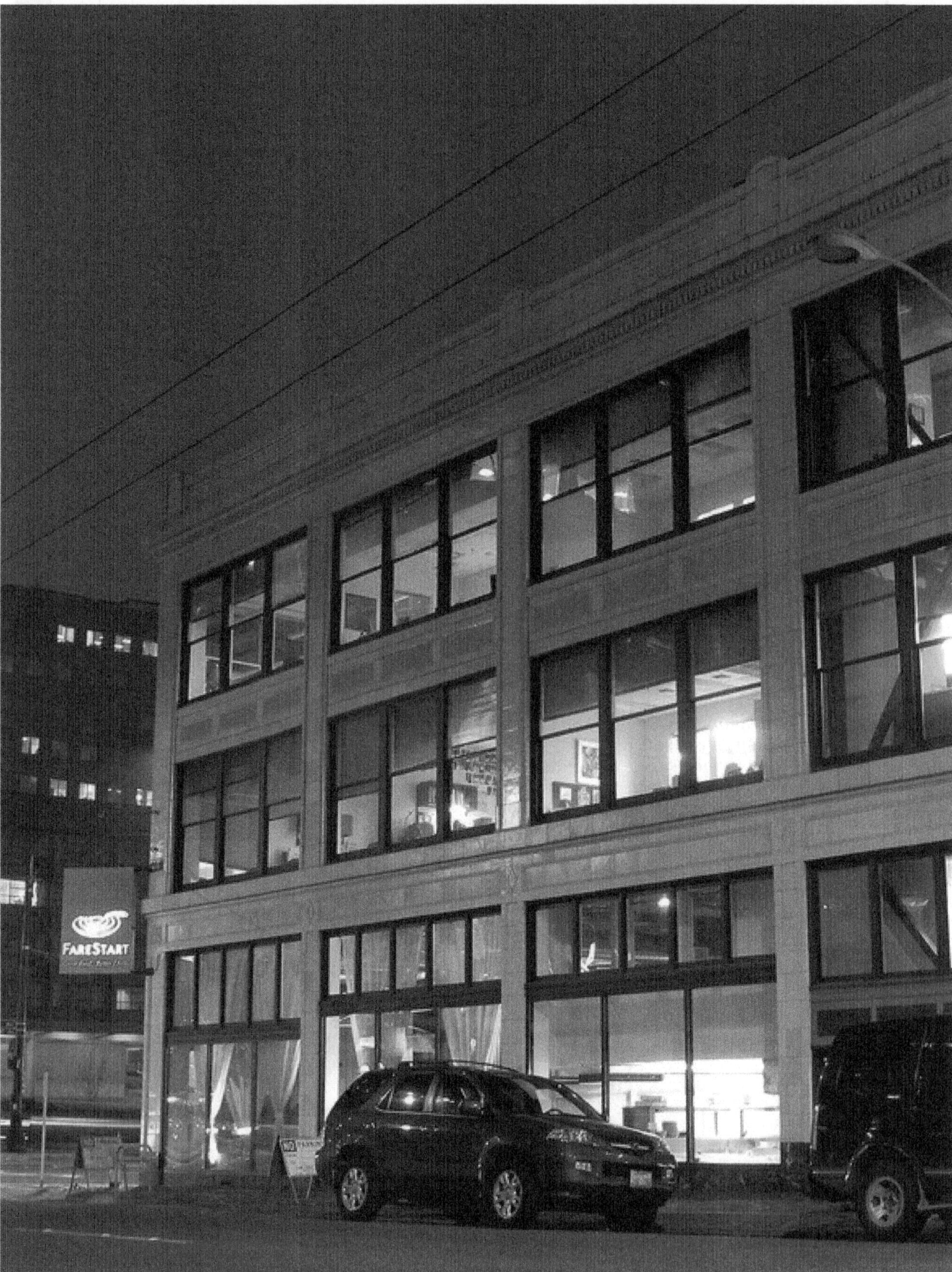
FARESTART

Vegetable Polenta Sunny-Side Up

FareStart is a culinary job training and placement program for homeless and disadvantaged individuals. Over the past 19 years, FareStart has provided opportunities for nearly 5,000 people to transform their lives, while also serving over 4.5 million meals to disadvantaged men, women, and children.

6 C. water (or vegetable or chicken stock)
2 tsp salt
1¼ C. yellow cornmeal (medium grind)
3 tbsp unsalted butter
½ C. grated parmesan cheese
4 eggs, cooked sunny-side up
1 C. packed kale, sautéed in oil with chopped garlic
marinara sauce
roasted vegetables and blue cheese, for topping

1. Bring 6 cups of water or stock to a boil in a large sauce pan. Add 2 teaspoons of salt. Gradually whisk in the cornmeal.

2. Reduce the heat to low and cook until the mixture thickens to desired consistency and the cornmeal is tender, stirring often, about 15-20 minutes.

3. Turn off the heat. Add the butter and cheese and stir until melted. Adjust seasoning as desired.

4. Spoon some polenta onto a plate and top each serving with warm marinara sauce, sautéed kale, and an egg, sunny-side up. Top with roasted vegetable and blue cheese, if desired.

FareStart
700 Virginia Street

"Food history is as important as a baroque church. Governments should recognize cultural heritage and protect traditional foods. A cheese is as worthy of preserving as a sixteenth-century building."
Carlo Petrini

Pancetta and Salmon Kebabs with Parsley Vinaigrette

As we move into our 15th year we still delight in the fact that every night at Flying Fish we have something new and exciting for our guests to discover. Whether it's Monkfish from Maine, Opaka Paka from Hawaii, or Steelhead from the Olympic Peninsula, we change our menu every day to provide our guests with what's fresh, what's in season and well…what just tastes really good. The idea for Flying Fish was born on a beach in Thailand. While traveling there I stopped for awhile on Koh Samui, an island in the Gulf of Thailand. There were several beach restaurants that served the catch-of-the-day simply grilled at tables perched in the sand on the water's edge. You could pick your fish out of the ice and it would reappear half an hour later in cooked form. It was so direct and so simple. It just seemed like a good idea.

5 tbsp good quality extra virgin olive oil, divided
2 tbsp good quality red wine vinegar
1 small garlic clove, minced
½ tsp kosher salt
½ tsp coarsely ground pepper, divided
1½ lb. skinned king or coho salmon fillet (1-inch thick), cut into 1½-inch chunks
4 oz. thinly sliced pancetta
3 tbsp coarsely chopped flat leaf parsley
bamboo skewers soaked in water for 30 minutes

1. Prepare the vinaigrette by combining 4 tbsp. oil, the vinegar, garlic, salt, and ¼ tsp. of pepper in a bowl. Set aside.

2. Heat grill to high (450-550°F). In a large bowl, combine remaining 1 tbsp. of oil with remaining ¼ tsp. of pepper. Turn salmon in oil to coat.

3. Set out rows of 3 salmon chunks on a work surface. Unroll pancetta slices into strips and wrap strips once or twice around salmon. Skewer each row of salmon leaving some space between the pieces of fish.

4. Oil cooking grate, using tongs and a piece of oiled paper towels. Set kebabs on grate, then grill, covered, turning once, until fish is barely cooked through, 4 minutes.

5. Arrange kebabs on plates. Stir parsley into the vinaigrette; spoon on top of kebabs. Serve with warm, crusty bread for dunking.

Flying Fish Restaurant

300 Westlake Avenue

"Nothing would be more tiresome than eating and drinking if God had not made them a pleasure as well as a necessity."
Voltaire

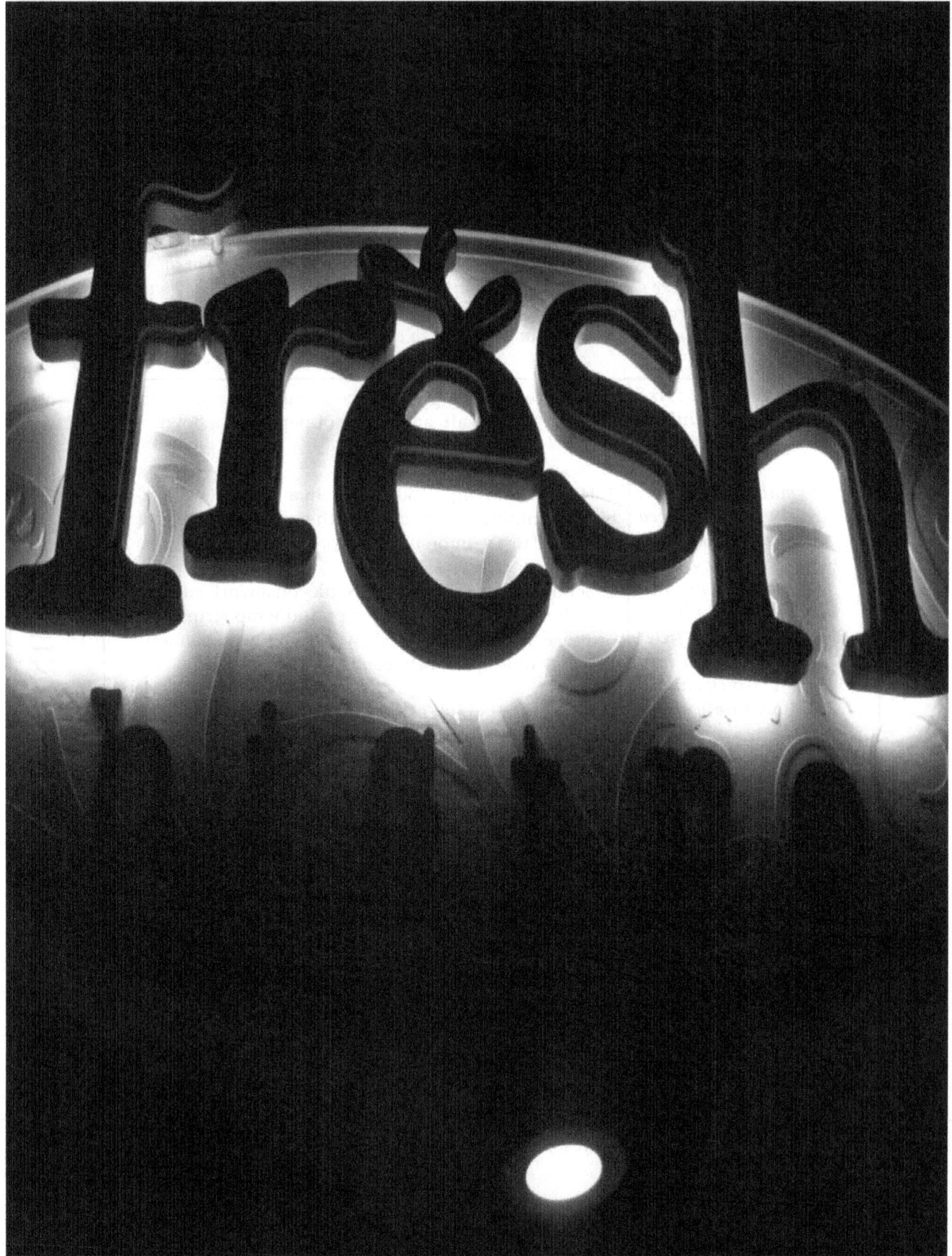
fresh

Star Anise-Brined Cornish Hens with a Quince Reduction

Fresh Bistro is the quintessential neighborhood restaurant: plates of fresh farm-to-table food, comfortable but not cutting-edge décor and a quiet, older lunch crowd make it a good choice when you're in the mood for relaxed, Northwest food without a fussy scene. There's nothing fussy about the ambiance, leaving room for you to focus on the plate: the food here is decidedly local and in-season, festooned with at least a half dozen ingredients. Mains are divided between classic comfort foods (spaghetti and meatballs and lamb burgers), more upscale seafood dishes (seared scallops with grapefruit beurre blanc) and vegetarian items (wild mushroom risotto with caramelized onions, smoked curado, and black garlic). Soups, sandwiches, and salads are offered at lunch, and patrons favor the pork belly slider during happy hour.

Brine:
2 C. vegetable stock, warmed
½ C. Kosher salt
1 C. ice water
2 pieces star anise
2 tbsp candied ginger

Quince Reduction:
(maybe be prepared ahead and reheated)
½ C. sugar
1 quince, seeded with skin on, medium dice
1 C. apple cider vinegar
1 C. chicken stock

2 Cornish game hens, each split in half
1 tbsp chopped thyme
2 tbsp olive oil
2 tbsp butter
salt and pepper, to taste

Brine:
1. In a gallon-size bucket or other large container, combine warm vegetable stock, salt, star anise, and candied ginger, and stir to dissolve salt.
2. Add ice water and game hens to the brine and place in refrigerator for up to 3 hours.

Quince Reduction:
1. Put sugar in a medium-sized sauce pan and cook over medium-high heat until the sugar begins to caramelize, stirring slowly to keep the sugar from burning. Once the sugar turns golden brown, add the quince and cook for 3-5 minutes.
2. Add vinegar and chicken stock and simmer sauce until it is reduced by 25 percent. You will end up with a syrup-like sauce. Let it cool, then transfer to a blender and puree until smooth. Pass sauce through a strainer and set aside.
3. Before removing the hens from the brine, preheat oven to 425°F. Pat hens completely dry with paper towels and season lightly with salt and pepper.
4. In a hot, medium-size sauté pan set over medium-high heat, drizzle oil, and place hens in the hot pan, breast-side down, and fry for 2 minutes.
5. Turn birds breast-side up and sprinkle the thyme on the hens. Add butter to the pan and put it in the oven. Cook, basting occasionally with the butter, until the hens reach an internal temperature of 160°F. Remove from the oven and let rest for 3-5 minutes.
6. Place hens on plates, breast-side up, and drizzle re-heated quince reduction over the top.

Fresh Bistro
4725 42nd Avenue

"Shipping is a terrible thing to do to vegetables. They probably get jet-lagged, just like people."
Elizabeth Berry

Georgian Lobster Bisque

The Georgian, now celebrating its 20th year rated as a AAA 4 Diamond restaurant, features French-inspired Northwest cuisine prepared by Executive Chef Gavin Stephenson in Seattle's premier dining room. The Georgian offers The Petite, an exclusive private dining room with seating for up to twelve guests, which is perfect for an intimate get together. The Georgian also features live jazz music Friday and Saturday evenings from 6:00 pm to 10:00 pm.

2 crushed lobster bodies
2 tbsp olive oil
½ C. celery
½ C. onion
½ C. carrot
1 tbsp fresh tarragon
2 sprigs fresh thyme
1 oz. tomato paste
¼ C. rice
2 oz. cognac
5 C. reduced lobster stock or water
½ C. heavy cream

1. In large sauce pot, add olive oil and sauté crushed lobster bodies over medium-high heat until all liquid is reduced.

2. Lower heat to medium and add celery, onion, carrot, tarragon, and thyme and cook until vegetables are lightly caramelized, being careful not to burn.

3. Add tomato paste and cook for 10 minutes.

4. Deglaze pot with cognac, reduce.

5. Add rice and lobster stock and simmer for 1 hour.

6. Finish with heavy cream and simmer bisque for 20 minutes and strain through cheesecloth.

The Georgian Restaurant
411 University Street

"No man in the world has more courage than the man who can stop after eating one peanut."
Channing Pollock

BON BON CHICKEN & NOODLE SALAD

We are a fresh, locally grown company dedicated to the craft of artisan baking and scratch cooking. Led by a unique mixture of family and friends along with some of the region's most talented bakers and cooks, Grand Central Bakery features a vibrant wholesale artisan bread line and a friendly collection of neighborhood bakeries in Seattle and Portland. The best way to get to know us is by eating our products. Visit one of our neighborhood bakeries, eat at a restaurant that serves Grand Central bread or find us at your favorite grocer. One delicious bite will reveal everything you need to know!

3 lb. chicken breast, boneless, skinless
as needed, water to cover

Pasta:
2 gallons water
¼ C. kosher salt
¾ lb. linguini, dry
¾ tbsp peanut oil

Bon Bon Sauce:
¼ C. ginger, fresh, minced
¼ C. garlic, fresh, minced
1¼ tbsp white pepper, ground
1¼ tbsp Kosher salt
2 C. creamy peanut butter
1 C. soy sauce
1 C. cider vinegar
6 tbsp sesame oil
2 tbsp hot pepper oil

½ C. granulated sugar
1½ lb. English cucumber cut in long julienne
1½ C. fresh cilantro leaves
1½ C. scallion, ½-inch bias-sliced

Chicken:
1. Place chicken in a large pot and pour water over to cover chicken by 1 inch. Place on medium-high heat and bring to a boil. Reduce heat and simmer until chicken is cooked through (to a minimun internal temperature of 165°F).
2. Remove chicken and discard the water. Cool and cut chicken into ½-inch long strips.

Pasta:
1. Add water and salt to a large pot and bring to a boil over high heat.
2. Add linguini and return to a boil, stirring to separate strands of pasta. Cook for 8-10 minutes until pasta is cooked al dente. Drain; rinse well with cold water. Toss pasta with oil and refrigerate.

Bon Bon Sauce:
1. Combine all ingredients in a blender or food processor fitted with a metal blade. Pulse for 15-20 seconds and scrape down the sides. Purèe to a smooth consistency. Chill in the refrigerator.

To Serve:
1. Arrange 4 oz. pasta on a plate and place a nest of 1 oz. of cucumber in the center. Top cucumber with 1½ oz. of shredded chicken and drizzle 3 tbsp. of Bon Bon Sauce over salad.
2. Garnish with 1 tbsp. each of cilantro leaves and scallion.
3. Serve immediately.

GRAND CENTRAL BAKERY
1616 EASTLAKE AVENUE

"It would be nice if the Food and Drug Administration stopped issuing warnings about toxic substances and just gave me the names of one or two things still safe to eat."
Robert Fuoss

VINE

Cabello de Angel

With just eight counter stools and a half-dozen chairs around three tiny tables, seating demand far outstrips supply. Regulars don't seem to mind standing around sipping sherry until seats open up, and many spurn opportunities for table seats because they want to sit at the counter, inches away from the affable owner, Joseba Jimenez de Jimenez, while he prepares the tapas.

1 spaghetti squash
2 to 3 C. sugar
1 lemon
2 cinnamon sticks

1. Cut the spaghetti squash in half and scoop out the seeds. Put in a pot and cover completely with water. Cook over high heat just until the water is at a bare simmer.

2. Remove one of the halves of squash and test with a fork to see if the stringy pulp can be scraped out. If the squash is too hard, return it to the water and cook just until it can be scraped from the outer shell. The strands will be al dente.

3. Put the the stringy pulp into a heavy-bottomed pot. Zest the lemon over the pot. Juice the lemon and add the strained juice. Add the sugar and cinnamon sticks. Allow this mixture to sit a few minutes until the squash releases some of its water to help dissolve the sugar. Cook over medium heat, stirring occasionally until the strands turn glassy. Taste for sweetness and texture. Adjust as necessary.

NOTE: With the larger amount of sugar, the preserves will last for about 2 months in the refrigerator, less if the lower amount is used.

Harvest Vine
2701 East Madison Street

"Good to eat, and wholesome to digest, as a worm to a toad, a toad to a snake, a snake to a pig, a pig to a man, and a man to a worm."
Ambrose Bierce

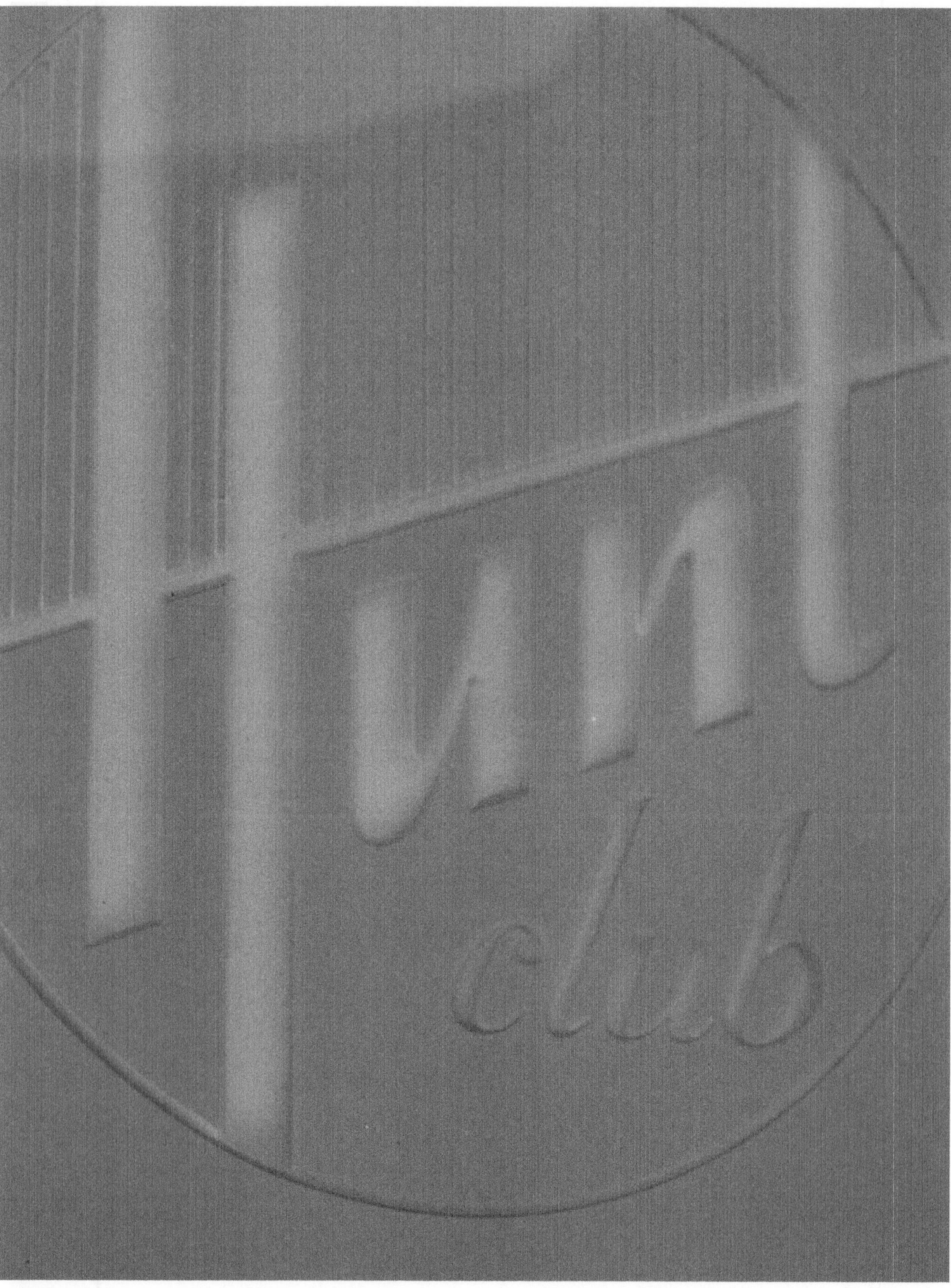
club

Grilled New York Steak with Fingerling Potatoes and Glazed Carrots

Beautiful mahogany pillars draped with silk curtains falling into deep folds give this hotel-based institution a rich, quiet elegance not found in most of Seattle's dining establishments. Voices – even from the staff – are quiet and pleasant; if there's a party happening, chances are it's a private affair, not a happy hour.

Hunt Club at the Sorrento Hotel
900 Madison Street

4 to 6 (10-oz.) New York strip steaks
3 lb. tri-colored fingerling potatoes
olive oil
¼ C. chopped thyme, rosemary, and sage
2 tbsp butter
3 lb. baby carrots
1 tsp chopped garlic
1 tsp chopped shallots
¼ C. chicken stock

1. Wash potatoes, cut them in half and blanch. Allow time for potatoes to dry before final cooking. Set aside.

2. Place baby carrots in cool, salted water and boil. Cook until tender and the peels wipe off with rough side of a kitchen towel. Cool carrots in ice water and pat dry. Set aside.

3. Preheat grill for steaks. While the steaks are on the grill, heat two large sauté pans to medium heat and pour a thin layer of olive oil into each pan.

4. When you turn the steaks for the first time, place the potatoes into one pan. Turn the flame to high until the pan regains temperature and then turn back to medium heat and add chopped herbs and butter.

5. In the other sauté pan, toss in the chopped garlic and shallots followed by the carrots.

6. After flipping the steaks, add the chicken stock and butter to the carrots and reduce the heat until they have a nice glaze.

7. Serve steaks with potatoes and baby carrots.

"We are all dietetic sinners; only a small percent of what we eat nourishes us; the balance goes to waste and loss of energy."
William Osler

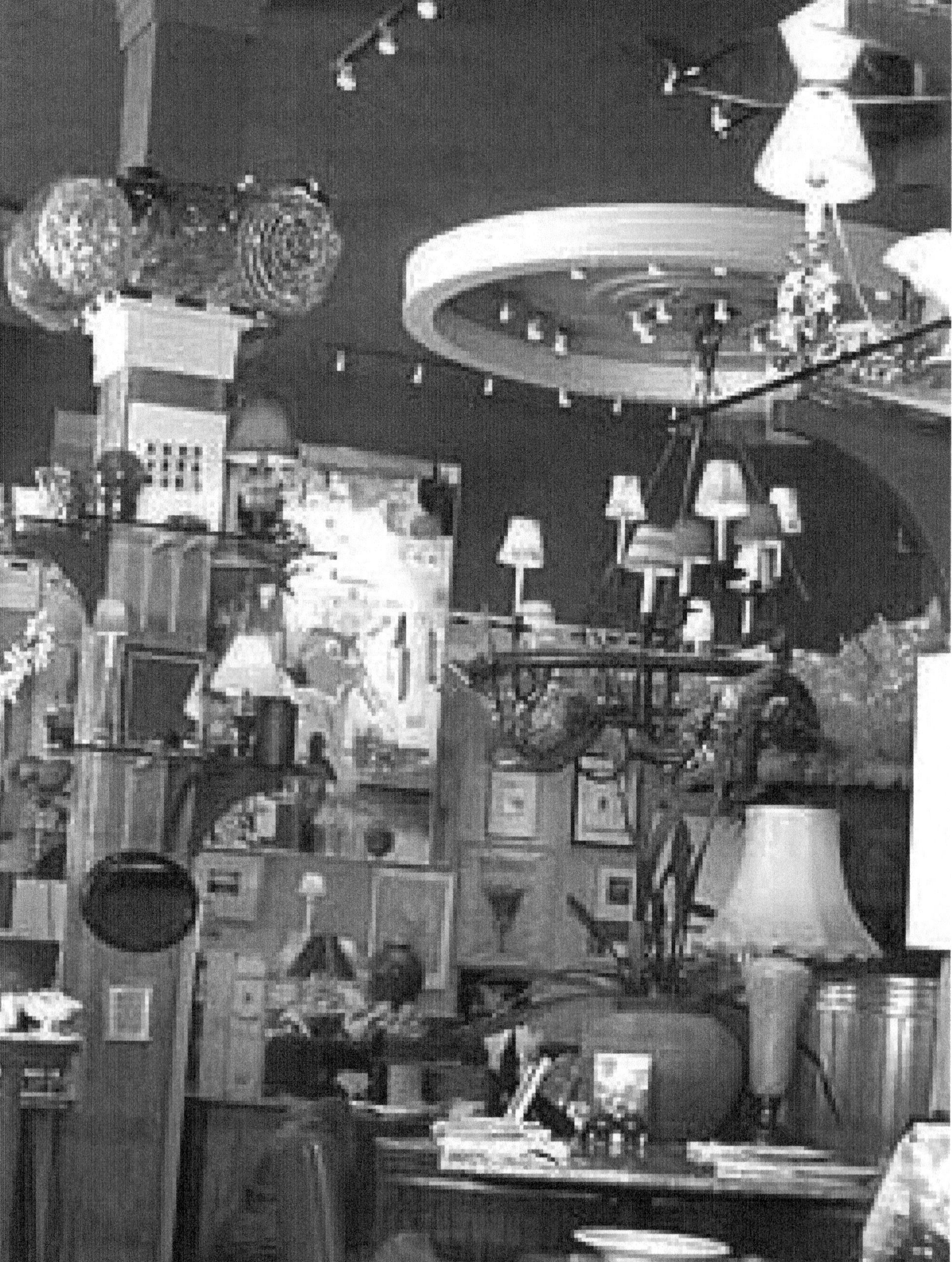

Candy Cane Cake

The Icon Grill is the ultimate destination for comfort food – in the style of the 60's – with a modern twist. The service is impeccable, and yes, the hostess will open the door for you and treat you as if you are the owner of the restaurant.

White Chocolate Cake:
2 oz. white chocolate
4 tbsp unsalted butter
¾ C. sugar
½ tsp vanilla extract
1 C.+ 2 tbsp sifted cake flour
½ tbsp baking powder
¼ tsp salt
2 egg whites
⅓ C. + 2 tbsp milk

Red Velvet Cake:
1 tsp white vinegar
1 tsp baking soda
1½ C. sugar
½ C. unsalted butter, softened
2 eggs
1 tsp cocoa powder
1 tsp salt
1 tsp vanilla extract
1¼ C. sifted cake flour
1 C. buttermilk
3 tbsp red food coloring

Peppermint Cream Cheese Frosting:
1 lb. cream cheese
½ lb. unsalted butter
2 lb. confectioners' sugar
1 tsp peppermint extract

Peppermint Simple Syrup:
½ C. boiling water
½ C. sugar
¼ C. peppermint schnapps

Assembly:
½ C. crushed peppermint candies
mint leaves
maraschino cherries, with stems

White Chocolate Cake:
1. Preheat oven to 300°F. Melt white chocolate in a small glass bowl over a pan of simmering water. Set aside to cool. Whip butter and sugar until fluffy with an electric mixer. Add vanilla and mix thoroughly. Sift together flour, baking powder, and salt in another bowl. Add egg whites to butter and sugar mixture and mix on low speed. Add half the milk and mix on low speed. Scrape the bottom of the bowl with a spatula. Add the remaining sifted flour mixture, a little at a time, then add the remaining milk. Do not over mix. Slowly pour in the melted white chocolate with the mixer on low speed. Pour batter into one 9-inch buttered and floured cake pan. Bake for 25-35 minutes or until a cake tester comes out clean. Place on a cooling rack.

Red Velvet Cake:
1. Preheat oven to 300°F. Mix vinegar and baking soda and let settle; set aside. Cream together butter and sugar until fluffy, scraping down the sides of the bowl thoroughly. Add eggs, one at a time, allowing each addition to mix completely before adding the next. Add cocoa, salt, and vanilla and beat until fluffy. Alternately mix in flour and buttermilk. Stir in red food coloring until well combined. Fold in vinegar mixture at the end. Pour batter into one 9-inch buttered and floured cake pan and bake for 40-45 minutes. Rotate cake as necessary during baking, cooking until a cake tester comes out clean.

Peppermint Cream Cheese Frosting:
1. Beat butter and cream cheese in an electric mixer until light and fluffy. Scrape the sides of the bowl. Begin adding the powered sugar on low speed, mixing thoroughly before the next addition. Finish by adding the peppermint extract and whip for 10 minutes on high speed.

Peppermint Simple Syrup:
1. Pour boiling water over sugar and schnapps and mix until sugar is dissolved. Cool completely.

Assembly:
1. Cool both cake layers thoroughly and cut each horizontally into 3 equal sized parts, for a total of 6 layers. Place a layer on a serving platter and lightly brush with the peppermint simple syrup. Frost, repeat for all layers and frost the outside of the cake. Garnish with peppermint candies and use mint leaves and stemmed maraschino cherries to create a "holly effect."

ICON GRILL
1933 5TH AVENUE

"A bad review is like baking a cake with all the best ingredients and having someone sit on it."
Danielle Steele

Clam Chowder

The Northwest dining legacy that is Ivar's began in 1938 with one very entrepreneurial spirit, the late Ivar Haglund. His future in music and entertaining took a slight detour when his waterfront aquarium needed a venue to feed its guests. Using his classic Northwest seafood recipes, Ivar's was born. This dining destination has since spawned many more restaurants to delight future generations. View the Ivar's timeline, see "our flounder's" wacky and never-ending promotional antics, and take a glimpse at Ivar's amazing, full life.

2 (6½-oz.) cans minced clams
1 C. finely chopped onions
1 C. finely diced celery
2 C. finely diced potatoes
¾ C. butter
¾ C. flour
4 C. warmed half and half
1 tsp. salt, to taste
1 dash pepper, to taste
¼ to ½ tsp sugar

1. Open the canned clams and drain the juice into a medium sauce pan. Set the reserved clams aside.

2. Add the onions, celery, and potatoes, to the sauce pan with clam juice and add enough water to just cover solids. Simmer, covered, over medium heat until the potatoes are tender, about 20 minutes.

3. Meanwhile, in a large sauce pan melt the butter over medium heat, then stir in the flour and cook until it becomes a roux and is golden.

4. Gradually whisk the half and half into the roux. Cook, whisking, until smooth and thick, about 5 minutes. (for a thinner chowder add ½ to ¾ C. water, chicken broth, or clam broth.)

5. Add the cooked vegetables with their liquid, the reserved clams, salt, pepper, and sugar. Stir well to combine and adjust seasonings to taste.

Ivar's
13448 Aurora Avenue N

"The greatest delight the fields and woods minister is the suggestion of an occult relation between man and the vegetable. I am not alone and unacknowledged. They nod to me and I to them."
Ralph Waldo Emerson

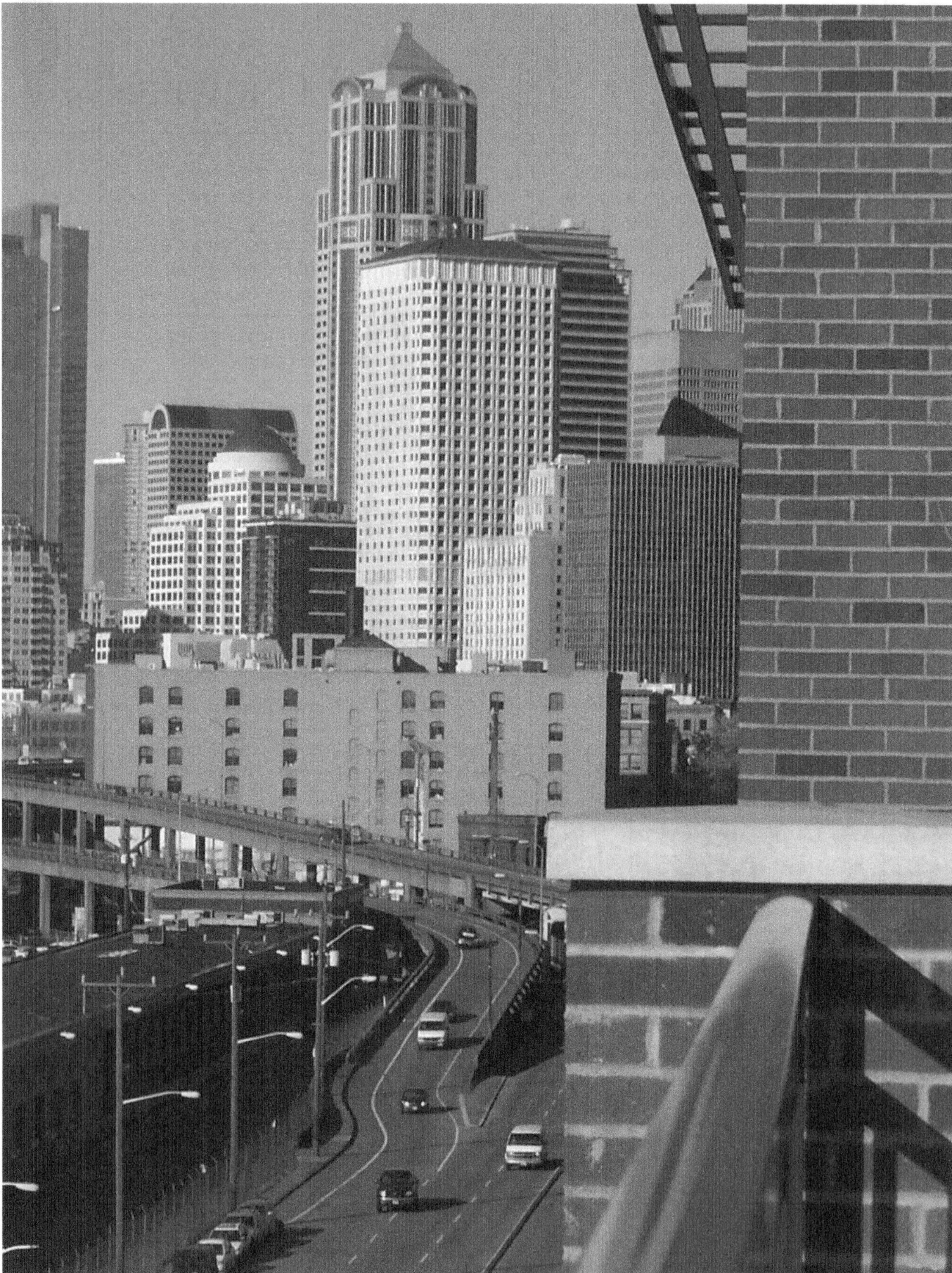

Bacon Wrapped Hot Dog

Founded in 1980, Silver Cloud Inns & Hotels is proud to celebrate over 30 years of providing outstanding guest service. Following the simple premise of offering our guests "Friendliness and Cleanliness", we have become the symbol of hospitality in the Pacific Northwest. Our reputation in these two areas exemplifies why our guests return again and again. Silver Cloud Inns & Hotels remain locally owned and operated and we continue to put extraordinary customer service and trust at the center of all we do.

1 Premium Beef Hot Dog
2 slices of applewood bacon, thick-sliced
1 whole wheat hot dog bun
3 oz. mozzarella cheese
1 tbsp herbed butter
2 oz. caramelized fennel and onions

Caramelized Fennel and Onions:
¼ C. onions, sliced
¼ C. fennel bulb, sliced
2 tbsp oil
salt and pepper, to taste

1. Brush herbed butter on the inside of the bun and toast in a frying pan.

2. Wrap 1-2 slices of bacon around the hot dog, affixing with wodden toothpicks.

3. Deep fry the hot dog until internal temperature of 150ºF is reached.

4. Remove toothpicks and place bacon-wrapped hot dog in the toasted bun.

5. Top with mozzarella cheese and place under a broiler to brown.

6. Serve hot dog with caramelized fennel and onions and fries as a side.

Caramelized Fennel and Onions:
1. In a medium sauté pan, caramelize the onions, fennel, and oil over medium heat, about 15 minutes.

Jimmy's at the Silver Cloud
Multiple Locations Around the City

"Only in America do we buy hot dogs in packages of ten and buns in packages of eight."
American quote

Asparagus with Green Garlic and Duck Eggs

Every aspect of Joule's food shows the chefs' care. Their branzino, a Mediterranean sea bass, is grilled until its flesh firms up and the skin crackles; then they set a translucent ring of potent black-olive tapenade and pickled green grapes in orbit around it. Their bison hanger steak is grilled to the perfect point between rare and medium-rare, sliced on the bias into even one-half-inch slices, and set on a pool of emerald green chimichurri sauce – and fine shavings of pickled garlic are appointed at just the right frequency to add one sliver to every slice.

1 large bunch asparagus, ends trimmed
½ C. soy sauce
¼ C. rice vinegar
1 tbsp sesame oil
1 tsp smoked chili paste or crushed chili flakes
2 tbsp canola oil, divided
3 bulbs green garlic, white parts only, thinly sliced
4 duck eggs

1. Blanch asparagus spears in a large pot of salted boiling water for 2 minutes; set aside.

2. Whisk soy sauce, rice vinegar, sesame oil, and chili paste (or chili flakes) together in a small bowl; set aside.

3. Heat a large skillet over medium-high heat. When hot, add 1 tbsp. canola oil, then add the garlic and sauté for a few minutes until soft. Add asparagus and cook for about 1 minute, shaking the pan until warmed through.

4. Meanwhile, in another pan, cook duck eggs sunny-side up in the remaining oil.

5. Arrange asparagus on plates, top with eggs, and drizzle sauce on top.

Joule Restaurant
1913 North 45th Street

"The way you cut your meat reflects the way you live."
Confucius

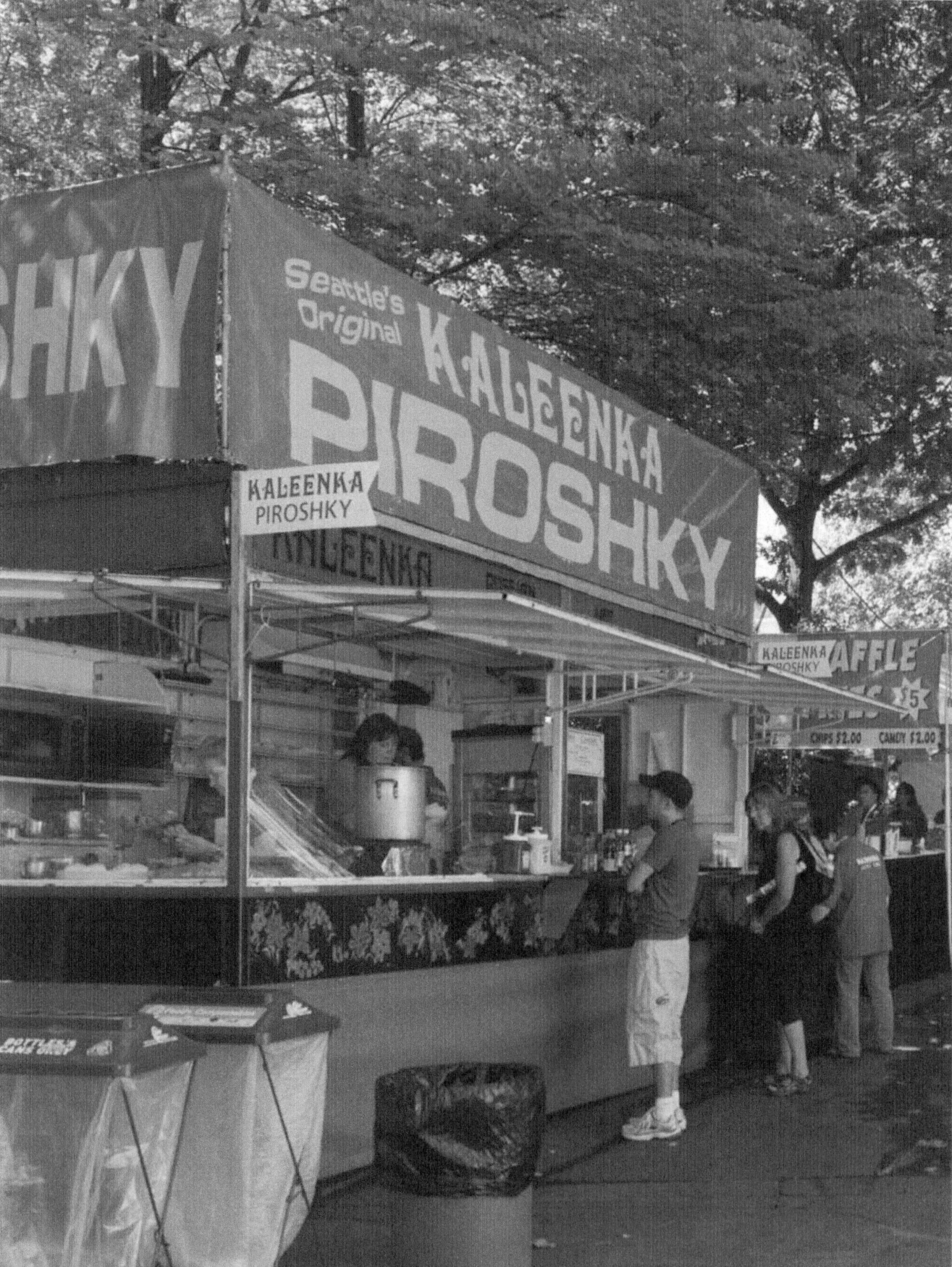
SHKY
Seattle's Original
KALEENKA
PIROSHKY
KALEENKA
PIROSHKY
KALEENKA
$5
CHIPS $2.00
CANDY $2.00

THE KALEENKA PIROSHKY

Seattle's Kaleenka Piroshky has become a favorite food at Washington State festivals for nearly 30 years. Freshly made bread dough and authentic fillings have earned the Kaleenka many "Best Entree" awards. The business is run by Steven, Lydia's youngest, and he is known as the Piroshky Guy; a name that was given to him by many happy customers. His family and wonderful Russian team help Steven run the business.

Dough:
1 (½-oz.) package dry yeast
¼ C. warm water
2 tbsp sugar
1 tsp salt
1½ C. milk
1 egg
¼ C. oil or ¼ C. butter
4½ C. flour

Filling:
2 tbsp butter
1 medium onion, chopped
1 garlic clove, minced
2 lb. ground beef
1 garlic clove, minced
salt
pepper

1 egg, beaten

Dough:
1. Dissolve yeast in water and let stand 10 minutes.
2. In a large bowl, combine flour, sugar, and salt. Make a well in the flour and add milk, egg, oil, and yeast. Combine to make a soft dough. Knead about 10 minutes. Return to the bowl and let dough rise 30 mintues to 1 hour.

Filling:
1. Melt butter in a medium sauté pan and brown chopped onion and garlic.
2. In another pan, brown the ground beef. Season with salt, pepper and add the browned garlic and onion. Cool meat mixture and remove solidified fat.

Assembly:
1. Pinch a golf-ball sized piece of dough, flatten with fingers or roll out to ⅛-thickness. Place 2 tbsp filling in center and bring opposite edges of circle together. Pinch securely to seal edges. (The traditional shape is a plump center with tapering ends.).
2. Let piroshkys rise seam-side down for 30 minutes.

To Cook:
1. Preheat oven to 350°F.
2. Brush piroshkys with egg and bake until golden brown and heated through, about 20 minutes depending on size.

NOTE: The piroshkys may also be deep fried in 350°F oil until golden (omit egg wash).

KALEENKA
MULTIPLE LOCATIONS

"The olive tree is surely the richest gift of Heaven, I can scarcely expect bread."
Thomas Jefferson

Kaspar's
BlueWing PHOTOS

Duck Breast with Grape and Black Peppercorn Sauce

Family owned and operated, Kaspar's Special Events & Catering is celebrating our 20th Anniversary this year! Our passion is to provide creative, fresh cuisine and superior service at a reasonable price. We cater to groups of all sizes, both within Kaspar's as well as off-site including private homes and other locations. We know our success is based on your success so we take the time to understand the special intricacies necessary to exceed your expectations and create an extraordinary experience you and your guests will always remember.

4 (7-oz.) Muscovy duck breasts
salt and pepper, to taste
1 tbsp olive oil
1 tbsp shallots, finely chopped
1 tsp black peppercorns, crushed
⅓ C. port wine
⅔ C. demi-glace
1 tsp honey
20 green California seedless grapes, halved

1. Season duck breasts with salt and pepper.

2. Heat olive oil in a frying pan over medium heat. Sauté duck breast, skin-side down, for approximately 7 minutes or until skin is golden brown and crispy. Turn duck breast over and sauté for 4 minutes. Remove duck from pan, set aside, and keep warm.

3. Discard fat from pan and place shallots and peppercorns in frying pan and deglaze with port wine, add the demi-glace and simmer until sauce is reduced by half.

4. Add honey and grapes to sauce and pour over duck breasts.

NOTE: The duck breast should still be a little pink in the middle. If you desire it well done, simmer duck breast in the sauce for a few more minutes. May be served either in one piece or sliced in thirds.

Kaspar's
19 W Harrison Street

"This is every cook's opinion—no savory dish without an onion, but lest your kissing should be spoiled your onions must be fully boiled."
Jonathan Swift

THE
KINGFISH
CAFE & PUB
KINGFISH
CAFE
NO
DRINKS
OUTSIDE

Coconut Cake

Southern cooking is a testament to both our past and present. Reunions, holidays, and other special occasions are times when the menu is just as important as the guest list. With that in mind, during the spring of 1997, we opened The Kingfish Café – a tribute to our family and the food we grew up on. The restaurant name comes from George "Kingfish" Stevens, a character on the 1950's Television show Amos 'n Andy; his business ventures were many, and often chaotic, but always comical. Like "Kingfish," we encountered a myriad of challenges on our journey, but the largest was our lack of restaurant experience and formal culinary training.

2¾ C. all-purpose flour
1 tsp baking powder
½ tsp baking soda
½ tsp salt
1¾ C. sugar
1 C. unsalted butter, softened
1 C. canned sweetened cream of coconut (such as Coco Lopez)
¼ C. fresh squeezed orange juice
4 large eggs, separated
1 tsp vanilla extract
1 C. buttermilk
pinch of salt

Cream Cheese Frosting:
2 (8-oz.) packages of cream cheese, softened
½ C. butter, softened
2 C. sifted confectioners' sugar
1 tsp vanilla extract
4 C. sweetened shredded coconut

1. Preheat oven to 350°F. Butter and flour two 9-inch cake pans with 2-inch-high sides.
2. In a medium bowl, whisk flour, baking powder, baking soda, and ½ tsp. salt together.
3. Using an electric mixer, beat together sugar, butter, sweetened cream of coconut, and orange juice in large bowl until fluffy.
4. Beat in egg yolks and vanilla extract.
5. On low speed, add in dry ingredients until just blended. Then mix in buttermilk until just blended.
6. Using clean, dry beaters, beat egg whites with a pinch of salt in another large bowl until stiff but not dry. Fold beaten egg whites into batter.
7. Divide cake batter between prepared pans. Bake cakes until tester inserted into center comes out clean, about 45 minutes. Cool cakes in pans on rack 10 minutes. Run small sharp knife around pan sides to loosen cakes. Turn cakes out onto racks and cool completely.
8. Place 1 cake layer on cake plate. Spread 1 C. Cream Cheese Frosting over cake layer. Sprinkle 1 C. sweetened shredded coconut over. Top with second cake layer. Spread remaining frosting over top and sides of cake.
9. Sprinkle remaining coconut over cake, gently pressing into sides to adhere. (Coconut Cake can be prepared up to 1 day ahead. Cover with plastic wrap and refrigerate. Let stand at room temperature 2 hours before serving.)

Cream Cheese Frosting:
1. Beat the cream cheese and butter together with a mixer until light and fluffy. Mix in the vanilla. Stir in the confectioners' sugar until smooth. Refrigerate until ready to use.

Kingfish Café
602 19th Avenue East

"We are living in a world today where lemonade is made from artificial flavors and furniture polish is made from real lemons."
Alfred E. Newman

cuisine of oaxaca, mexico

LA CARTA DE OAXACA

TAQUERIA · TEQUILA

5431 ballard ave

www.lacartadeoaxaca.com

Mole Negro

La Carta serves one of the most authentic delicious Mexican food in Seattle. Great food, good atmosphere, great location, and super cheerful bartender and waiter. La Carta de Oaxaca offers an authentic flavor of Oaxaca Mexico with traditional dishes like albondigas, tacos carne asada and mole negro Oaxaqueno, the house specialty. An excellent break from all of the other Mexican restaurants in town that seem to serve the same stuff from the same region of Mexico.

8 mulato chiles
8 pasilla mexicano chiles
4 chilhuacle chiles
4 tbsp lard
¼ C. raisins
¼ C. almonds
¼ C. pecans
¼ C. peanuts with skins
¼ C. pumpkin seeds
¼ C. sesame seeds
2 cinnamon sticks
¼ tsp anise
3 whole cloves
¼ tsp cumin
3 whole black peppercorns
4 slices of egg bread (semisweet), torn in pieces
2 plantains, sliced
¼ tsp dried thyme
¼ tsp dried marjoram
¼ tsp dried oregano
1 tomato, roasted
3 tomatillos, roasted
3 cloves of garlic, roasted
½ medium onion, roasted
4 C. chicken broth
3 tbsp sugar
½ C. Oaxacan chocolate
4 avocado leaves
salt, to taste
8 pcs. of boiled chicken

1. Clean the dried chilies with a damp cloth. Open the chilies by making a lengthwise slit down one side. Take out the seeds, veins, and stems.

2. Heat 3 tablespoons of the lard in a sauce pan and then fry the chilies. Remove chilies as soon as they begin to change color and become crispy; place in a bowl lined with paper towels.

3. In another pan, heat the remaining lard and fry the raisins until they puff up and brown a bit. Remove the raisins and then add the almonds, pecans, and peanuts; fry for 5 minutes until they are dark brown. Remove from the pan. Fry the pumpkin seeds, sesame seeds, cinnamon, anise, cloves, cumin, and black peppercorns in the same pan until they are dark brown. Remove from the pan and then fry the bread pieces in the remaining hot lard and remove.

4. Fry the plantains in a new pan in clean oil until they are golden.

5. Place the thyme, marjoram, oregano, roasted tomato and tomatillos, garlic, 1 plantain, and 1 C. of chicken broth into a blender. Blend until smooth. Place in bowl and set aside.

6. Place the fried chiles and 1½ C. of chicken broth into the blender, and blend into a smooth paste.

7. Pour remaining lard from the pan into a deep pot, heat and then add the blended chilies. Cook for 3 minutes; then add the spice and nut mixtures and bread and cook for 3 minutes more. Add the sugar and chocolate and stir, cook for 5 minutes until chocolate is melted.

8. When fat rises to the top of the mixture, add the rest of the chicken broth and the avocado leaves. Season with salt. Cook the mole negro for 3 minutes over medium heat.

9. Add chicken pieces before serving and garnish with remaining plantain slices.

La Carta De Oaxaca
5431 Ballard Avenue

"There is one thing more exasperating than a wife who can cook and won't, and that's a wife who can't cook and will."
Robert Frost

la Spiga

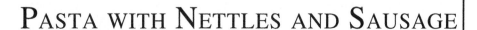

Pasta with Nettles and Sausage

Renowned for its Northern Italian cuisine, La Spiga is authentic enough in both food and ambiance to make you feel a wave of nostalgia, even if you've never been to Emilia-Romagna. Chef and co-owner Sabrina Tinsley crafts the Romagnola cuisine to make it genuine, yet hers alone. Using the very finest ingredients, menus are changed seasonally to reflect what is freshest in local markets. As co-owner and host Pietro Borghesi says, "An evening at La Spiga is like dining in Italy – without the plane fare."

1 lb. fresh nettles
2 tbsp olive oil
1 medium onion, finely chopped
2 cloves garlic, sliced
4 thin slices (about ¼ lb.) pancetta, cut into strips
2 mild Italian sausages without fennel (about ½ lb.), casing removed
28 oz. can whole peeled tomatoes
2-4 C. chicken broth
1 lb. bite-sized pasta, such as penne
salt, pepper, and cayenne pepper, to taste

1. Bring a large pot of water to a boil. Wearing kitchen gloves or with tongs, dump the nettles into the water without touching them. Cook, stirring with tongs, for a few minutes, until wilted, at which point they will be safe to touch. Drain, cool, and squeeze the water out of them. Coarsely chop and set aside.
2. Heat a large high-sided sauce pan (or heavy soup pot) over low heat. Add olive oil, then onion and garlic, and cook, stirring frequently, until tender and translucent.
3. Increase heat to medium, add pancetta, and cook, stirring, for about 5 minutes, until the pancetta begins to crisp.
4. Crumble the sausage into the pan in bite-sized pieces and cook, stirring occasionally and breaking up the sausage with a spoon, for 10 minutes, or until cooked through.
5. Drain the tomato juices into the pan. Pour canned tomatoes into a medium-size bowl crush them into small pieces. Add tomatoes to the pan along with the reserved nettles and 2 C. of the chicken broth. Cook until the tomatoes break down and the nettles are tender, about 30 to 40 minutes, adding broth as necessary to maintain a thin, juicy consistency.
6. When the sauce is almost done, cook pasta according to package directions.
7. Season the sauce with salt, pepper, and cayenne to taste, and serve piping hot over the pasta.

La Spiga
1429 12th Avenue

"If God had intended us to follow recipes, He wouldn't have given us grandmothers."
Linda Henley

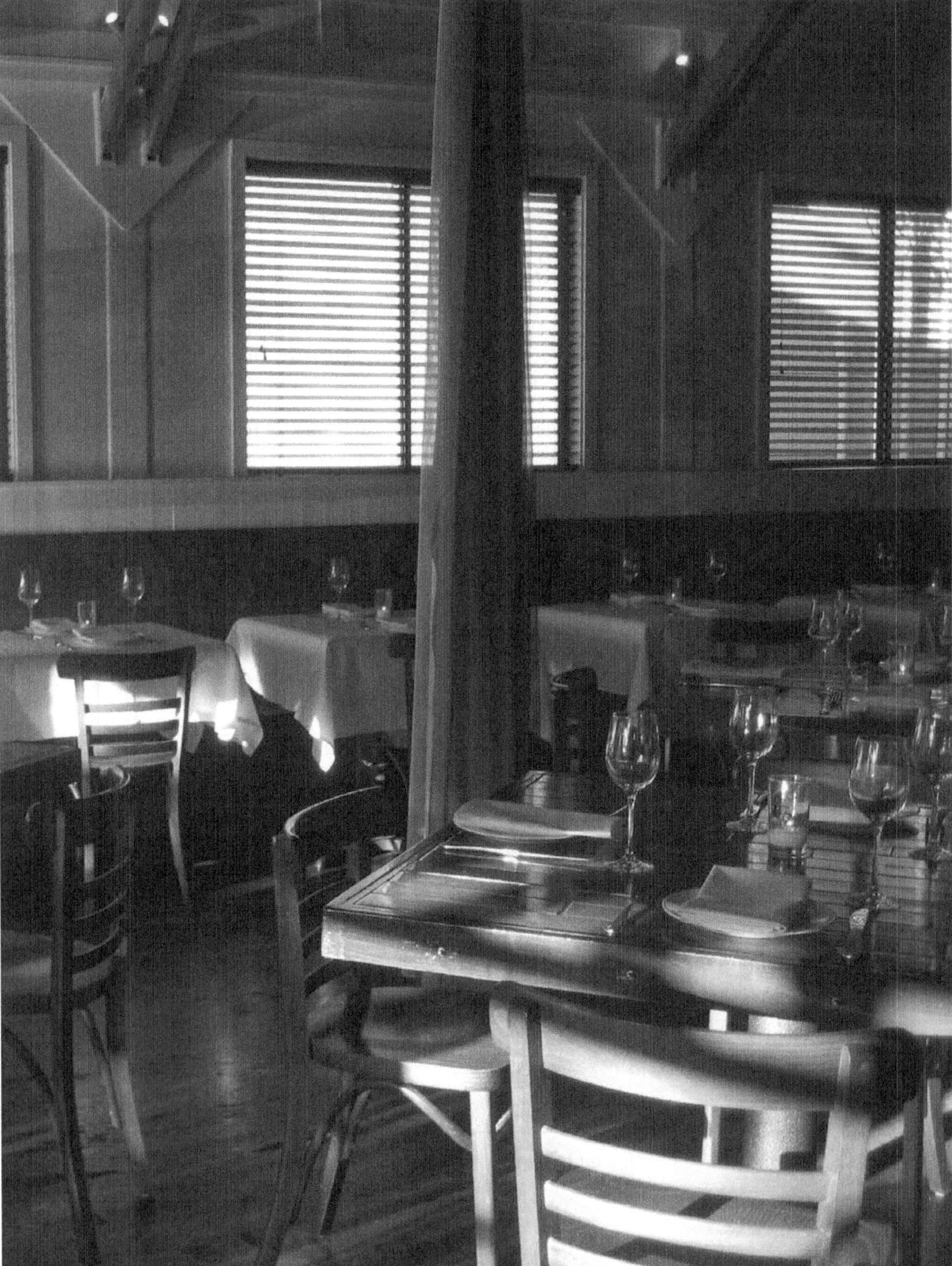

Razor Clam Chowder with Turnip, Truffle & Thyme

Welcome to Chef John Sundstrom's Lark, one of the Pacific Northwest's premier, artisan-focused restaurants. Located in Seattle's Capitol Hill neighborhood, Lark offers a warm dining experience meant to be shared with friends and family. Our menu features small plates of locally-produced and organic cheese, charcuterie, vegetables, grains, fish, and meats, all prepared with a signature focus on flavor and quality. We work with local artisans, farmers, and foragers to serve the best of each season, bright and intense with summer and spring, rich and heartening in the winter and fall.

Clam Stock:
1 tbsp butter
½ C. yellow onion, diced
½ C. leek whites, washed and sliced
½ C. fennel bulb, sliced
2 lb. Manila clams
2 C. dry white wine
3 C. water
1 head garlic, cracked
3 branches thyme
1 bay leaf
10 black peppercorns

Soup:
1 tbsp butter
¼ C. turnips, peeled and diced
¼ C. celery root, peeled and diced
¼ C. Yukon gold potatoes, peeled and diced
2 C. reserved clam stock
1 C. heavy cream
6 branches thyme, washed, dried, and picked
¼ lb. razor clams, chopped
¼ lb. reserved Manila clams
salt and pepper, to taste
1 black truffle, shaved thin
1 tbsp black truffle oil

Clam Stock:

1. Melt butter in a large pot over medium heat. Add onion, leek, and fennel, and sweat gently.

2. Add clams and white wine; reduce by half.

3. Add water and aromatics; simmer gently for 15 minutes.

4. Strain liquid through a fine chinoise and reserve.

5. Shuck clams and reserve.

Soup:

1. Melt butter in a large pot over medium heat. Sweat turnip, celery root, and potato without coloring.

2. Add reserved clam stock, heavy cream, and thyme. Simmer until vegetables are tender.

3. Add razor and manila clams, cooking for about 30 seconds. Season to taste with salt and pepper.

4. Ladle soup into serving bowls, drizzle with truffle oil and top with truffle shavings.

Lark
926 12th Avenue

"Rice is born in water and must die in wine."
Italian Proverb

Tarte Belle-Hélène

Le Panier, created by Hubert Loevenbruck and a group of French bakers, opened its doors in 1983. Pike Place Market was the perfect location to share the authentic style of a classic boulangerie and patisserie with the people of Seattle. Along with these artisan bakers, he brought French equipment and technology to help in the daily bread-making process. The aroma of fresh-baked bread has delighted our neighborhood and the many passers-by for over 25 years.

Almond Cream:
½ C. ground almond meal
¼ C. granulated sugar
1 egg
3 tbsp butter, softened
¾ tsp vanilla extract
1 tsp rum aroma paste
1 tbsp all-purpose flour

6 egg yolks
100 g. sugar
100 g. dark chocolate, chopped
2 tbsp crème fraîche
3 large pears, peeled, halved, seeded
250 g. shortcrust pastry
2 tbsp almond powder
200 g. flaky pastry

1 tsp of icing (castor) sugar
1 egg white, for glaze

Almond Cream:
1. Using a food processor, combine all the ingredients until a smooth, creamy paste forms.

Assembly:
1. Preheat oven to 350°F.
2. Cream the egg yolks with the sugar using a mixer set on high speed.
3. Slowly melt the chocolate in a bain-marie or in the microwave. Pour the melted chocolate into the creamed yolks and sugar.
4. Add the crème fraîche and mix well. Cool to room temperature.
5. Using a tart mold, press the shortcrust pastry into the mold, leaving the pastry edges untrimmed and hanging over the edge of the mold.
6. Sprinkle almond powder on the bottom of the mold. Spread the chocolate mixture on top of the almond powder in the bottom of the mold.
7. Line the pears in the tart mold, heads toward the center.
8. Cover with the almond cream.
9. Roll out a disk of flaky pastry to fit the diameter of the mold. Place flaky pastry over the tart mold.
10. Glaze the surface using egg white and fold the sides of the lower shortcrust pastry over the flaky pastry to seal. Glaze the sides and sprinkle the surface of the tart with castor sugar.
11. Bake for about 30 minutes. When finished, cool a bit and sprinkle with extra castor sugar. Serve warm.

Le Panier
1902 Pike Place

"It is, in my view, the duty of an apple to be crisp and crunchable, but a pear should have such a texture as leads to silent consumption."
Edward Bunyard

Gâteau au Foie de Volaille

Americans often conjure up heavy sauces, heavy draperies and high prices when we think of French cuisine. Not that those are bad things, but there are folks around town who offer a more realistic, modern view of French food. Two of those people are Jim Drohman and Joanne Herron of Le Pichet and Café Presse.

1½ cups Madeira
1 bay leaf
1 tsp whole black peppercorns
1 piece dried orange peel

1 lb. fresh organic chicken livers
2½ cups heavy cream
4 whole farm eggs
1 tsp sugar
2 tbsp Kosher salt

1. Preheat oven to 375°F.

2. Put the Madeira, bay leaf, peppercorns, and orange peel in a small sauce pan. Reduce over high heat until only about ¼ cup of liquid remains. Strain and cool.

3. While the Madeira is reducing, put the livers into the work bowl of a food processor and process until smooth. Pass the liver puree though a drum sieve and into a large mixing bowl.

4. Put the eggs and cream into the unwashed processor bowl and pulse until well mixed. Pass this mixture through the drum sieve into the liver puree. Mix in the sugar, salt, and cooled Madeira reduction.

5. Line a loaf pan with plastic film. Fill the loaf pan with the liver mixture. Bake the gâteau in a water bath until just set in the center. This should take about 60 minutes. Remove the gâteau from the water bath and cool completely.

6. Turn the cooled gâteau onto a serving plate and unmold. Remove the plastic and cut with a hot knife. Serve with crusty bread, mustards, and cornichons.

Le Pichet
1933 1st Avenue

"A good cook is the peculiar gift of the gods. He must be a perfect creature from the brain to the palate, from the palate to the finger's end."
Walter Savage Landor

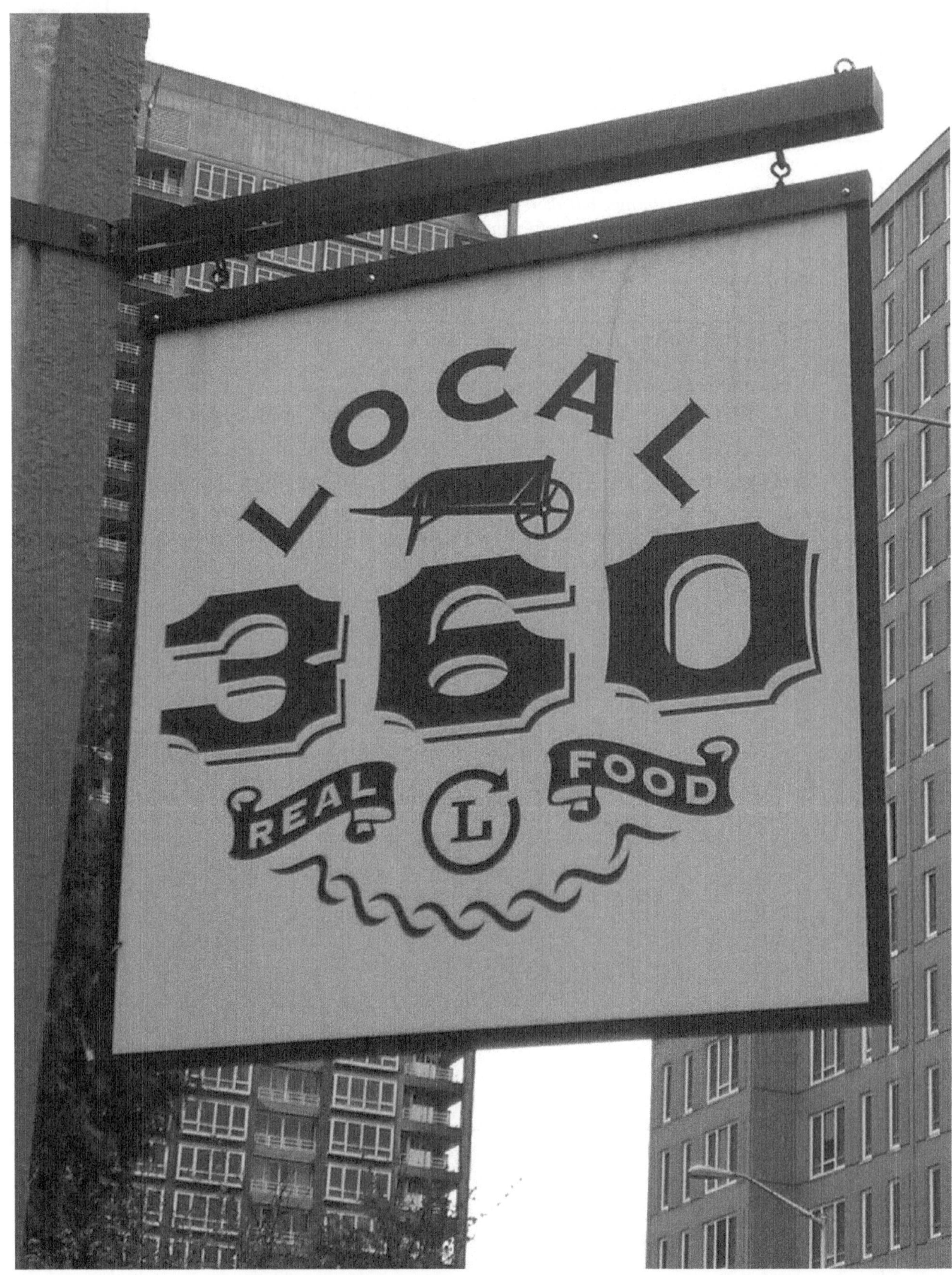
LOCAL
360
REAL
L
FOOD

Fried Chicken

Local 360 is a sustainable restaurant and food producer, based in the heart of downtown at the corner of 1st and Bell. We care about where our ingredients come from, and how they are produced. From arugula to zucchini, our goal is to source everything we use from within a 360 mile radius of Seattle. At times, this will not be possible – in spite of its popularity, coffee still does not grow in the great Pacific Northwest, and we have yet to find a sugarcane field in our neck of the woods. We believe that local produce, meat, and grains are more than mere vehicles for nutrients, but vital parts of the intricate system that supports our environment and the good folks who live here.

Chicken Roulade:
2 qt. water
½ C. Kosher salt
6 garlic cloves
1 bunch of fresh thyme
3 tbsp peppercorns
½ C. granulated sugar
3 bay leaves
4 single-lobed chicken breasts, skin on
4 oz. bacon, cubed
3 egg whites
½ C. heavy whipping cream

Breading:
1 C. all-purpose flour
4 eggs, beaten
2 C. panko bread crumbs
2 tbsp salt
2 tbsp ground pepper

canola oil

1. First make a brine for the chicken by placing 2 qt. of water, all but 3 tbsp. of the salt, 4 cloves of garlic, ½ bunch of thyme, peppercorns, sugar, and bay leaves together in a large pot and bring to a boil. Set aside to cool. Place the chicken breasts in the brine and refrigerate for 24 hours. Remove chicken from the brine and lay on a dry kitchen towel and pat until completely dry.
2. For the filling, add bacon, the 2 remaining cloves of garlic, the rest of the thyme (chopped), and the remaining salt into the bowl of a food processor. Pulse the bacon mixture until smooth. Scrape the sides down and add the egg whites and heavy cream. Pulse again just until bacon-mousse mixture comes together.
3. On a flat surface, roll out a 2-foot-long strip of plastic wrap with a second layer directly over top the first. Rub hands across plastic wrap to adhere the two pieces. Place chicken breasts in the center, skin side down, and place 2 more layers of plastic wrap over the top. Pound the breasts gently until there is an even layer of chicken. Remove the top layer of plastic wrap and arrange the chicken breasts tightly together on the plastic wrap creating an even layer. Spread a 3-inch layer of bacon mousse across the breasts (left to right). Roll the bottom of the breasts up to the top as you would a sushi roll creating a tight cylinder. Tightly roll the plastic wrap around the cylinder and poke holes in to allow air to escape. Tie off one end with a knot, reroll the cylinder two more times until the roll is evenly shaped and tie off the other end. Lay down two more layers of plastic wrap and repeat the process to form a second layer but do not poke holes in this layer; tie off ends.
4. In pot large enough to hold the roulade, add cold water and submerge roulade and heat over medium-high heat. Lay a plate on top of the roulade so that it stays submerged during the cooking process. Cook in simmering water until the center reaches 153°F. When the temperature is reached, immediately place the roulade in an ice bath for one hour.
5. Preheat oven to 350°F. Cut plastic off of the roulade and cut into 2-inch thick slices, discarding the ends. Dredge each piece in flour, then egg, then press into panko (seasoned with salt and pepper).
6. Heat canola oil to 375°F in a deep fying pan and fry the roulade for 4 minutes per side until golden brown. Place in 350°F oven for 5-10 minutes or until internal temperature reaches 165°F.

LOCAL 360
2234 1ST AVENUE

"The difference between 'involvement' and 'commitment' is like an eggs-and-ham breakfast: the chicken was 'involved' - the pig was 'committed'."
American Quote

Lola
Lola

Roasted Leg of Lamb

Chef Liam Spence presents rustic Mediterranean cuisine at Lola, another in the Tom Douglas family of exceptional downtown restaurants. Don't miss our ouzo sizzling kebabs, steaming savory tagines or our grilled to order pita bread, brought to us fresh from our own Dahlia bread bakery right across the street, twice daily. Located in the heart of the bustling Belltown neighborhood, Lola offers the perfect urban dining experience in it's upbeat environment, just minutes from downtown shopping and theater to the south and great music and night life to the north on Fourth Avenue. We're committed to a green community, composting 75% of waste and supporting our local growers.

1 leg American lamb
½ bunch Greek oregano, crushed
½ bunch rosemary, finely chopped
4 tbsp Kosher salt
2 tbsp pepper
2 lemons, juiced
2 oz. extra virgin olive oil

1. Remove the bone from the leg of lamb and open up the lamb leg; remove all visible silver skin. Lightly score the inside of the leg and fat cap.

2. Combine the oregano, rosemary, salt, and pepper in a small bowl. Rub the mixture onto the lamb, then tie back together. Refrigerate for one day before roasting for optimal flavor.

3. Preheat the oven to 325°F.

4. Roast leg of lamb until it reaches an internal temperature of 130°F, basting every half hour with olive oil and lemon juice.

5. After the lamb reaches 130°F, let it sit in a cool oven for 20 minutes before slicing.

Lola
2000 Fourth Avenue

"The breakfast slimes, angel food cake, doughnuts and coffee, white bread and gravy cannot build an enduring nation."
Martin H. Fischer

MACRINA
Bakery Cafe

Corn Chowder with Pink Potatoes & Cream

The idea for Macrina Bakery & Café existed long before we opened our doors. The seed was planted while Leslie Mackie was in cooking school and continued to take root throughout her early restaurant career and during her travels.

2 tbsp olive oil
1 medium yellow onion, diced
2 garlic cloves, finely diced
8 to 10 C. water
Kosher salt
4 ears fresh corn, shucked and cut in half crosswise
¼ C. heavy cream
4 medium red new potatoes, washed and chopped into ¼-inch pieces
1 tbsp chopped fresh thyme
freshly ground black pepper
½ C. sour cream
2 tbsp freshly squeezed lime juice

1. Pour the olive oil into a large, heavy-bottomed soup pot. Add onion, cover, and cook for 15 minutes over medium-low heat to sweat the onion, stirring occasionally, until the onion is translucent.

2. Add garlic and continue cooking over medium-low heat for 1 minute, or until garlic smells sweet but is not brown.

3. Add 8 C. of the water and ½ tsp. salt. Bring to a boil. Carefully drop in the ears of corn and cook until kernels are tender, 4 to 6 minutes. Remove corn and set aside to cool for 5 minutes. Remove kernels from the cobs with a knife, then place the cobs and half of the kernels back in the soup pot. Cook over medium heat for 30 minutes, then remove the cobs and discard.

4. Add the heavy cream, potatoes, and thyme. Simmer over medium heat until potatoes are tender, adding more water as needed (about 15 minutes). Season to taste with salt and pepper. Add the remaining kernels of corn just before serving.

5. In a small bowl, combine ½ tsp. salt, sour cream, and lime juice. Mix well and drizzle over steaming bowls of soup.

Macrina Bakery
1943 First Avenue South

"Bread appears as the Sun, anew each day to keep away the darkness and make the earth grow."
Leslie Mackie, Owner

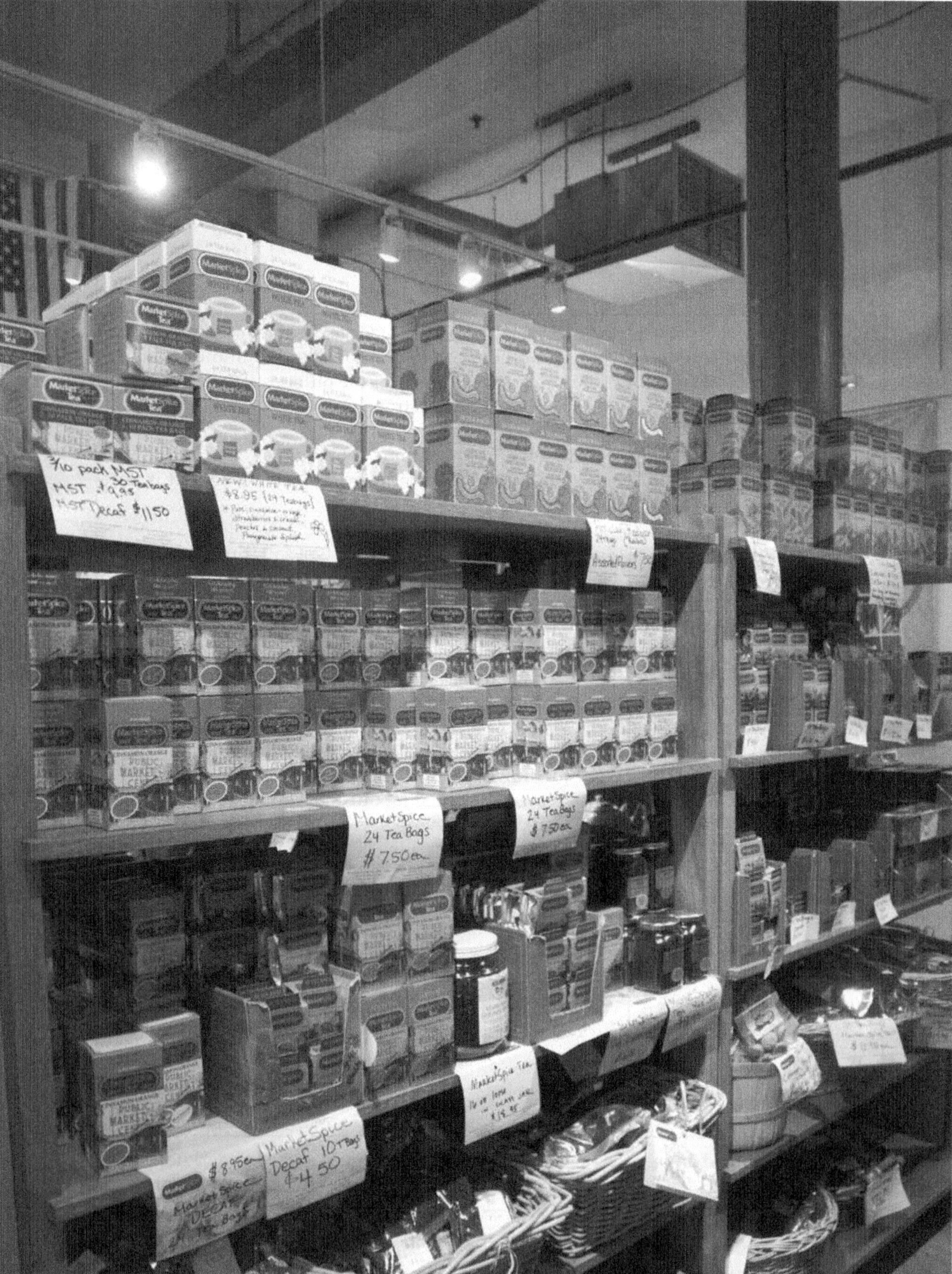
3/10 pack MST
MST 30 Teabags $9.95
MST Decaf $11.50
NEW! WHITE TEA
$8.95 (24 Teabags)
MarketSpice
24 Tea Bags
$7.50 ea.
MarketSpice
24 Tea Bags
$7.50 ea.
MarketSpice
Decaf 10 T Bags
$4.50
$8.95 ea.
MarketSpice
DECAF
Tea Bags

THREE MEAT CHILI

The history of MarketSpice can be traced back to a small tea and spice shop established in Seattle's historic Pike Place Market in 1911. MarketSpice Tea is our "Signature" blend of black tea with spices and cinnamon-orange flavorings. Known the world over for its wonderful aroma and natural sweetness, MarketSpice Tea is perfect anytime. Because of it's spicy, sweet taste, our tea is also delicious iced.

2 tbsp olive oil
2 lb. sirloin steak, cut into 1-inch cubes
1 lb. ground beef
1 (12-oz.) chorizo sausage, casing removed, cut into ¼-inch cubes
1 large onion, chopped
¼ C. chili powder, regular
1 tbsp garlic salt
2 tsp ground cumin
1 tsp whole basil
3½ C. beef broth
2 (15-oz.) cans whole tomatoes, drained
1 C. cilantro, chopped
1 (6-inch) cinnamon stick
3 whole bay leaves
2 green jalapeños, split lengthwise 3 times each
1 tbsp yellow cornmeal
salt and pepper, to taste
shredded cheese
sour cream

1. Place oil in a large, heavy pot over medium heat. Brown the sirloin in batches. Remove to a bowl.

2. Add ground beef, chorizo, and onions to the pot and brown. Make sure to break up the meat. Drain out the fat.

3. Return sirloin to the pot. Stir in the remaining ingredients except for the cheese and sour cream.

4. Bring to a boil, reduce heat and simmer for 2 hours. Stir occasionally and break up tomatoes.

5. Before serving discard cinnamon stick, bay leaves, and jalapeños. Serve with shredded cheese and/or sour cream.

MARKET SPICE
85 PIKE STREET

"Fresh-caught fried fish without hush-puppies are as man without woman, a beautiful woman without kindness, law without policemen."
Marjorie Kinnan Rawlings

matt's

IN THE MARKET

LUNCH • DINNER • PRIVATE PARTIES

LUNCH 11:30 - 2:30 MONDAY - SATURDAY

DINNER 5:30 - 10:00 MONDAY - SATURDAY

CLOSED SUNDAYS

MATTSINTHEMARKET.COM

206.467.7909 94 PIKE STREET SUITE 32

Salmon Chowder

Many say that Pike Place Market is the heart of Seattle. Located on the third floor of the Corner Market building, Matt's in the Market is in the center of it all. Offering spectacular views of Elliott Bay, the Olympics, and the Market's famous clock through it's charming arched windows, Matt's intimate setting makes you feel your are a part of the ceaseless ebb and flow of the market, witness to the very heartbeat of our beautiful city. Savoring every morsel of this blissfully delicious food, you realize that here in the heart of Seattle, you have discovered its soul.

Shell Stock:
1 tbsp canola oil
20 prawn shells
½ onion, diced
¼ bunch fresh thyme
2 bay leaves
1 tbsp black peppercorns
1 lemon, peeled
1 Roma tomato, seeded and diced
½ C. white wine
4½ C. water

Chowder:
2 tbsp canola oil
2 large sweet onions, large dice
½ lb. bacon, cooked and cut into ¼-inch cubes
½ stalk celery, large dice
4 Yukon gold potatoes, large dice
1 tsp minced fresh thyme
1 C. heavy cream
2 lb. wild king salmon, cut into ¾-inch cubes
salt and black pepper
2 tbsp lemon juice
1 tsp minced tarragon
1 tsp minced fresh chives

Shell Stock:
1. In a large sauce pan over low heat, add the oil and sweat the prawn shells with the onion, thyme, bay leaves, peppercorns, lemon, and tomato for 2-3 minutes.

2. Add the white wine and water and simmer for 45 minutes. Strain and reserve.

Chowder:
1. In a large sauce pan over low heat, add the oil and sweat the onions with the bacon and celery for 5-6 minutes.

2. Add the potatoes and sweat for another 5 minutes.

3. Add the thyme, reserved shell stock, and heavy cream and bring to a simmer for 15 to 20 minutes.

4. Add the salmon and season with salt, pepper, and lemon juice.

5. For service, garnish with tarragon and chives.

Matt's in the Market
94 Pike Street, Suite 32

"Fishiest of all places was the Try Pots, which well deserved its name; for the pots there were always boiling chowders. Chowder for breakfast, and chowder for dinner, and chowder for supper, till you began to look for fish-bones coming through your clothes."
Herman Melville, 'Moby Dick'

McCORMICK
& SCHMICK'S
SEAFOOD
RESTAURANT

Crème Brûlée with Strawberries

Since teaming up in the early 1970s, Bill McCormick and Doug Schmick have established more than 80 restaurants and catering operations throughout the country – an extraordinary feat in a business with the highest attrition rate of any in the United States. The two men, very different yet surprisingly compatible, have established themselves as entrepreneurs with one collective vision, to run the nation's premier family of seafood restaurants. The combination of an open imagination and a respect for tradition are what makes McCormick & Schmick's the classic and successful business that it is today.

2 C. whole strawberries
2 tbsp granulated sugar
1 qt. heavy cream
½ vanilla bean
10 egg yolks
1 pinch Kosher salt
4 oz. granulated sugar
1 tsp granulated sugar for each, to caramelize

1. Preheat oven to 325°F.

2. Reserve a couple of small, nice looking strawberries for garnish. Wash, hull, and slice the remaining strawberries and toss in the 2 tbsp. of sugar. Set the berries aside to macerate while you prepare the custard.

3. Scald the cream in a heavy-bottomed pan. Scrape out the vanilla bean and add to the scalded cream. Add the macerated strawberries and their syrup to the mixture and whisk for 1 minute.

4. Combine the yolks, a pinch of salt, and 4 oz. of sugar in a mixing bowl and mix well. Slowly pour the scalded cream-strawberry-vanilla mixture into the sugar and eggs while whisking.

5. Strain the mixture, skim the froth, and portion into individual custard cups or shallow brûlée dishes. Bake covered in a water bath for 30 minutes at 325°F or until the centers are just set. Cool slightly or completely before caramelizing the tops.

6. Sprinkle the top of each crème brûlée with 1 tsp. of sugar and caramelize with a pastry torch immediately before serving. Before the crust cools, place a strawberry on top for garnish.

McCormick & Schmick's
1103 First Ave.

"Strawberries are the angels of the earth, innocent and sweet with green leafy wings reaching heavenward."
Terri Guillemets

Metropolitan
"THE BEST STEAK IN

Cheddar Cheese and Beer Sauce

The moment you step inside Metropolitan Grill, you will know you have entered a classic steakhouse. Rich in tradition, The Met is housed inside the historic Marion Building, which dates to 1903. Guests pass under The Met's signature green awning and enter through the tall mahogany doors to be greeted by our tuxedo-clad maître d'. In the front entry, a glass display showcases The Met's cuts of beef. Twenty-foot columns reach to the ceiling, trimmed with the original crown moldings. Tables and railings are adorned with mahogany and brass, and the plush booths are oversized.

¼ C. salad oil
2 tbsp finely chopped parsley
¼ green onion, finely chopped
¼ C. flour
2 C. milk, warmed
¾ C. your favorite beer
¼ tsp dry mustard
½ tsp Worcestershire sauce
1¼ C. shredded cheddar
¼ tsp salt
pinch white pepper
pinch cayenne pepper
pinch granulated garlic

1. Heat oil in a large sauce pot. Add chopped parsley and green onions. Lower heat, add flour to make a roux, and cook over medium heat, stirring frequently, for 10 minutes.

2. Add milk, beer, mustard, and Worcestershire to the roux and stir over medium heat until thickened.

3. Remove pot from the heat, then stir in the cheese until melted and add final seasonings, to taste.

Metropolitan Grill
820 2nd Avenue

"We load up on oat bran in the morning so we'll live forever. Then we spend the rest of the day living like there's no tomorrow."
Lee Iacocca

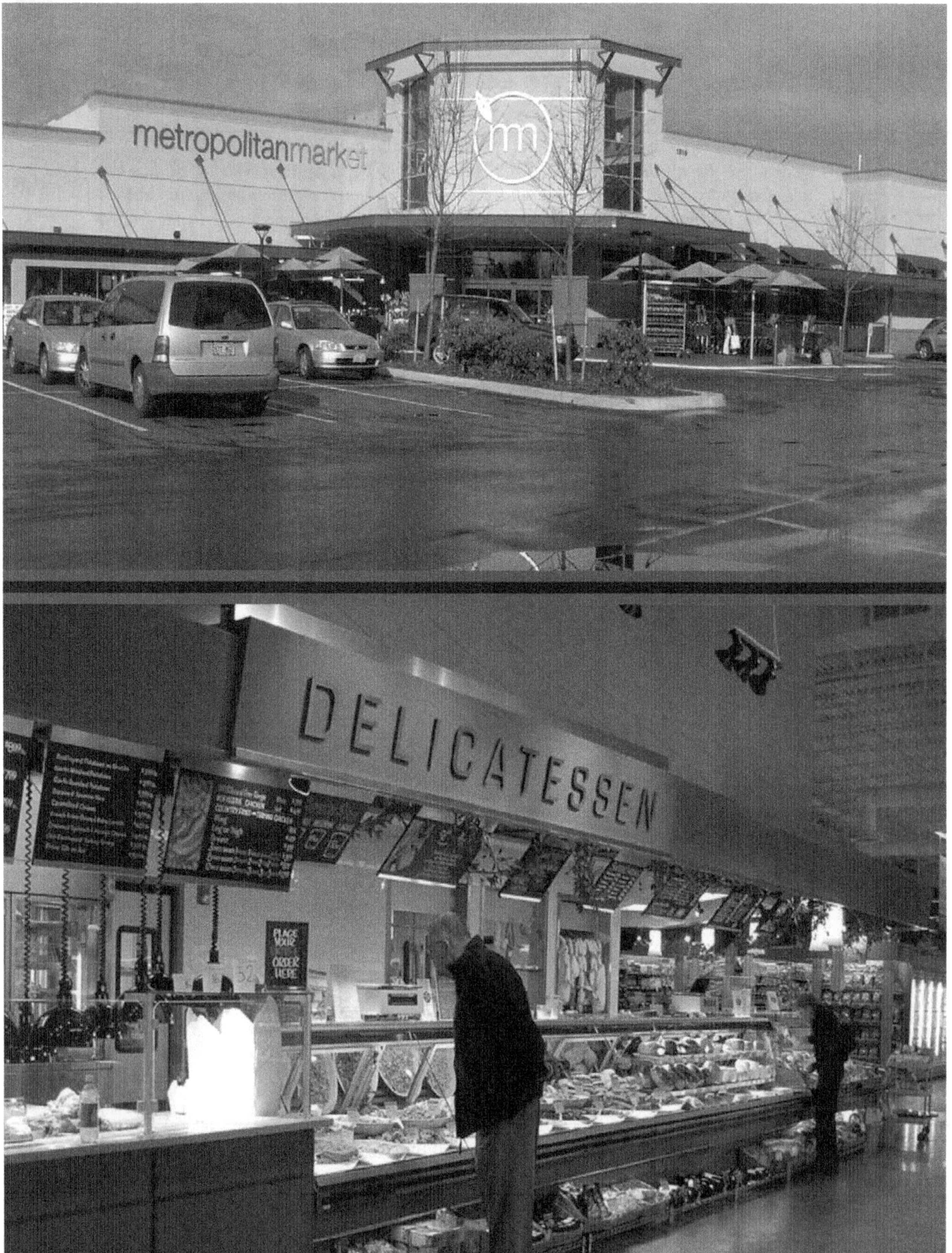
metropolitanmarket
DELICATESSEN
PLACE YOUR ORDER HERE

Salmon with Pinot Noir Sauce

It all began in 1971 with one store location in Seattle. Today, Metropolitan Market has become an award-winning grocery store with multiple locations throughout Seattle. It has always been our goal as the area's leading progressive, independent grocer to always be the first to bring you the best. Our specialists travel the world to find unique products of the highest quality that will satisfy even the most discriminating palate. Everything in our stores reflects this passion for food, from our knowledgeable specialist in each department, to the thousands of Good Cuisine recipes we've developed and our culinary kiosks.

4 (6-oz.) fillets of salmon
¼ C. (2-3 oz.) shallots, chopped
1½ C. Pinot Noir
¼ C. whipping cream
4 tbsp butter
1 C. Pinot Noir grapes, (or Champagne, ¼ globe or black grapes)
⅛ tsp salt and pepper
dill or chervil, to garnish
wild rice or baby bok choy, optional

1. Heat a large skillet over medium heat and sprinkle the shallots on the bottom, then place the salmon fillets on top.

2. Add the wine, cover with lid or parchment paper and bring to a boil, then turn down the heat and simmer for 10 minutes, or until salmon is just cooked through.

3. Remove the salmon to a warm serving platter.

4. Turn up the heat and reduce the poaching liquid by half, add the cream and reduce by half again.

5. Off the heat and whisk in the butter a little at a time. Add the salt and pepper.

6. Strain the sauce, return it to the pan, then add the grapes and bring to a simmer, then pour the sauce over the salmon. Garnish with sprigs of dill or chervil.

7. Serve with steamed wild rice or baby bok choy.

Metropolitan Market
Multiple Locations throughout the City

"There is but one season of the year when salmon should be served hot at a choice repast; that is in the spring and early summer, and even then it is too satisfying, but sufficiently delicate. The man who gives salmon during the winter, I care not what sauce he serves with it, does an injury to himself and his guests."
Ward McAllister, 'Society As I Have Found It'

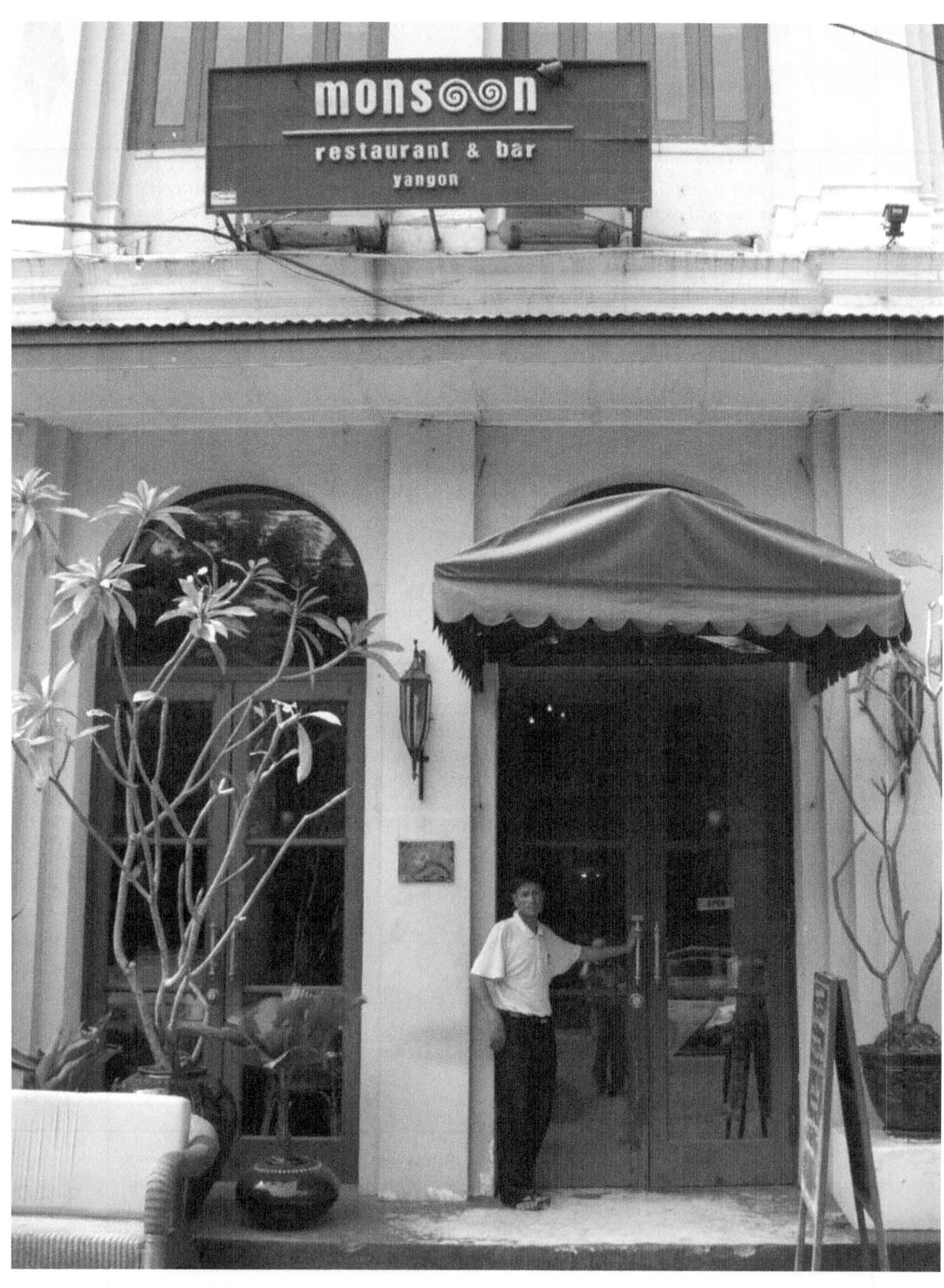
monsoon
restaurant & bar
yangon

Vietnamese Pork Belly

A fixture of Seattle's vibrant Capitol Hill neighborhood since 1999, Monsoon marries traditional Vietnamese cuisine with Pacific Northwest innovation and serves it up with one of the best wine lists in the region. We use organic vegetables when available and support small farms when possible. Everything is fresh.

2 tsp Kosher salt
1 tbsp whole black peppercorns
1 large piece pork belly (3½–4 lb.)

Braise:
juice of 3 young coconuts (or 20 oz. canned coconut juice)
2 C. chicken stock
5 cloves garlic
2 tbsp Kosher salt
¼ C. fish sauce
2 tbsp caramelized sugar (available in Asian markets) or dark brown sugar
10 hard-cooked eggs, peeled (optional)

1. Place pork belly on a small sheet pan. Coat with salt and peppercorns. Cover pan tightly with plastic wrap. Let cure in refrigerator for at least 1 day, and up to 3 days.

2. Preheat oven to 350°F.

3. In a large pan, sear pork on both sides over medium-high heat until browned, about 5 minutes per side. (For easier browning, cut meat into 3 or 4 pieces.) Set aside.

4. Meanwhile, in a deep roasting pan or braising pot, combine coconut juice, chicken stock, garlic, salt, fish sauce, and sugar. Stir to combine. Add pork belly.

5. Cover the belly and braising liquid with a sheet of parchment paper to regulate temperature, then place a tight-fitting lid on top. Braise in oven for about 3 hours. Add eggs after 1 hour.

6. When the belly is tender, it can be served immediately. Cut into 3-by-1-inch pieces. Spoon each serving into a shallow bowl and drizzle in some of the brasing liquid over top. Place 1 egg on top. Serve with cornichons or pickled leeks on the side.

Monsoon
615 19th Avenue East

"Wine is a precarious aphrodisiac, and its fumes have blighted many a mating."
Norman Douglas

MORTON'S
THE STEAKHOUSE

Bacon-Wrapped Sea Scallops with Apricot Chutney

Morton's The Steakhouse Seattle is located in the heart of downtown Seattle, on 6th Avenue between Pike and Pine Streets, within walking distance from Pike Place Market, theaters, retail shops, the Benaroya Symphony Hall, and the Washington State Convention and Trade Center. Nearby hotels include the Westin Seattle, Sheraton Seattle, The Grand Hyatt, the Fairmont Olympic Hotel, W Hotel, and the Hilton Seattle. Richly appointed dark wood interiors make Morton's an elegant yet inviting atmosphere to relax in the bar with a martini or enjoy a meal in the dining room. Every detail, from the succulent steaks and seafood and vast wine selections to the seamless service, makes Morton's the best dining experience in Seattle.

6 slices of bacon
6 large sea scallops, connective tissue removed

Apricot Chutney:
1 tsp freshly ground black pepper
¼ C. strained prepared horseradish
½ C. apricot preserves

bamboo skewers, soaked in water

1. Preheat oven to 500°F.

2. Place six bacon strips on a sheet pan and bake for approximately 10 minutes (remove before bacon is crispy).

3. Place cooked bacon into a pie tin and cover with plastic wrap to keep bacon pliable. Wrap one bacon strip around each scallop.

4. Using a cutting board as a flat surface, line up three scallops and run a bamboo skewer through each scallop to keep the bacon in place. Repeat with remaining scallops.

5. Place scallops on a greased sheet pan and bake in a 500°F oven, until scallops are cooked through and bacon is crisp, approximately five minutes per side.

Apricot Chutney:
1. Combine all ingredients in a mixing bowl and mix thoroughly with a wire whisk. Use to accompany scallops.

Morton's The Steakhouse
1511 6th Avenue

"Part of the secret of success in life is to eat what you like and let the food fight it out inside."
Mark Twain

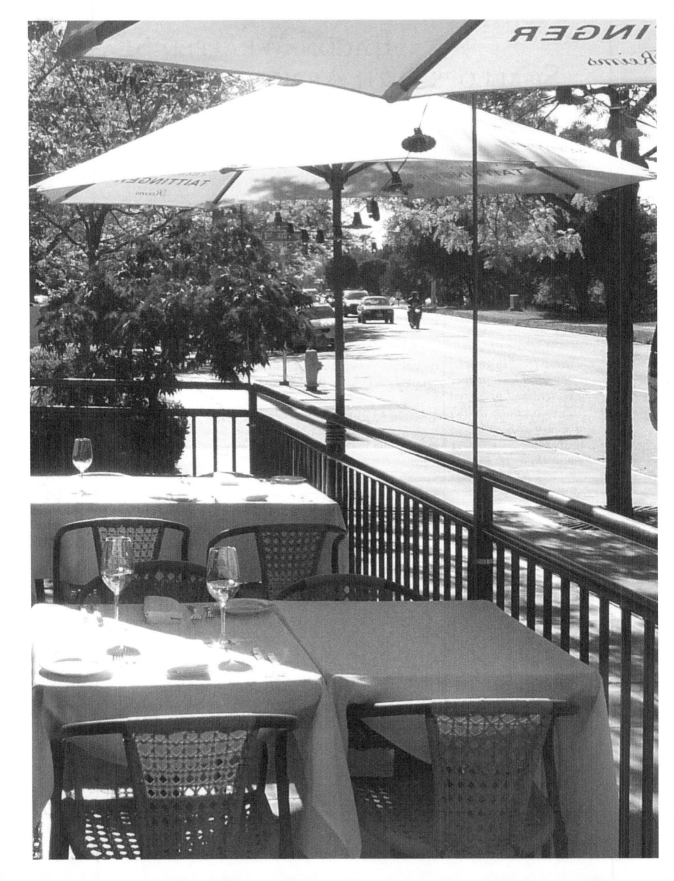
TAITTINGER

Almond Gazpacho with Grapes

When dining at Nell's you can choose from our current seasonal fare or enjoy our sumptuous five course tasting menu, the finest of what we offer from appetizer through dessert, at a single fixed price. Nell's menus are designed to pair beautifully with your wine selection from our hand picked wine list. We also offer vegetarian and vegan options on request.

4 thick slices of bread, crusts removed
5 oz. almonds, lightly toasted
2 cloves garlic
½ cucumber, peeled and deseeded
1 C. extra virgin olive oil
2 oz. sherry vinegar
3 tsp salt
½ tsp pepper
1 C. green California seedless grapes, washed and cut in half

1. Moisten bread in a little water and soak for approximately one hour.

2. Squeeze some of the water from the pieces of bread and place in a blender. Add almonds, garlic, and cucumber.

3. Process to a smooth consistency, adding water as needed. Slowly add oil, then vinegar, salt, and pepper. Add remaining water as needed to get proper thickness.

4. Check seasonings for salt, pepper, and vinegar. Chill. Ladle into serving bowls and top each portion with grapes.

Nell's Restaurant
6804 East Green Lake Way North

"Condensed milk is wonderful. I don't see how they can get a cow to sit down on those little cans."
Fred Allen

Tomato Basil Soup

The cafe is located on the third floor of the flagship Nordstrom department store located on 5th and Pine. There is a varied selection of light fare and it is a pleasant place to come for a quick lunch with an inviting atmosphere.The friendly staff at Nordstrom Café are committed to serving sustainable, natural, and organic dishes.

1 C. olive oil
3 lb. carrots, chopped
3 lb. onions, chopped

4 tbsp dry basil
4 tbsp Kosher salt
4 tbsp black pepper
12 C. canned peeled plum tomatoes
1 lb. chicken base
2 gal. water
3 qt. heavy cream

1. In a large stock pot, sauté the olive oil, carrots, and onions over medium heat for 15 minutes. Add the basil, salt, pepper, and tomatoes and bring to a simmer.

2. In a large bowl, whisk the chicken base into the water until dissolved. Add the chicken base mixture to the stock pot, bring to a boil, and simmer for 45 minutes.

3. Puree the soup using a hand blender while adding the heavy cream until it reaches a thin consistency.

Nordstrom Café
500 Pine Street

"Always eat grapes downward – that is eat the best grapes first; in this way there will be none better left on the bunch, and each grape will seem good down to the last. If you eat the other way, you will not have a good grape in the lot."
Samuel Butler

Kale and Farro Salad

The Pike/Pine corridor's living room for homemade baked goods, market salads, roast chicken or a Manhattan. Oddfellows is a place to enjoy breakfast, lunch and dinner, plus a late night café and bar serving seasonal, rustic fare in the heart of Capitol Hill's most dynamic neighborhood.

1 lb. (dry weight) farro
1 bunch kale, julienned
1 bunch parsley, roughly chopped
1 red pepper, small dice
1 yellow pepper, small dice
1 fennel bulb, julienned

Dressing:
1½ tsp black pepper
1½ tsp salt
1½ tsp minced garlic
½ C. lemon juice
3 tbsp extra virgin olive oil

1. Cook the farro until bloomed but still slighly chewy; set aside to chill.

2. Once the farro is chilled, toss with the vegetables in a large bowl.

3. In a small bowl, mix together the salt, pepper, garlic, and lemon juice. Add the oil in a small stream while whisking constantly to combine.

4. Mix salad with the dressing and top with shaved parmesan, if desired.

Oddfellows Café & Bar

1525 10th Avenue

"I won't eat anything that has intelligent life, but I'd gladly eat a network executive or a politician."
Marty Feldman

Olivar

GNOCCHI

Olivar, the Spanish word for "olive grove," is the theme of this cozy new spot reminiscent of a quaint bistro that one would discover while exploring France and Spain. Olivar combines Chef Philippe Thomelin's deep roots from growing up in the Loire Valley of France, the influence of his Catalan grandmother, and his love of all things Spanish to create dishes that reflect his philosophy of using the freshest, most seasonal seafood, meat and produce to create high quality food in a relaxed and welcoming environment.

2 large russet potatoes
1 egg
1 C. flour
Kosher salt

1. Bake the potatoes on a sheet pan with salt at 375°F for 1 hour.

2. When the potatoes are cooked, cut in half and spoon out the pulp and pass potatoes through a ricer.

3. Working the dough quickly, so it stays warm and soft, add ¼ C. of flour and the egg. Mix it together and add the flour only as necessary until it doesn't stick to your fingers, and roll it into a big bread-loaf shape.

4. Cutting a small amount of dough at a time, roll it into small cylinder, about ½ inch or less, and then cut into small pieces, and roll the dumplings gently in some flour.

5. Working in small batches, boil the gnocchi in hot salted water for two minutes, or until they float to the top, and cool down quickly in iced water.

6. Drain and add some olive oil, the gnocchi are then ready to be fried quickly in hot olive oil and topped with any seasonal garnish.

OLIVAR RESTAURANT
806 EAST ROY STREET

"Everything I eat has been proved by some doctor or other to be a deadly poison, and everything I don't eat has been proved to be indispensable for life. But I go marching on."
George Bernard Shaw

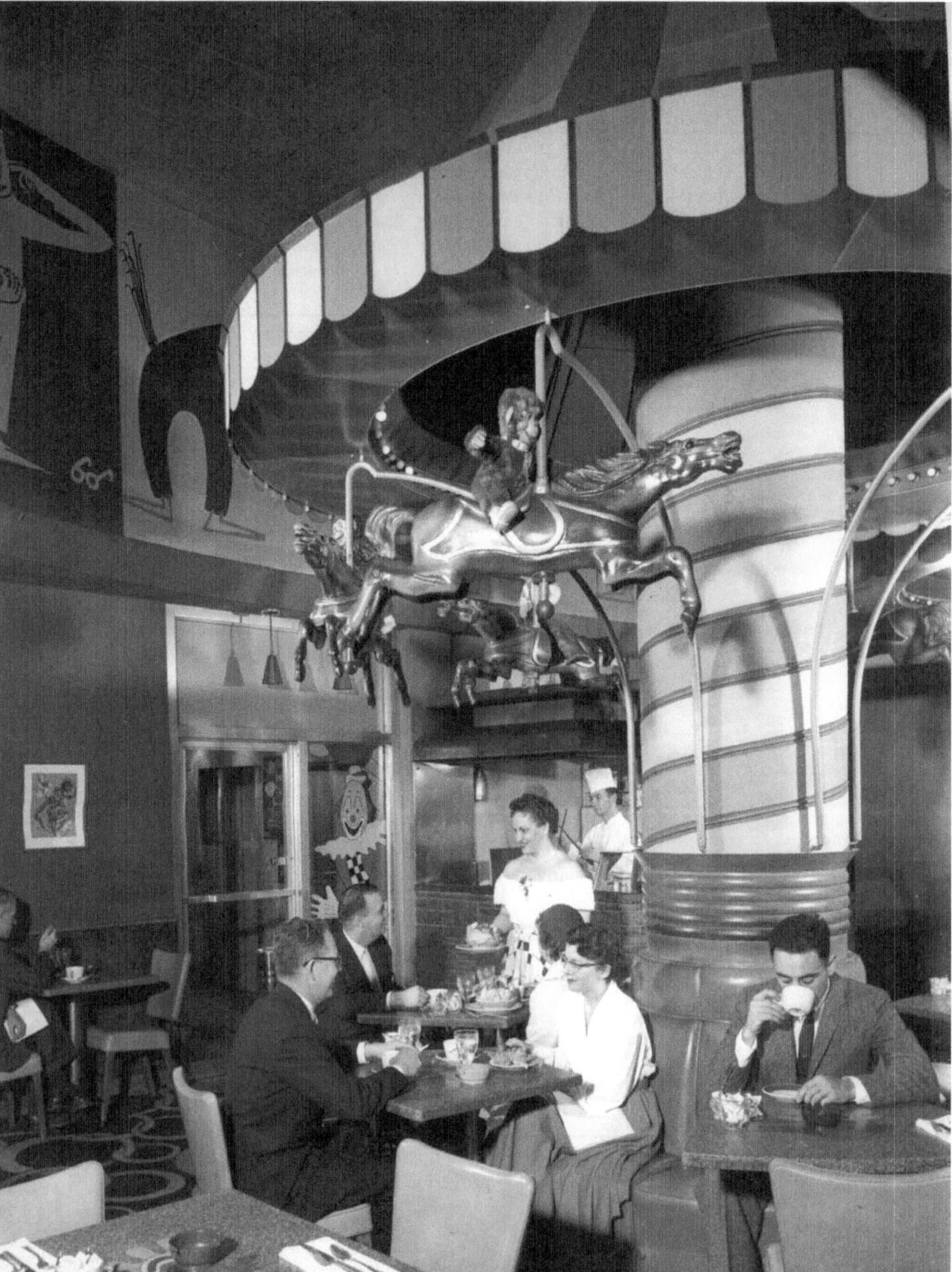

Paradigm Shift and Silver Belle

Oliver's is the perfect place to unwind and soak up the stunning cityscape. An elegant downtown bar, Oliver's provides a casual setting for lunch, snacks or your favorite cocktail. Located in the Mayflower Park hotel, Oliver's offers award-winning cocktail creations such as these contest winners, under the watchful eye of master artisan Patrick Donnelly, Jr. The Mayflower began life as the Bergonian Hotel, built by local owners. Eighty years later, it is still locally owned and a landmark location for the city.

Paradigm Shift:
wedge of fresh grapefruit
1½ oz. Skyy vodka
½ oz. Bombay Sapphire gin
¼ oz. Campari
¼ oz. raspberry-infused sour mix
fresh raspberries

Paradigm Shift:

1. Squeeze the grapefruit into a cocktail shaker filled with ice.

2. Add remaining ingredients and shake vigorously.

3. Strain into a chilled martini glass.

4. Garnish with skewered raspberries.

Silver Belle:
1 oz. Grey Goose vodka
½ oz. St. Germaine liqueur
¼ oz. fresh lemon juice
float of champagne
twist of lemon

Silver Belle:

1. Combine the first 3 ingredients into a cocktail shaker filled with ice.

2. Shake and strain into a champagne flute.

3. Float champagne on top.

4. Garnish with a twist of lemon.

Oliver's Lounge
405 Olive Way

"A woman drove me to drink and I didn't even have the decency to thank her."
W. C. Fields

Grilled Marinated Steak

This is Seattle's classic landmark restaurant perched on the water's edge with a breathtaking view through the expanse of windows out over Elliott Bay with the city and Olympic Mountains as a backdrop. Whether for special business or a romantic occasion or just for a break from the day, come enjoy a cocktail in our elevated piano bar next to the indoor waterfall.

Steak Marinade:
2 tbsp + 1 tsp garlic, minced
1 C. canola oil
3½ oz. red wine vinegar
2 tbsp Lawry's seasoning
4 tsp Durkees hot sauce
2 tbsp Worcestershire sauce

1 (10-12 oz.) flank or sirloin steak

3 oz. red potatoes, blanched & quartered

4 oz. assorted vegetables-smoked in a tin basket
lemon juice
olive oil

1. Whisk ingredients for marinade together in a medium-sized bowl. Ladle on the steaks and refrigerate for 1-5 hours. Reserve 1-2 tbsp. of the marinade for the potatoes.

2. Place marinated steaks on a hot grill and cook to desired temperature. Let rest and then slice.

3. For the potatoes, toss in 1-2 tbsp. of the marinade and grill until just tender.

4. For the vegetables, toss assorted vegetables in lemon juice and olive oil to taste. Place in an aluminum pan and poke holes through it. Meanwhile put any flavor of wood chips on the coals of the grill and let smoke. Place the pan of vegetables on the grill. Pour water over the chips and let the vegetables simmer until the smoke has stopped.

5. Serve the sliced steak with the grilled potatoes and smoked vegetables.

Palisade Restaurant
2601 West Marina Place

"Training is everything. The peach was once a bitter almond; cauliflower is nothing but cabbage with a college education."
Mark Twain

Cuban Roasted Pork Sandwiches

Paseo has been featured in several publications across the nation. Some of our accolades over the years include being the top-ranked Seattle restaurant on UrbanSpoon, and making it on Esquire Magazine's list of "Best Sandwiches in America."

1 pork shoulder (4-5 lb. to ensure lots of leftovers), bone-in
20 cloves garlic
2 tsp salt
1 onion, diced
1 tsp dried oregano
1 C. orange juice
¼ C. lemon juice
¼ C. lime juice
1½ C. olive oil

For the Sandwich:
toasted baguette
caramelized onions (recipe follows)
aïoli or mayonnaise
fresh cilantro sprigs
romaine leaves, washed and dried
pickled jalepeños

Caramelized Onions:
2 tsp butter
1 tbsp olive oil
2 large yellow onions, peeled and cut into ¼-inch half moon strips
salt
½ tsp sugar

1. Place pork shoulder in a deep dish. Using a sharp knife or fork, pierce the meat multiple times on all sides. Set aside.
2. In the work bowl of a food processor, pulse the garlic and salt until finely chopped. Add the onion, oregano, and juices; pulse until thoroughly mixed.
3. In a medium sauce pan, heat the olive oil over medium heat then whisk in the marinade and heat through. Pour marinade over the pork shoulder; cover and refrigerate 4 hours or overnight.
4. Preheat oven to 325°F. Remove the pork from the marinade (reserve marinade) and place, fat side up, in a Dutch oven. Transfer to oven and let roast, uncovered, for roughly 1 hour per pound, basting occasionally with some of the reserved marinade. Pork should easily fall apart when done. Remove from oven and transfer to a cutting board; let rest for 15 minutes. Drain the accumulated fat from the Dutch oven. Set aside.
5. Using a sharp knife and/or two forks, shred pork into bite-sized pieces. Add it back to the Dutch oven and mix with browned bits on the bottom.
6. Skim the fat off the reserved marinade and strain over the shredded pork. Bring to a simmer, partially covered, over medium heat and cook for about 10 minutes, adding water as necessary. Season with salt to taste.
7. To assemble sandwiches: generously slather both sides of the toasted baguette with aïoli or mayonnaise and pile on the shredded pork, caramelized onions, pickled jalepeños, cilantro, and romaine leaves. Serve immediately.

Caramelized Onions:
1. In a large skillet over medium heat, melt butter with oil. Add onions and sauté, stirring occasionally, for 10 minutes. Sprinkle with salt and sugar and continue cooking for another 15-20 minutes or until onions are very soft and have a deep caramel color.

Paseo Caribbean
4225 Fremont Avenue North

"A fruit is a vegetable with looks and money. Plus, if you let fruit rot, it turns into wine, something Brussels sprouts never do."
P.J. O'Rourke

The No-Name Cocktail

Peso's adds an air of romance and sophistication to the mystique of Mexico and Latin infused cuisine. Featuring over 115 different kinds of tequila in a dark, candle-lit lounge with gothic chandeliers and high-arched floor to ceiling windows, Peso's promises to ease even the most stressful of days. The food, as any Seattlite will tell you, is incredible, but its the happy hour that makes this one of the signature spots in the city. This cocktail has no name, as long-time bartender Ethan Silvera refuses to name any of his masterful creations.

1½ oz. cucumber vodka
½ oz. triple sec
1 oz. water
1 oz. Sprite
splash of Pimm's

1. Combine all ingredients over ice in a glass.

2. Garnish with a wedge of lime.

NOTE: Water is added to this cocktail to soften the alcohol and sugar. Furthermore, it helps to release the flavor of the vodka.

Peso's Kitchen & Lounge
605 Queen Anne Avenue North

"The chief reason for drinking is the desire to behave in a certain way, and to be able to blame it on alcohol."
Mignon McLaughlin

Spinach Lasagna

Along the quaint Post Alley of Seattle's Pike Place Market awaits a seductive netherworld fronted by a mysterious, milky rose portal better known as The Pink Door. Enter through it, and the tides of reality wash away into the sea of the sublime. Welcome! The Pink Door tempts with homespun Italian-American food, conversation that flows as liberally as the Barolo, provocative - always free - live entertainment, and a warm, lively respite from the ordinary world. From the trapeze artist swinging over guests in the dining room to the couples entwined on the patio taking in the Elliot Bay view, what's not to love.

Spinach Pasta Dough:
½ lb. fresh spinach or ½ (10-oz.) package of frozen spinach, thawed, well drained
1½ C. bread flour
2 large eggs
3 tbsp butter
¼ tsp nutmeg
2 tbsp flour
3 C. heavy cream, milk or half and half
½ C. ricotta
¼ C. pesto sauce
2 C. packed fresh baby spinach, to layer in lasagna
salt and pepper, to taste
1 C. marinara sauce

1. Preheat oven to 375°F.

2. Cook (or thaw) spinach and drain. Squeeze out all excess liquid. Chop very fine.

3. Pour the flour on to a work surface and shape it into a mound with a deep hollow in the center. Break eggs into the hollow, add cooked spinach, and whisk together. Slowly incoporate the flour into the egg/spinach mixture until dough is formed. Knead by hand or by machine until smooth. Wrap in plastic wrap and let dough rest for 30 minutes. Pass dough through a pasta roller a few times to form long, thin sheets. Cut pasta into 4-inch lasagna noodles. Cook noodles for 2 minutes in lightly salted boiling water, drain, and set aside, covered with a clean, damp kitchen towel.

4. In a sauce pan set over medium heat, melt the butter and whisk in the flour until completely incorporated. Add nutmeg and cream and turn heat to high, stir until thickened. Add ricotta and pesto and stir. If béchemel sauce is too thick, thin with more cream. Season to taste with salt and pepper.

5. Layer the lasgana in 2 (12-oz.) casserole dishes. Start with a thin layer of béchamel on the bottom, then add a layer of noodles, then a layer of fresh baby spinach, top with more béchamel, and finish with another noodle. Repeat process in second casserole (or use a larger dish to make 6 layers). Completely cover the entire top layer with marinara sauce and bake, covered with foil, for 20 minutes, then remove foil and continue to cook for 10 minutes more, until lasagna is bubbling.

Pink Door
1919 Post Alley

"This special feeling towards fruit, its glory and abundance, is I would say universal....We respond to strawberry fields or cherry orchards with a delight that a cabbage patch or even an elegant vegetable garden cannot provoke."
Jane Grigson

3014

Ponti

SEAFOOD GRILL

Open Daily 4:00PM

Private Dining Rooms
Catering

Dinner
From 5:00PM Daily

Bar
From 4:00PM DAILY
Happy Hour
4:00PM - 6:30PM
9:00PM - Close

Lunch
Open for Private Dining
and
The Month of December

pontiseafoodgrill.com
206 • 284 • 3000

Shellfish Miso Soup with Penn Cove Mussels, Manila Clams and Prawns

When Richard and Sharon Malia opened the doors of Ponti Seafood Grill to Seattle in 1990, they revealed a modern mosaic restaurant. Ponti, meaning "bridge" in Italian is built in the style of a Mediterranean villa featuring warm Tuscan inspired colors and waterside patios. Located on Seattle's Ship Canal, four private dining rooms and two outdoor patios showcase vistas of the water and the Fremont and Aurora bridges.

2 qt. water
1 C. miso
1 tbsp canola oil
1 tbsp finely minced ginger
1 tbsp finely minced garlic
1 tbsp finely minced shallot
1 large carrot sliced into thin match sticks
4 green onions sliced into rings
1 lb. Manila clams
1 lb. Penn Cove mussels
18 medium-sized prawns
1 tsp red chili flakes
2 tbsp unsalted butter
2 C. sake
salt and pepper, to taste
1 C. coconut milk
2 tbsp thinly-sliced basil
1 large lime

1. Bring water to a boil and whisk in miso, then turn down temperature; hold hot.

2. Heat a 6-quart pot over medium-high heat and add the oil. Add ginger, garlic, and shallots. Sauté for about 30 seconds. Add carrots, green onions, clams, mussels, and prawns. Stir the ingredients in the pot; this will ensure that all of the seafood cooks evenly.

3. Add chili flakes, butter, sake, salt, and pepper; stir and cover. Cook until shellfish opens (toss out any shells that are unopened).

4. Add hot miso, coconut milk, and basil. Finish with freshly squeezed lime juice, to taste.

Ponti Seafood Grill

3014 3rd Avenue North

"Cooking is like love. It should be entered into with abandon or not at all."
Harriet van Horne

poppy

Coffee Cake with Orange-Rhubarb Compote

Jerry Traunfeld's Capitol Hill restaurant brings a new style of dining to the Northwest. Jerry's inspiration comes from the "thali," a platter served to each guest holding a variety of small dishes. Poppy's menu borrows the idea of the thali to present Jerry's own style of Northwest cooking, highlighting seasonal ingredients, fresh herbs, and spices. It's a modern Northwest tasting menu served all at once.

Streusel:
1/3 C. all-purpose flour
1/3 C. (packed) brown sugar
1/4 tsp salt
1/4 tsp baking powder
1 tsp cinnamon
4 tbsp unsalted butter, very cold

Cake:
Cake ingredients must be at room temperature
1½ C. all-purpose flour
1½ tsp baking powder
1/4 tsp Kosher salt
½ C. unsalted butter
½ C. sugar
2 large eggs, separated
1/4 C. sour cream
½ C. milk
1 tsp vanilla extract

Compote:
1 lb. rhubarb, cut into ½-inch cubes
3/4 C. sugar
2 tbsp unsalted butter
2 tbsp orange liqueur
zest of 1 orange

1. Preheat oven to 350°F. Grease a 9-inch round baking pan and line with parchment paper.

Streusel:
1. Mix dry ingredients in a bowl.
2. Cut butter into mixture until small crumbles form.

Cake:
1. Sift dry ingredients together; set aside.
2. Cream butter and sugar together with an electric mixer until light and fluffy, about 5 minutes. Add egg yolks and sour cream, mix 1 minute more. Set mixer to low and add dry mixture in 3 parts, alternating with milk and vanilla extract.
3. In a separate bowl, whip egg whites to medium peaks, then carefully fold into batter.
4. Spread batter into pan and sprinkle streusel on top. Bake for 30 to 45 minutes.

Compote:
1. Toss rhubarb with sugar.
2. Melt butter in a heavy-bottomed sauce pan over medium heat; add rhubarb, liqueur, and orange zest. Cook, stirring occasionally, for 10 to 15 minutes, until viscous.
3. Top cake with compote and serve warm with whipped cream.

Poppy
622 Broadway East

"A man may be a pessimistic determinist before lunch and an optimistic believer in the will's freedom after it."
Aldous Huxley

PORTAGE BAY
CAFE

Chicken Ballotine with Wild Mushrooms and Pickled Butternut Squash Salad

With three Seattle restaurants, we were one of the very first to focus our menus on local, organic, and seasonal ingredients in a casual setting. We strive to offer the widest array of food sourced from local, clean, and sustainable farms and producers. On the wall are pictures of some of our local sources including Full Circle organic farm, Oxbow organic farm, Fonte organic coffee, Bluebird Farms organic grains, and Painted Hills Natural Beef. Most of the producers work within a few miles of the restaurant. This ensures that the food you get is fresh, ripe when picked, and only minutes traveling time from where it is produced. This also means we know the people who make your food and we trust them to bring us the best product.

Pickled Butternut Squash:
1 butternut squash
1 C. white vinegar
1 C. sugar
1 C. water
salt
garlic
dried chilies

Chicken Ballotine:
1 (3-lb.) chicken
1 C. cream
1 egg
2 sprigs thyme
½ lb. wild mushrooms
1 minced shallot
1 tbsp minced chives
salt and pepper, to taste
truffle oil (optional)
caul fat

To Serve:
1 head frisée
olive oil
aged sherry vinegar
salt and pepper

Pickled Butternut Squash:
1. Peel and dice squash.
2. In a pot, combine vinegar, sugar, water, salt, garlic, and dried chilies to taste. Add squash, bring to a simmer, remove from heat, and let cool. Remove squash from liquid when cool and reserve for salad.

Ballotine:
1. Remove skin from chicken, keeping skin in tact as one piece as much as possible.
2. Cut breasts from chicken and remove and reserve the tenders (the extra flaps of meat on the side of the breast). Remove rest of meat from chicken and place with breasts in a food processor with cream and egg. Blend until smooth.
3. Transfer ground chicken to a bowl and add thyme leaves, mushrooms, shallot, and chives and mix with a spatula until incorporated.
4. Preheat oven to 425°F. Lay caul fat on a flat surface. Season chicken skin with salt and pepper, and place on one end of the caul fat. Spoon a layer of chicken mousse in a horizontal line across the chicken skin. Lay reserved chicken tenders down the center of the mousse, and top with the remaining mousse.
5. Lift edges of caul fat (as though it's plastic wrap) and use it to wrap the mousse in chicken skin and shape the mousse into a log.
6. When ballotine is shaped, pull back caul fat and trim it with a knife so you have just enough to wrap the ballotine.
7. Heat an oven-safe pan with a small amount of oil. Wrap caul fat around the ballotine (like it's a package) and transfer to the pan, seam side-down. Brown seam side then rotate to brown the ballotine on all sides. Transfer to the oven and roast for 15 minutes per lb. (about 30 minutes). Let rest at least 1 hour and serve at room temperature.

To Serve:
1. Slice ballotine into half-inch slices. Toss squash and frisée with olive oil and sherry vinegar and season with salt and pepper. Plate salad and lay two slices of ballotine on top.

Portage Bay Café
4130 Roosevelt Way NE

"But when the time comes that a man has had his dinner, then the true man comes to the surface."
Mark Twain

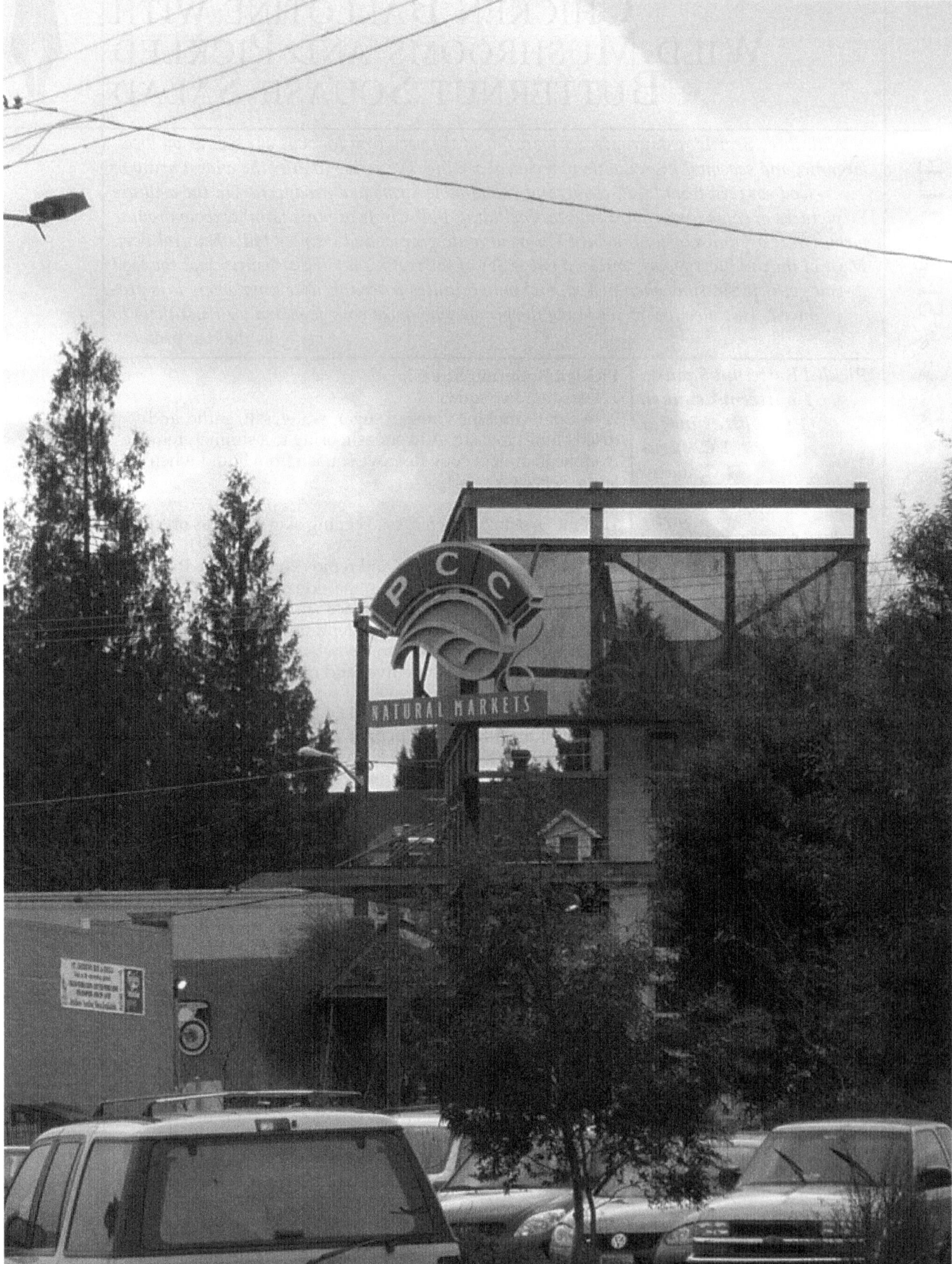
PCC
NATURAL MARKETS

Coconut Fish Curry with Charred Chiles & Lime

PCC Natural Markets began as a food-buying club of 15 families in 1953. Today, it's the largest consumer-owned natural food retail co-operative in the United States. PCC has nine stores in the Puget Sound region and is owned by nearly 45,000 members who shop (along with thousands of non-members) in our neighborhood locations.

2 jalapeños, seeds and membranes removed
2 stalks lemongrass, chopped (use bottom 5 inches)
½ C. chopped shallots
¼ C. cilantro stems (save the leaves)
1 garlic clove
2 tbsp chopped ginger
1 tsp ground coriander seed
1 tsp ground cumin seed
¼ tsp salt
¼ tsp dried turmeric (or 1 tsp grated fresh turmeric
5 Kaffir lime leaves, grind 1 for use in the curry paste, reserve the rest whole (or substitute with the zest from 2 limes)
stock or water, up to ¼ C.
1 tbsp vegetable oil
1 (14-oz.) can coconut milk
1 tbsp fish sauce
½ lb. halibut, cut in to chunks
toasted sesame seeds, for garnish

Chile-Lime Topping:
1 tsp vegetable oil
4 Fresno chiles, seeded and minced
2 tbsp diced red onion
½ C. chopped cilantro leaves
2 limes, rind removed, roughly chopped
salt, to taste

1. Put jalapeños, lemongrass, shallots, cilantro stems, garlic, ginger, coriander, cumin, salt, turmeric, and ground Kaffir lime leaf (or zest from 1 lime) in a food processor, and blend to create a curry paste. Use up to ¼ C. of the stock or water to help achieve a smooth puree. Blend well, at least 3 minutes.

2. Heat oil in a small sauce pan over medium-high heat. Add curry paste and fry the paste for 2-3 minutes. Add coconut milk, the rest of the Kaffir lime leaves or zest, and the fish sauce. Bring to a boil, reduce to a simmer and cook for 10 minutes.

3. Add the halibut and turn the heat off. Let the residual heat gently cook the fish. After 5 minutes it will be ready to serve. Top with sesame seeds. Serve this dish with rice and sautéed greens.

Chile-Lime Topping:

1. Heat the oil in a small sauté pan over medium-high heat. Fry the chiles and onion until caramelized.

2. Remove from heat and stir in the cilantro leaves, lime pieces, and salt. Place a spoonful on top of each serving.

PCC Natural Markets
600 North 34th Street

"An empty stomach is not a good political advisor."
Albert Einstein

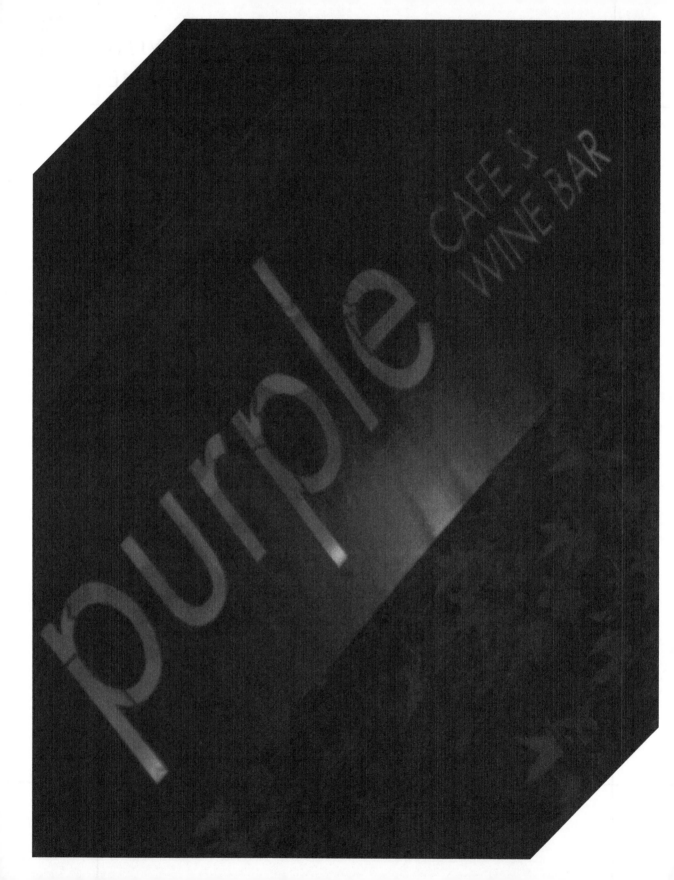
purple
CAFE &
WINE BAR

Boucheron Goat Cheese Appetizer

Founded by Seattle-based couple Larry and Tabitha Kurofsky, we're the management team behind Purple, Barrio, and Lot No. 3 restaurants. The business began in 2001, when Larry and Tabitha opened the first Purple Café & Wine Bar in Woodinville, Washington (if you're curious, Larry worked the bar and Tabitha served tables) with the goal of providing an experience that delivered "approachable expertise." Purple paired a global wine selection with Northwest cuisine made from local seasonal ingredients – all in an informal atmosphere. All menu items were designed to be enhanced by wine pairings and vice versa. In addition, all the staff not only were trained to be knowledgeable about the pairings, but to make recommendations for guests in a very comfortable, accessible way.

10-12 oz. of Boucheron goat cheese, cut into ½-inch thick rounds
¼ C. fireweed honey
3 tbsp dried cranberries, chopped
1 tsp lemon thyme (or regular thyme), picked
artisanal crackers for serving

1. Preheat oven to 350°F.

2. Place the disks of cheese in an oven safe dish and bake for 6-8 minutes or until the cheese is bubbling and beginning to turn golden brown.

3. Remove cheese from the oven and drizzle with fireweed honey. Sprinkle with chopped cranberries and picked lemon thyme.

4. Serve immediately with artisanal crackers.

Purple Café & Wine Bar

1225 4th Avenue

"Soup and fish explain half the emotions of human life."
Sydney Smith

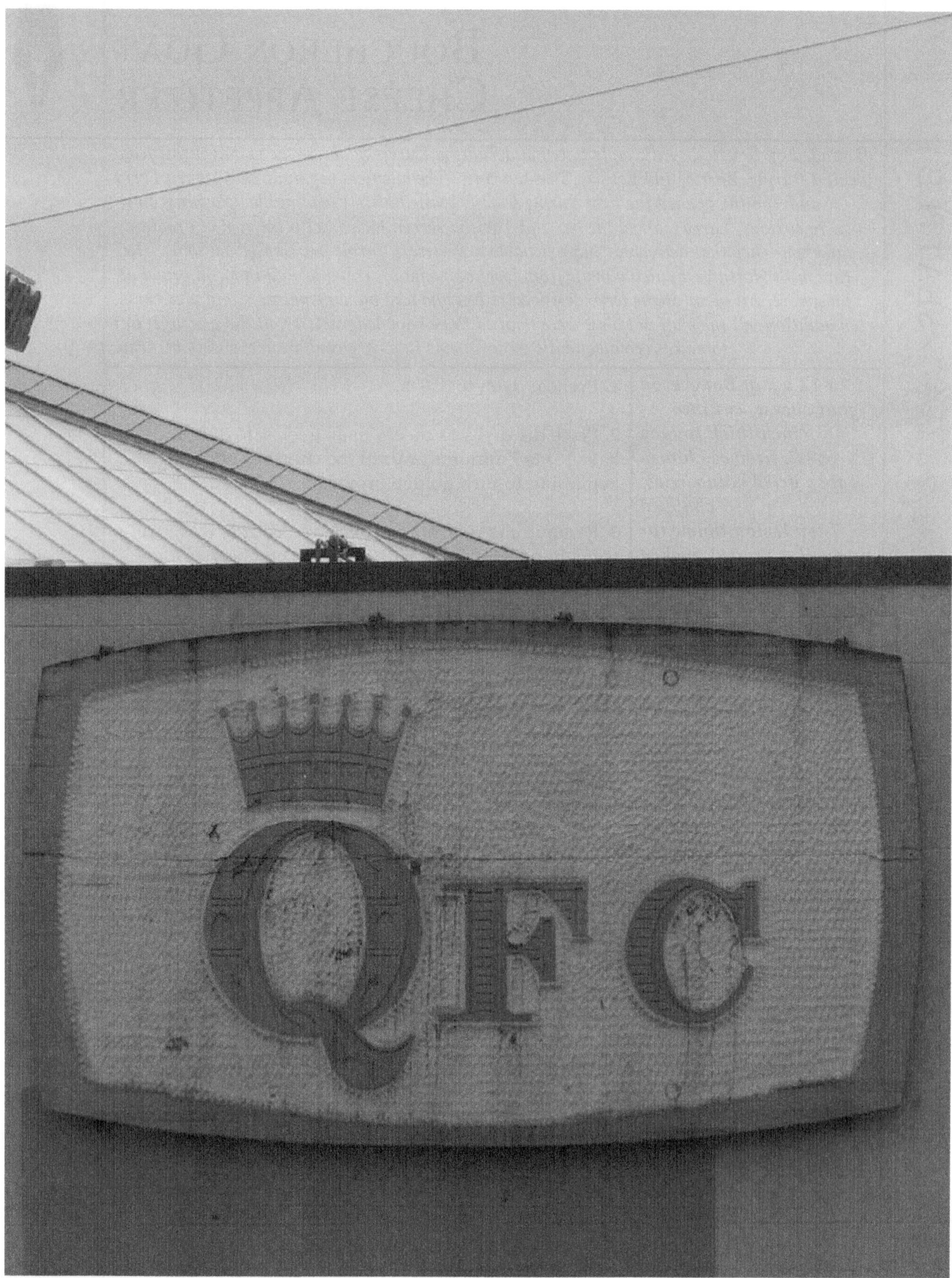
QFC

Bacon, Cheddar & Chive Scones

This is the QFC flagship store! Customer service is always great. They have a fabulous wine department. Their seafood and meat department carries fresh and quality cuts. They also carry a wide array of Kosher food.

2 C. all-purpose flour
2 tsp baking powder
¼ C. butter, chilled
3 eggs, divided
½ C. light cream
1½ C. sharp cheddar cheese, shredded
8 slices bacon, crisply cooked, crumbled
1 tbsp chopped fresh chives
1 tbsp water

1. Preheat oven to 425°F.

2. Mix flour and baking powder in a large bowl. Cut in butter until mixture resembles coarse crumbs.

3. Beat 2 of the eggs and cream in a medium bowl. Add to flour mixture; stir just until moistened.

4. Stir in cheese, bacon, and chives. Shape into a ball. Knead dough 10 times on lightly floured surface. Roll out to 12x6-inch rectangle. Cut into 8 (3-inch) squares; cut each square in half diagonally. Place scones on a lightly greased cookie sheet.

5. Mix remaining egg and water in a small bowl; brush over tops of scones.

6. Bake for 14 to 16 minutes or until lightly browned. Serve warm.

QFC-Quality Food Centers
417 Broadway East

"There has always been a food processor in the kitchen. But once upon a time she was usually called the missus or Mom."
Sue Berkman

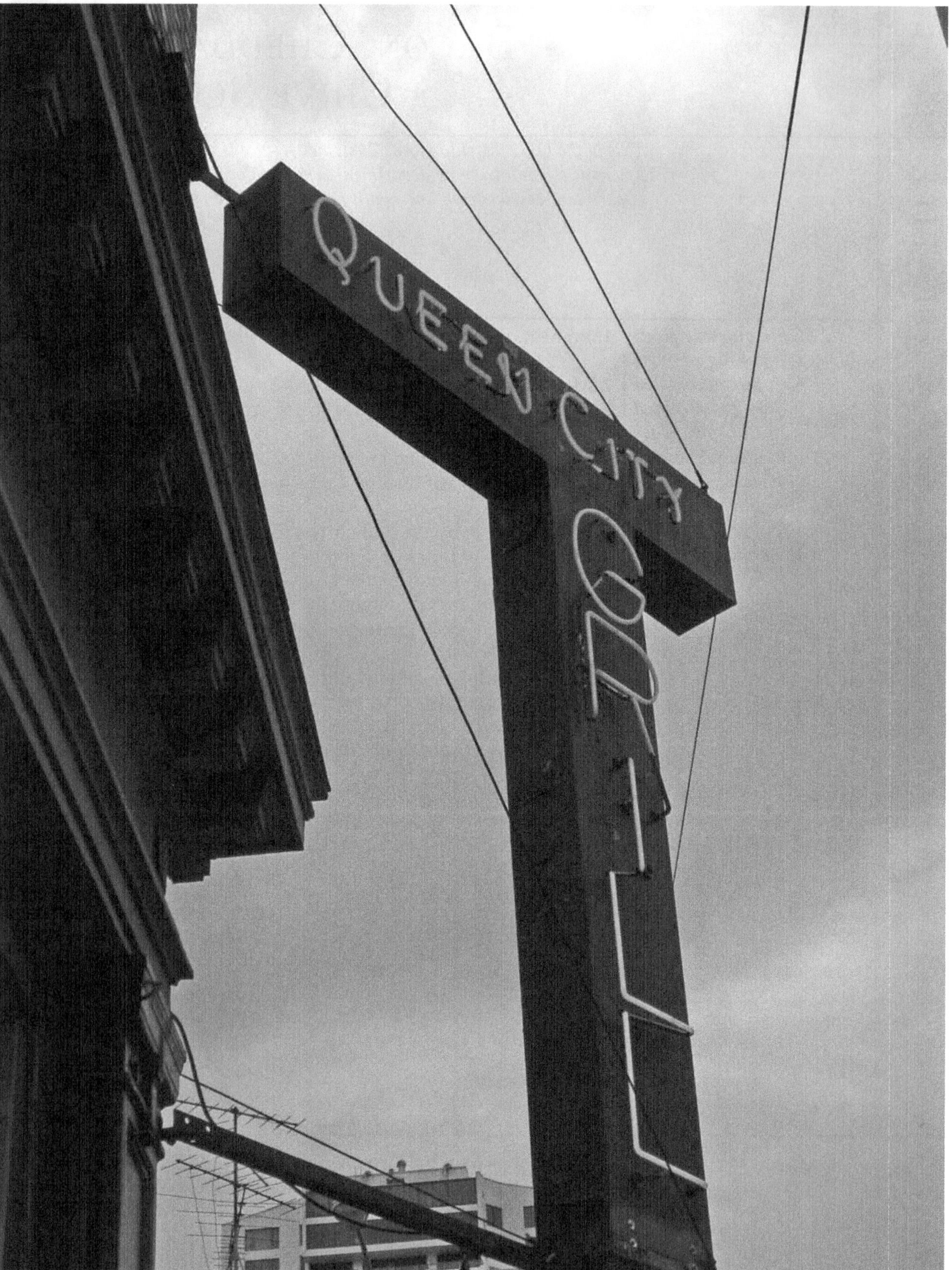
QUEEN CITY

Seared Sweetbreads with Roasted-Corn Polenta

Located in the heart of vibrant Belltown, the Queen City Grill specializes in fresh, simply grilled Northwest seafood. Settle into one of our high backed wooden booths surrounded by the glow of warm tangerine lighting and enjoy outstanding service, our award-winning 500-label wine list and classic cocktails handcrafted by some of Seattle's finest bartenders.

Polenta:
4 C. water
1 C. 2% milk
¼ salted butter
1½ C. polenta
2 C. roasted corn
½ C. grated parmesan
salt and pepper, to taste

Sweetbreads:
1½-2 lb. veal sweet breads (ask for heart lobe)
8 C. water
2 C. white wine
2 bay leaves
5 whole black peppercorns

For Serving:
prepared vinaigrette
balsamic reduction

Polenta:
1. Combine water, milk, and butter in sauce pot and bring to a boil. Whisk in polenta and reduce heat to medium-low, stir constantly.
2. When polenta is close to desired consistency add corn, parmesan, salt, and pepper. Pour out onto a sheet pan, smooth the top and refrigerate.
3. When cooled, turn sheet pan over onto cutting board and tap out polenta. Cut portions into desired shape. Can be prepared 1 day ahead.

Sweetbreads:
1. In a medium sauce pot bring water, wine, bay leaves, and black peppercorns to a boil. Add the sweetbreads, reduce the heat and simmer for about 3 minutes.
2. Remove the sweetbreads and cool completely in an ice bath. Drain and pat dry. Remove any excess membrane or fat.
3. Line a large plate or sheet pan with parchment paper. Cut portions from the lobe and place on parchment paper. Once portioned, cover with another piece of parchment paper and put another plate or sheet pan on top and weigh down sweetbreads for about an hour. They should compress a bit, but not be flattened. Remove weight and pat dry. Refrigerate overnight.

To Serve:
1. Brush oil on one side of the polenta and start with that side first to brown or mark your presentation side, then reheat polenta on a grill or in a sauté pan.
2. While the polenta is browning heat a sauté pan until very hot. Dredge the sweetbreads in flour and shake off excess. When pan is hot, add some oil and a bit of butter. Lay the sweetbreads in the pan, being careful not to crowd them. Brown well on the first side and then flip and quickly finish on second side. Remove and let rest on a paper towel to release some of the oil.
3. On each plate make a medium-sized pool of vinaigrette, place the polenta next to it and lean the sweetbreads against polenta into the vinaigrette.
4. With a spoon, drizzle the balsamic reduction over everything, especially the sweetbreads, and serve.

Queen City Grill
2201 1st Ave #1

"Don't forget that the flavors of wine and cheese depend upon the types of infecting microorganisms."
Martin H. Fischer

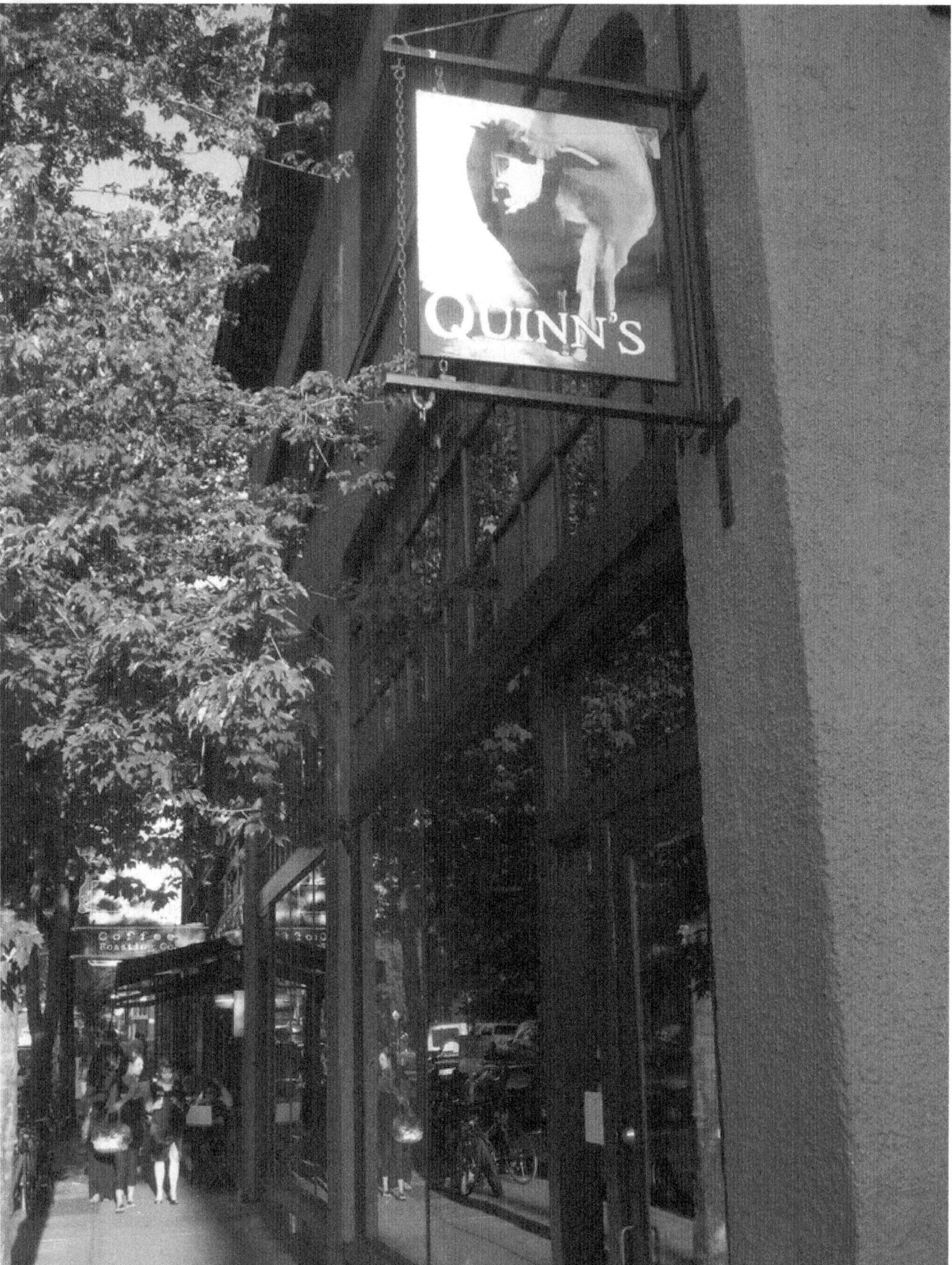
QUINN'S

Buffalo Duck Wings with Cumin-Scented Blue Cheese Dip

Welcome to Quinns – Scott and Heather Staples (owners of Restaurant Zoë) new gastropub located at 10th and Pike on Capitol Hill. Our menu features slow-roasted pork ribs, pan-roasted Idaho trout, fish and chips, and a great burger. We have 14 beers on tap including several Trapist ales, and, of course, a full bar.

Cumin-Scented Blue Cheese Dip:
2 tbsp chives, finely chopped
1 tsp Worcestershire
½ tbsp sherry vinegar
¼ C. mayonnaise
1 tsp Dijon mustard
½ tsp horseradish
1⅓ C. heavy cream
¾ C. Gorgonzola crumbles
3 tbsp crème fraîche
pinch cayenne
pinch cumin
salt and pepper, to taste

Duck Wings:
12 duck wings
6 qt. melted duck fat
8 oz. Frank's RedHot sauce
1 tsp smoked paprika
¼ C. butter
2 tbsp honey
salt

Cumin-Scented Blue Cheese Dip:
1. Combine dip ingredients in blender or food processor and blend thoroughly.

Duck Wings:
1. Place raw duck wings and fat in a pot large enough to cover wings with ½ inch of the melted duck fat. Bring the wings and fat to 200°F and simmer for 45 minutes or until tender and almost falling off the bone.

2. Remove wings from the duck fat (save for another use) and let cool on a sheet tray.

3. When the wings are cool enough to handle, toss them with the Frank's RedHot, a pinch of salt, and smoked paprika. Let marinate for 30 minutes.

4. In a separate pan, melt the butter and whisk in the honey until combined and set aside.

5. Put wings on a hot grill until the skin is crispy. Before removing from the grill, brush with the butter and honey mixture.

6. Serve with cumin-scented blue cheese dip.

Quinn's Pub
1001 East Pike Street

"To the old saying that man built the house but woman made of it a "home" might be added the modern supplement that woman accepted cooking as a chore but man has made of it a recreation."
Emily Post

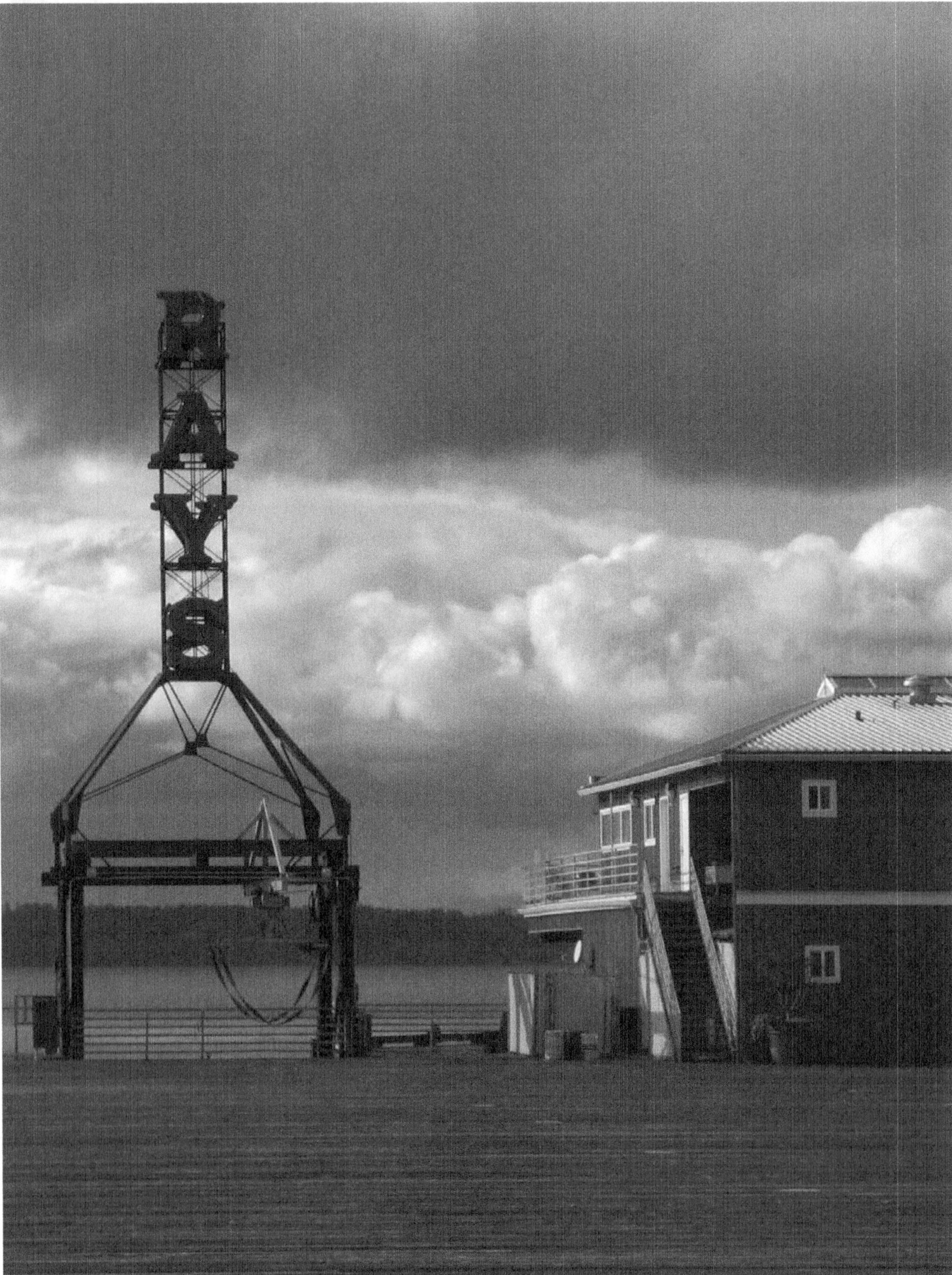

Oven Roasted Alaskan Ling Cod

Widely regarded as a "must visit" by locals and travelers alike, Ray's Boathouse is world-renowned for its impeccably fresh Northwest seafood. Our culinary professionals hand select the best products from local purveyors and then prepare them simply to enhance the naturally fresh, clean flavors and succulent textures. The menu changes weekly to reflect what is seasonally and locally available. Combined with our spectacular bayside view of the Olympic Mountains over Puget Sound, Ray's Boathouse is the quintessential Northwest seafood experience. Complementing Ray's cuisine is our award-winning wine list of more than 700 selections, with an emphasis on Northwest vineyards.

4 (6-oz.) Ling cod fillets (or any meaty whitefish, such as halibut)
Kosher salt
freshly ground black pepper
2 tbsp olive oil
12 red new potatoes, blanched and shocked
4 oz. Spanish chorizo
20 Manila clams
8 oz. calamari, tubes and tentacles
2 medium bell peppers, julienned
20-25 small green beans
2 C. white wine
4 tbsp unsalted butter, in one whole piece

1. Preheat oven to 350°F.

2. Season flesh side of the cod with salt and pepper. Heat the olive oil in a large non-stick sauté pan over medium-high heat. Add the ling cod, seasoned side down, and sear 2 to 3 minutes. Turn cod over and cook for another 1-2 minutes.

3. Transfer cod to an oven-proof baking dish and bake for 10-12 minutes.

4. While cod is baking, in the same sauté pan, reheat the remaining olive oil and fish juices. Add the potatoes and cook 2-3 minutes, turning occasionally. Add the chorizo and clams and cook for another 3-4 minutes. Add the calamari, peppers, and beans and cook for additional 2-3 minutes.

5. Deglaze the pan with white wine and let simmer for 1 minute. Turn off the heat and add the butter, swirling the pan to melt.

6. Divide the mixture into the middle of four plates or shallow bowls and pour the white-wine butter sauce over top. Top with ling cod fillets. Serve immediately.

Ray's Boathouse
6049 Seaview Avenue NW

"I eat so poorly during the stressful part of my day I need to have a vegetable orgy for dinner just to make up for it."
Carrie Latet

Masa Onion Rings

The original Red Mill was located in the Capitol Hill neighborhood in Seattle and opened in 1937. It closed in 1967. It was known as a diner and ice creamery with table and counter service. The current Red Mills were opened first in the Phinney Ridge neighborhood in 1994 and the second location in the Interbay neighborhood in 1998.

2 onions (about 1½ lb.)
4 C. all-purpose flour
2 C. buttermilk
1 C. medium-ground yellow cornmeal
¼ C. masa harina
1 tbsp. paprika
1 tbsp Kosher salt
2 tsp cayenne pepper
1 tsp dried thyme
½ tsp freshly ground black pepper
peanut oil for deep-frying

1. Peel onions and and cut into ½-inch-thick slices. Separate the onions into rings. Discard the inner center pieces, which are too small, or reserve for another use.
2. You will need three bowls for breading the onion rings. Place two cups of flour in the first bowl. Pour the buttermilk into the second bowl. In the third bowl, combine the remaining two cups of flour with the cornmeal, masa harina, paprika, salt, cayenne, thyme, and black pepper.
3. Line two baking sheets with parchment or wax paper.
4. In batches, dip the onions in flour, then buttermilk, and then seasoned flour mix. When necessary, to keep the flour clean and easy to work with, sift the seasoned flour mix and discard any clumps of batter. Place the breaded rings on the baking sheets and place the sheets in the refrigerator for one hour to set.
5. Preheat oven to 350°F and heat a straight-sided pan with at least two inches of oil, no more than halfway up the sides, to 350°F.
6. Fry the onion rings without crowding them until golden yellow, then drain on paper towels. The onion rings should be light in color; be careful not to burn.
7. Season to taste with salt and serve immediately.

NOTE: If you are frying the onion rings in batches, you can hold them on a baking sheet in a 350°F oven while you finish frying all of them. Don't leave them in the oven too long, or they will get soggy.

Red Mill Totem House
3058 Northwest 54th Street

"Banish (the onion) from the kitchen and the pleasure flies with it. Its presence lends color and enchantment to the most modest dish; its absence reduces the rarest delicacy to hopeless insipidity, and dinner to despair."
Elizabeth Robbins Pennell

Fettucine Carbonara

In two decades as a Capitol Hill favorite, Machiavelli has earned a reputation for bringing people together and making them feel like family. Under Tom and Linda's steady guidance, the restaurant has nurtured devoted and loyal customers as well as a devoted and loyal staff. Upon celebrating Machiavelli's 20-year anniversary in August 2008, Tom and Linda have brought on two longtime staff members as partners so they can relax and enjoy life just a bit more. Suzette Jarding has been with Machiavelli for 10 years, serving customers in every imaginable position at the front of the house. Javier Arevalo has been the backbone of the kitchen and Linda's right-hand man in preparing consistent and dependable dishes night after night.

1 lb. fettucine noodles
4 eggs
1 C. parmesan cheese
freshly ground black pepper
8 slices of bacon, thick cut
1 tbsp garlic, chopped
½ tsp red pepper flakes, crushed
¼ C. white wine
2 tbsp butter

1. Bring a large pot of salted water to boil. Drop in noodles. Cook 10 minutes, or until al dente. Drain, reserving ½ cup of pasta cooking water.

2. In a bowl large enough to acommodate all the cooked noodles, crack the eggs. Add the cheese and a generous quantity of freshly ground pepper. Mix well with a fork. Set aside.

3. In a sauté pan, brown the bacon until three-quarters done. Remove bacon and set aside. Discard fat and clean pan.

4. Add bacon back to pan and cook until crisp. Add garlic and red pepper flakes and stir quickly so garlic does not burn. Add wine and butter and reduce. Remove pan from heat.

5. Place hot fettucine noodles and bacon mixture into the bowl with the eggs and toss quickly so that the eggs don't coagulate. Add ¼ cup of the reserved pasta water and mix, adding more water as necessary to make a creamy sauce.

NOTE: Noodles should have a creamy consistency with just the right amount of sauce clinging to them. There should not be a pool of sauce in bottom of the bowl.

Ristorante Machiavelli
1215 Pine Street

"Most of the food allergies die under garlic and onion."
Martin H. Fischer

RN74
1433
ONE WAY

Orecchiette with Fava Pesto

The cuisine at RN74 aims to be a perfect complement to the wines – creative, modern, but simple interpretations of regional French cuisine punctuated with seasonal, fresh ingredients and bold flavors, all executed with a signature original twist.

Pesto:
1 lb. fava leaves, stems removed
12 oz. canola oil
2 oz. Marcona almonds
1-2 garlic cloves
1 orange, zested and juiced

1 lb. fava beans

Spring Onion Confit:
2 spring onions
½ C. extra virgin olive oil

1 lb. orecchiette pasta
3-4 oz. fresh ricotta cheese
1 baguette from local bakery

Pesto:
1. Fill a large pot with salted water and bring to a boil.
2. Blanch the fava leaves for about 1 minute. Transfer to an ice bath to stop the cooking. Remove from the ice bath and squeeze out the excess water. Coarsely chop the blanched fava leaves and place into a blender.
3. Add the oil, almonds, and garlic to the blender and blend on high until smooth.
4. Place mixture in a bowl and stir in salt, pepper, orange juice and zest, to taste. Store cold until ready to use.

Fava Beans:
1. Open up the pod to remove the fava beans. Once all are cleaned, blanch the fava beans for 1-2 minutes until tender then place in ice water to stop the cooking.
2. Once the beans are cool, carefully peel off the outer skin layer to reveal the bright green beans.

Spring Onion Confit:
1. Remove the root end and cut the onions into ½-inch rings. Rinse well under cold water. Place the onions in a small pot and cover with the olive oil.
2. Cook on low heat until very tender and translucent.
3. Reserve oil from the cooking process.

Assembly:
1. Cook the pasta according to the package directions. When the pasta is done, drain well but do not rinse. Place the pasta back into the warm pot.
2. Toss in the fava beans, spring onion confit (do not add the reserved oil), and the pesto, as desired. Toss the pasta mixture well and adjust seasoning.
3. Place pasta into a large bowl and top with dollops of fresh ricotta cheese. Drizzle with the reserved spring onion confit oil. Top with additional chopped almonds, if desired. Serve with a fresh toasted baguette.

RN74
1433 4th Avenue

"Ever since Eve started it all by offering Adam the apple, woman's punishment has been to supply a man with food then suffer the consequences when it disagrees with him."
Helen Rowland

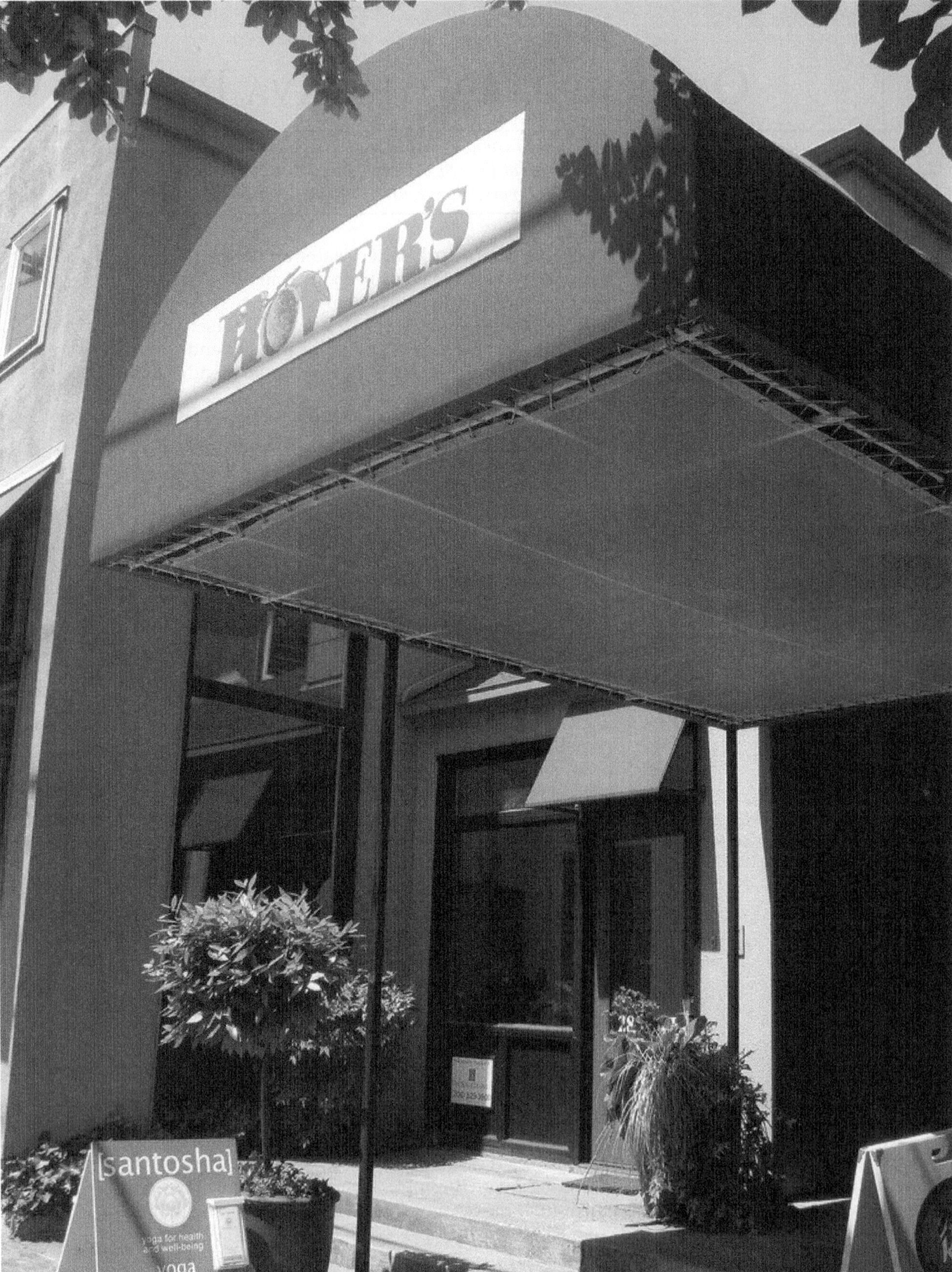
[santosha]
yoga for health
and well-being
yoga

Dungeness Crab Salad

Our menu is best described as the cuisine of the Pacific Northwest refined by a French accent. The Chef in the Hat provides the French accent while the bounty of the Pacific Northwest provides the raw ingredients. We do not serve classical French food; instead, we use traditional French techniques to tease out the many flavors of the region's best ingredients. Chef Thierry Rautureau is passionate about sourcing ingredients that are local, sustainable, organic, and seasonal.

1 head garlic
2 shallots
3 tbsp + 4 tsp olive oil
salt and freshly ground white pepper
4 slices thyme brioche or 8 slices baguette
¼ C. + 1 tsp pomegranate juice
¼ C. red wine vinegar
6 oz. Dungeness crabmeat
2 tsp minced chives
salt and freshly ground black pepper
small handful chervil leaves or baby watercress
1 tsp basil oil or extra virgin olive oil

1. Preheat the oven to 375°F.
2. Peel away the loose papery skin from the whole head of garlic and trim the root end to expose some of the garlic flesh.
3. Trim the root end from the shallots. Set the garlic and shallots in the center of a large piece of foil, drizzle them with 2 tsp. of the olive oil and season with salt and pepper.
4. Wrap the package securely and roast until tender when pressed between your fingers, 1 to 1¼ hours. Set aside until cool enough to handle. When cool, squeeze roasted garlic and shallots from their skins and coarsely chop. Toss garlic and shallots together and set aside.
5. Trim brioche slices into 4-inch rounds. Heat a medium skillet over medium heat, add 2 tsp. of olive oil. Add the brioche slices and toast well on each side, about 3 minutes total. Set aside on paper towels.
6. Combine ¼ C. pomegranate juice and the vinegar in a small sauce pan. Bring to a boil over medium-high heat and reduce to 2 tablespoons, 5 to 7 minutes. Remove pan from heat, whisk in 3 tbsp. of the olive oil and set aside.
7. Pick over crabmeat to remove any shell or cartilage. Set 4 large claw or leg portions aside for garnish. Put remaining crabmeat in a bowl. Add pomegranate vinaigrette and chives with salt and pepper to taste. Toss well to evenly mix.
8. Toss garlic and shallots with remaining tsp. of pomegranate juice and season to taste with salt and pepper.
9. To serve, spoon the garlic/shallot mixture onto the toasted brioche rounds and set them on individual plates. Form large quenelles of the crab salad and set them on top of the brioche. Top the crab salad with reserved claw or leg portions.
10. In a small bowl, toss the chervil with the basil oil and a pinch of salt. Add the chervil salad alongside and serve.

Rover's Restaurant
2808 East Madison Street

"Bread and butter, devoid of charm in the drawing-room, is ambrosia eating under a tree."
Elizabeth Russell

UPSTAIRS
at
SALTY'S

Dungeness Crab Macaroni and Cheese

Salty's Seafood Grill is truly in a class by itself. We bend over backwards to please you with our award-winning fresh Northwest seafood cuisine and attentive friendly service. Whether enjoying live Dungeness crab and Maine lobster (they're swimming in our salt-water tanks in the lobby) to our world-famous Alaskan salmon and halibut in season, oysters and clams from Northwest beaches or USDA prime-aged charbroiled steaks, pasta, chicken, or luncheon salads, and sandwiches, you will find many choices on our menus to please the most discriminating palette. Our award-winning Sunday brunch is like none you've ever seen elsewhere.

1½ C. macaroni, cooked
½ C. heavy cream
2 tbsp cream cheese
1 tbsp chèvre cheese
2 tbsp white cheddar cheese, grated
2 tbsp Beecher's cheese, grated
1 tbsp butter
1 pinch black pepper
1 pinch Kosher salt
3 oz. Dungeness crabmeat
1½ tbsp Beecher's Bread Crumbs (recipe follows)

Beecher's Bread Crumbs:
1 tbsp bread crumbs
2 tsp Beecher's cheese, finely grated
1 pinch garlic granules
1 pinch onion granules

fresh chopped Italian parsley, for garnish

1. Preheat broiler.

2. Place a sauté pan over medium heat, add heavy cream, cream cheese, chèvre cheese, white cheddar cheese, and Beecher's cheese. Bring to a simmer stirring constantly with a rubber spatula.

3. Add pre-cooked macaroni, butter, black pepper, Kosher salt and 2 oz. of crabmeat. Turn heat to medium high and stir until the mixture thickens, about 3-5 minutes.

4. Transfer macaroni to an oven-proof serving bowl, top with the Beecher's bread crumbs and place in broiler and cook for 2-3 minutes or until surface is browned.

5. Garnish with remaining 1 ounce of crabmeat and finish with chopped Italian parsley (optional).

Salty's Seafood Restaurant
1936 Harbor Avenue S.W.

"My soul is dark with stormy riot, directly traceable to diet."
Samuel Hoffenstein

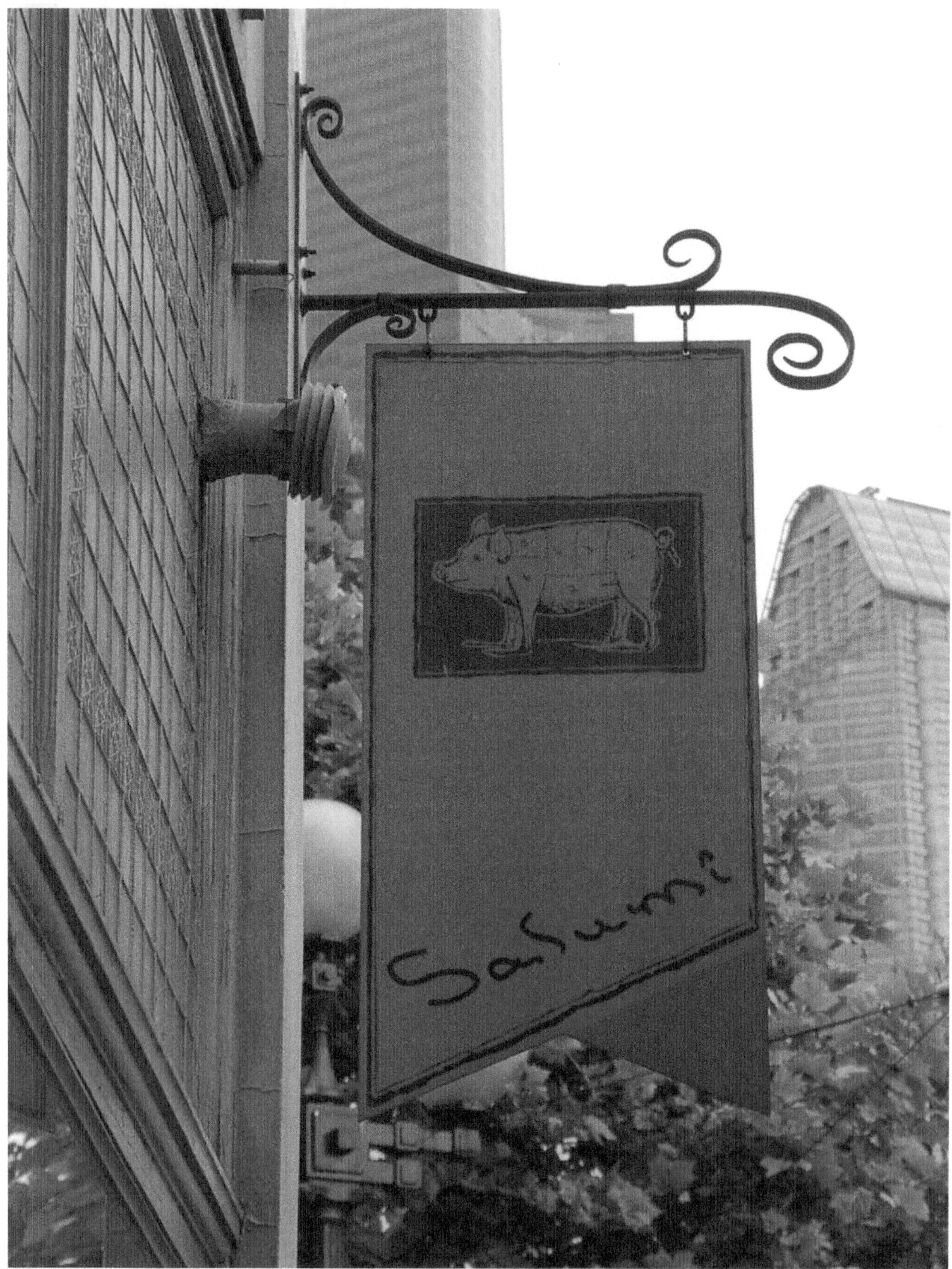
Salumi

Beef and Sausage Meatloaf with Mozzarella

Armandino Batali of Salumi in Seattle, writes: "My son, Mario Batali, may be the most recognizable foodie in the family, but the Batali's interest in Italian cooking and culture goes back generations. My grandfather opened Seattle's first Italian-food import store in 1903. It was located just a few steps from where my restaurant, Salumi, is now, and it's one of the things that inspired me to get into the business.The idea behind Salumi was to create a restaurant, deli, and meat factory in one place, just like the salumerias in Italy. We're known for homemade sausages and salami, but we also attract a large lunchtime crowd. Some of the specials, like the meatloaf and frittata, have been in our family for years. They're also easy to make at home. This Italian-inspired version is filled with sausage, mozzarella cheese, and basil.

2 lb. lean ground beef (15 percent fat)
1 lb. coarsely grated whole-milk mozzarella cheese
1 lb. sweet Italian sausages, casings removed, meat crumbled
2 C. chopped fresh basil
2 C. fresh bread crumbs made from crustless French bread
1 medium onion, chopped
1 C. chopped drained oil-packed sun-dried tomatoes
5 garlic cloves, minced
1½ tbsp dried oregano
2 tsp salt
1 tsp ground black pepper
1 C. tomato sauce, divided
3 large eggs, beaten to blend
½ C. dry red wine

1. Preheat oven to 375°F.

2. Combine all ingredients except the tomato sauce, eggs, and wine, in large bowl.

3. Gently mix in ½ C. tomato sauce, eggs, and wine. Place meat mixture on large rimmed baking sheet and shape into a free-form 16x4-inch loaf. Brush with remaining ½ C. tomato sauce.

4. Bake meatloaf until cooked through and thermometer inserted into center registers between 160°F and 170°F, about 1 hour 15 minutes.

Salumi
309 3rd Avenue South

"I'm trying to eat better. And, I do feel wise after drinking tea. After eating vegetables, I just feel hungry."
Carrie Latet

ZERAC
THE ROOSEVELT HOTEL

Salmon with Lemon Risotto and Morel Sauce

You come in, sit down and the first thing you notice are the napkin rings. The ones shaped like pigs....Or maybe it's the elegantly eccentric chandeliers, crafted by Seattle's own Grey Design Studios. Perhaps the Maya Romanoff flexible glass bead wall coverings catch your eye....This is Sazerac in downtown Seattle. Next to Hotel Monaco Seattle, it's a restaurant as personable and distinct as the Pacific Northwest is to the rest of the U.S.

6 (6-oz.) Copper River salmon fillets, brushed with olive oil and grilled

Risotto:
4 oz. olive oil
1 onion, diced
3 C. risotto rice
10 C. chicken stock, kept warm
3 lemons, zested
1 C. parmesan cheese
4 oz. butter
½ bunch thyme, picked

Morel Sauce:
2 tbsp butter
4 oz. morel mushrooms
2 shallots, sliced
3 cloves garlic, sliced
1 C. port
2 C. fish fumet
2 tbsp whole grain mustard
1 tsp butter
red wine vinegar, to taste
salt and pepper, to taste

Risotto:

1. In a heavy-bottomed pot, heat olive oil and onions over medium heat. Sweat the onion until translucent, 1-2 minutes.
2. Add risotto and stir well until rice is well coated.
3. Slowly add warm chicken stock about 1 cup at a time. Constantly stir risotto, adding more stock when liquid is nearly absorbed. Cook risotto until al dente, about 20 minutes. At this point, risotto should be creamy and smooth.
4. Add lemon zest, cheese, thyme, and butter. Season with salt and pepper.

Morel Sauce:

1. Add butter to a sauté pan and sauté shallots, morels, and garlic over medium heat until lightly browned.
2. Add port and reduce by half.
3. Add fish fumet and reduce by half.
4. Add in the butter and finish with whole grain mustard. Season with salt and pepper, to taste.

To Serve:

1. Serve lemon risotto with grilled salmon fillet over top, drizzle morel sauce over the salmon.

Sazerac
1101 4th Ave

"Life expectancy would grow by leaps and bounds if green vegetables smelled as good as bacon."
Doug Larson

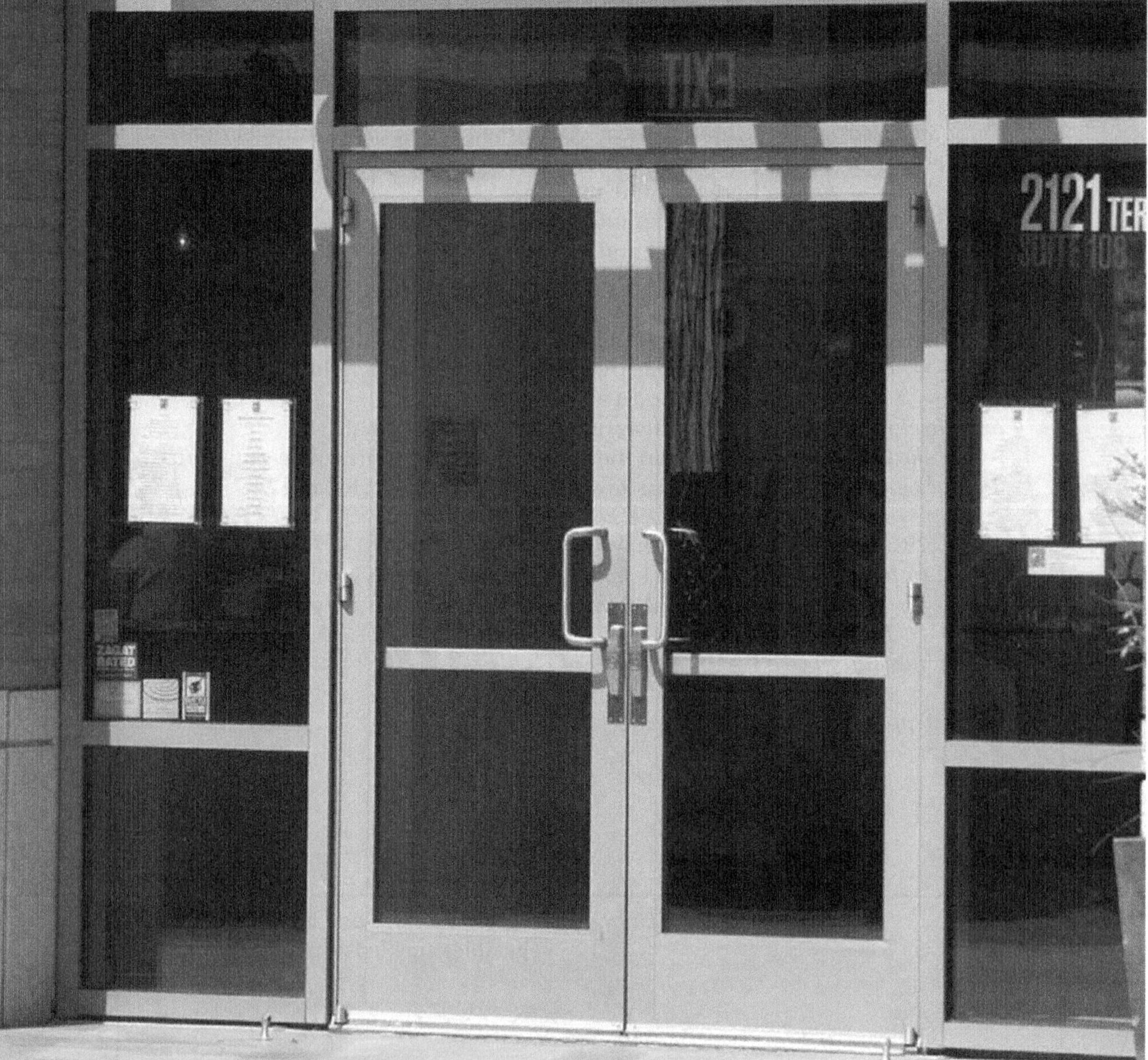
SEASTAR
restaurant and raw bar
2121

Steamed Clams with Pesto

Seastar is brought to you by renowned chef John Howie, formerly of Seattle's Palisade Restaurant. Seastar provides guests with an amazing array of freshly prepared seafood, great steaks, poultry, pastas and raw bar items. Enjoy the comfort of the luxurious Seastar dining room or the upbeat Raw Bar. Either way, Seastar's talented staff will help to make you feel right at home, and the food will keep you coming back for more.

Steamed Clams:
1½ tsp olive oil
⅜ tsp garlic, minced
⅛ tsp crushed red chilies
8 oz. clams in shells, small Manila or butter
1 tbsp clam juice
1 tbsp white wine
2 tbsp sweet basil pesto (recipe follows)
1½ tsp pine nuts, toasted
Parmigiano-Reggiano cheese, shaved

Sweet Basil Pesto:
½ C. packed fresh basil, coarsely chopped
½ oz. fresh parsley, coarsely chopped
1 tbsp garlic, minced
¼ C. pine nuts, toasted
½ tsp Kosher salt
3 tbsp Parmigiano-Reggiano cheese, grated
2 tbsp salted butter
⅓ C. olive oil

Steamed Clams:
1. Place the olive oil, chilies, and garlic over medium heat in a sauté pan. Sauté 1-2 minutes until garlic begins to turn golden.

2. Deglaze pan with clam juice and white wine.

3. When liquid begins to boil, add clams. Reduce heat to low and cover. Cook 2-3 minutes until clams just begin to open.

4. Add the sweet basil pesto and let cook until sauce begins to thicken.

5. Place clams and liquid in a heated bowl. Garnish with pine nuts and shaved Parmigiano-Reggiano.

Sweet Basil Pesto:
1. Combine all ingredients except butter and oil in a food processor and pulse until ingredients are finely chopped but not pureed.

2. Add the butter and oil and process to a thick paste.

Seastar Restaurant & Raw Bar
2121 Terry Ave, Suite 108

"Our countries are great friends. We have given you Lafayette and French fried potatoes"
O. Henry

Serafina
osteria & enoteca

Venetian Marinated Mussels

Serafina opened its doors in 1991 as an intimate neighborhood restaurant located along Eastlake between the University and Downtown. Its ochre walls, reminiscent of the Tuscan landscape, its intimate, sultry atmosphere, and its authentic Italian cuisine make it a favorite with diners from around the Puget Sound and beyond. Serafina's philosophy is simple: Offer the freshest, highest quality ingredients, present the food in an honest and inviting way, and provide the casual warmth and soothing ambiance that echoes the welcoming embrace of an Italian home.

1 lb. mussels, locally grown
1 C. white wine
1 shallot, julienned
¼ C. red onion, minced
3 tbsp champagne vinegar
1 lemon, zested
1 orange, zested
¼ C. red bell pepper, finely chopped
¼ C. yellow bell pepper, finely chopped
½ tbsp basil, chopped
½ tbsp parsley, chopped
½ tbsp chives, chopped
¼ C. extra virgin olive oil
salt and pepper, to taste

1. In a sauté pan, combine the mussels, white wine, shallot, 1 cup of water, salt and pepper to taste, and bring to a boil. When boiling, stir and cover. After 4 minutes, check to see if all the mussels have opened, if 20% are not open, cook a few more minutes.

2. When most of the shells are open, drain the mussels and chill. When cold, pull the mussels out of the shell and set aside. Twist shells apart for presentation on the half shell.

3. In a mixing bowl, combine the onion, the vinegar, and the zest and let sit for 15 minutes.

4. Add the diced peppers, herbs, and oil. Season with salt and pepper, to taste.

5. Add the cleaned mussels to the marinade and mix gently, but well.

6. Place 1 mussel back into each half shell for presentation. Serve on a bed of Kosher salt or finely chopped ice. Serve very cold with Prosecco or white wine.

Serafina Osteria and Enoteca
2043 Eastlake Avenue East

"Food for all is a necessity. Food should not be a merchandise, to be bought and sold as jewels are bought and sold by those who have the money to buy. Food is a human necessity, like water and air, it should be available."
Pearl Buck

Serious pie.

Pizza Margherita

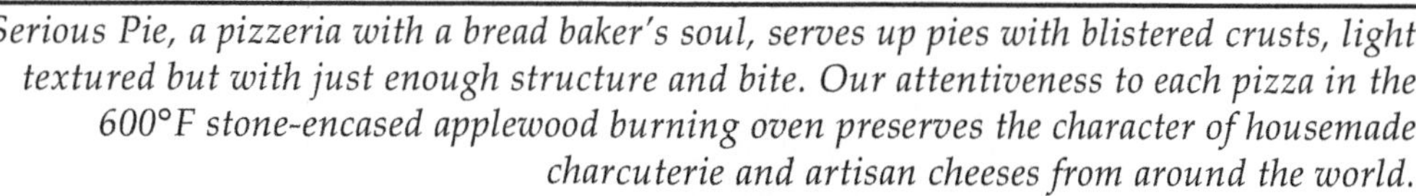

Serious Pie, a pizzeria with a bread baker's soul, serves up pies with blistered crusts, light textured but with just enough structure and bite. Our attentiveness to each pizza in the 600°F stone-encased applewood burning oven preserves the character of housemade charcuterie and artisan cheeses from around the world.

Basic Pizza Dough:
- *1½ C. water*
- *3 tbsp extra virgin olive oil*
- *3 C. unbleached all-purpose or bread flour*
- *1⅛ tsp table salt*
- *¾ tsp active dry yeast*

Pizza Margherita:
- *2 large ripe tomatoes*
- *2 tbsp extra virgin olive oil*
- *4 tsp balsamic vinegar*
- *1 tsp coarse salt*
- *8 oz. fresh mozzarella*
- *10 leaves fresh basil*
- *1 batch pizza dough at room temp (above)*
- *cornmeal for transferring pizza*
- *extra virgin olive oil for brushing dough*
- *additional salt, to taste*

Basic Pizza Dough:

1. Pour water and oil into bread machine pan. Add the flour, distributing it evenly over the water. Add the salt around the edges of the pan.

2. Make a slight indentation in the center of the flour and add the yeast. Set the pan in the bread machine and choose the "Dough" cycle.

3. When the dough cycle is done, punch it down and transfer to a well oiled storage bag. Store the dough in the refrigerator for at least 4 to 6 hours, preferably for a day or two.

4. Let the dough come to room temperature before shaping. Divide the dough in 2 equal portions.

Pizza Margherita:

1. Set baking stone on bottom rack of oven. Preheat the oven to 500°F for about an hour.

2. Core tomatoes, cut into half or quarters, then slice thinly. Gently toss tomatoes with olive oil, vinegar, and salt. Slice mozzarella thinly. Cut basil into thin ribbons.

3. Roll or stretch dough into two 12-14 inch rounds on a well-floured surface. Sprinkle a pizza peel or sheet pan generously with corn meal.

4. Transfer one of the shaped pizza doughs to the peel or sheet pan. Give the peel a shake to make sure dough slides easily. Add more cornmeal if it sticks. Let the dough rest 5 to 10 minutes before topping.

5. Pour about 1 tbsp. extra virgin olive oil onto the shaped pizza dough and use a brush (or back of spoon) to spread it out evenly. Scatter half the tomato pieces evenly over the dough, then place half the mozzarella evenly over the dough, followed by half the basil. Finally, top the pizza with a good sprinkling of coarse salt to taste.

6. Transfer pizza to baking stone. Bake for 8-10 minutes, or until dough is set and cheese is browned to your liking. Let the pizza cool for 10 minutes before slicing. Repeat with second pizza.

Serious Pie
316 Virginia St

"Food to a large extent is what holds a society together and eating is closely linked to deep spiritual experiences."
Peter Farb and George Armelagos

Sitka & Spruce

Muhammara

This intimate restaurant has a neighborhood bistro ambiance with bare wood tables, mismatched chairs and the menu and wine list, which change regularly, is hand-printed entirely on adjacent blackboards. Servers are knowledgeable and can recommend pairings. Items like the Halibut Crud and Haunch and Leg of Rabbit are served one plate at a time, meant for family-style sharing.

½ C. walnuts, toasted
1 tbsp chopped garlic
2 tbsp tomato paste
¾ C. fresh bread crumbs (from a Tall Grass Bakery baguette)
3 tbsp extra virgin olive oil
3 red bell peppers, roasted, skinned, seeded, pith removed, and drained
2 tbsp pomegranate molasses (available at Metropolitan Market)
2 tsp hot Spanish smoked paprika
¼ tsp smoked chipotle Tabasco
¼ tsp Chinese red pepper sauce
½ tsp ground cumin
salt, to taste

1. Pulse walnuts in a food processor until they are in very small pieces. Add garlic, tomato paste, bread-crumbs, and oil and pulse until it becomes a thick paste.

2. Add remaining ingredients except salt, and blend until it is thick and smooth. Taste and correct seasoning with salt.

3. Store, refrigerated in a covered container, for at least an hour so the flavors blend. Muhammara can be eaten as a dip with bread or as a sauce for kebabs, grilled meats, and fish.

Sitka & Spruce
1531 Melrose Ave.

"Do unto those downstream as you would have those upstream do unto you."
Wendell Berry

The Sitting Room

On the Slate Boards

Smoked Duck Breast and Red Grape-Hazelnut Salad

Inspired by the cafés, bars and bistros of France and old-world Europe, The Sitting Room opened its doors in December of 1998 and has become one of Seattle's most distinctive and charming evening destinations. Come experience our stylish, unhurried European ambiance where you will find great company, wonderful menu items and no televisions. Chic surroundings and warm countryside lighting offer a relaxing atmosphere. Sink into the antique sofa or sit at the authentic zinc bar with one of our signature fresh-herb or fruit cocktails. We also offer a carefully chosen selection of international wines, beers, premium spirits, and light cuisine fare.

Dressing:
¼ C. fresh orange juice
1 tsp orange zest
large splash of sherry vinegar
2-3 tsp pomegranate molasses
¼ C. olive oil
salt and pepper, to taste

Salad:
2 C. mixed greens
¾ lb. smoked duck breast, thinly sliced and warmed
2 C. red seedless California grapes, halved
½ C. hazelnuts, toasted
orange zest

Dressing:

1. In a small bowl, mix together all ingredients for dressing except the oil.

2. Add the oil in a thin stream, whisking until combined. Season with salt and pepper.

Salad:

1. Toss greens in dressing.

2. Arrange warmed duck slices and sliced grapes over dressed greens. Sprinkle hazelnuts over top. Garnish with orange zest.

The Sitting Room
108 West Roy Street

"Food without wine is a corpse; wine without food is a ghost; united and well matched they are as body and soul, living partners."
Andre Simon

RESERVED PARKING
FOR
ALPHA CINE LAB
CLIENTS & EMPLOYEES
M - F 6:AM - 6:PM
EVENINGS $3
WEEKENDS & HOL DAYS $3
PLUS TAX
lletstreetfood.com FOR
• CALENDARS
• MAPS
• MENUS
KETCHUP
skillet

Bacon Jam

The original street food business has become a brand but has not strayed from its roots. The thread is still there: great food prepared with care, technique and the best of ingredients; an innovative experience that consistently surprises and satisfies; and a feeling of being personally connected to Skillet, in all its manifestations. We see this as our mission – to continue to deliver on these themes and to continue to find new channels though which we can expand the brand and the family of loyal Skillet customers.

1 lb. Hempler's bacon
1 medium onion, chopped
4 cloves garlic, minced
½ C. lightly packed brown sugar (light)
1 C. freshly brewed coffee
¼ C. 100% pure maple syrup
¼ C. cider vinegar
1 tbsp Dijon mustard
2-5 drops of Tabasco sauce, or to taste
½ tsp ground black pepper

1. Using kitchen scissors, cut bacon into ½ inch pieces and put into a large, cold Dutch oven or large pot.

2. Cook bacon over medium heat until most of the fat has rendered and the bacon is starting to brown.

3. Using a slotted spoon, remove bacon and drain on paper towels. Pour off all but 1 tbsp. of the bacon fat.

4. Add the onions and garlic and sauté in the bacon fat until it is translucent. Add bacon back to the Dutch oven and then add remaining ingredients.

5. Bring to a simmer and then lower heat and continue to simmer, uncovered, for about 1 hour or until thick and jam-like, stirring occasionally.

6. Allow the jam to cool for 5 minutes then transfer to food processor. Pulse the mixture 8-10 times or until it reaches desired texture.

7. Put into a jar and cool, then cover and refrigerate.

Skillet Street Food
1400 East Union Street

"Food is not about impressing people. It's about making them feel comfortable."
Ina Garten

Mocha-Braised Short Ribs

Everything here is fresh, the food, the conversation, even the view! Yes, the entire restaurant moves 360 degrees allowing you to take in each course of the city as you take in each delicious course of your meal. The elevator ride and O Deck are on us when you dine! Try the Lunar Orbiter dessert served up since 1962.

6 meaty bone-in beef short ribs

Brine:
1 C. salt
2 C. water
2 C. brewed coffee (chilled)

Braise:
¼ C. olive oil
1 medium onion, sliced
3 cloves garlic, smashed
2½ C. red wine
2½ C. beef broth
1 C. bittersweet chocolate
2 bay leaves

Brine:
1. Mix ingredients for brine together in a large bowl and place beef short ribs in brine for 6 hours, or overnight, in the refrigerator.

Braise:
1. Preheat oven to 350°F.

2. In a heavy bottom braising pan, heat the olive oil over medium-high heat.

3. Pull ribs from brine and dry the meat. Season ribs with salt and pepper and brown the meat in the oil, working in batches. Remove ribs from pan and place on a large plate.

4. Add onion and garlic to the pan, sauté until onions are translucent. Deglaze with red wine, scrape up the browned bits, reduce slightly. Then add broth and reduce again.

5. Add ribs and accumulated juices back to pan and add chocolate, stir until chocolate is melted. Add bay leaves and cover pan with a lid and braise ribs for 3 hours or until very tender.

6. Remove from oven and let cool for 20 minutes. Remove ribs from liquid and keep warm.

7. Strain sauce back into the pan and reduce over medium-high heat, skim fat. Reduce sauce until it coats the back of a spoon. Serve ribs with sauce.

Sky City at the Space Needle
400 Broad Street

"Let your food be your medicine, and your medicine be your food."
Hippocrates

Zucchini Carpaccio with Salt-Broiled Shrimp

Chef Jason Stratton, late of Poppy and Café Juanita, recently took the helm at Cascina Spinasse, where Justin Neidermeyer had been the founding chef. When recently interviewed about the transition, Stratton shared his plans to meld his long-standing passion for Italian food with the bounty of seasonal ingredients from local farms. These days, Stratton says that what he is most excited about is zucchini--particularly the Italian heirloom varieties he's been getting from his friends Siri Erickson-Brown and Jason Salvo at Local Roots Farm.

Zucchini:
3 tbsp extra virgin olive oil, plus more for drizzling
2 zucchini (6 oz. each), sliced lengthwise ¼-in. thick
salt and freshly ground pepper
1 small onion, finely diced
3 garlic cloves, thinly sliced
large pinch of crushed red pepper
1 C. dry white wine
1 tbsp + 1 tsp red wine vinegar
¼ C. chopped parsley
2 tbsp chopped mint

Pine Nut Sauce:
1 C. pine nuts
2 C. low-sodium chicken broth
three 1-inch strips of lemon zest
½ tsp fresh lemon juice

Salt-Broiled Shrimp:
1½ cups coarse sea salt
¼ cup crumbled bay leaves
zest of 1 lemon, coarsely chopped
12 large shrimp in the shell

1. In a large skillet, heat 1 tablespoon of the oil. Add half of the zucchini slices and cook over moderately-high heat until browned in spots, about 1 minute. Turn and cook for 30 seconds longer, until barely tender. Season the zucchini with salt and pepper and transfer to a large plate. Repeat with 1 more tablespoon of oil and the remaining zucchini.
2. Add the remaining 1 tablespoon of oil to the skillet along with the onion and cook over moderate heat, stirring, until the onion is golden, 4 minutes. Add the garlic and crushed red pepper and cook until fragrant, 2 minutes. Add the wine and vinegar and boil over high heat until reduced by two-thirds, 5 minutes. Transfer the onion mixture to a bowl and let cool. Add the parsley and mint and season with salt and pepper.
3. Spoon one-third of the onion mixture into a shallow dish or glass pie plate. Arrange half of the zucchini on top, followed by another third of the onion mixture. Top with the remaining zucchini and onion mixture. Press lightly and drizzle with olive oil. Let the zucchini stand at room temperature for 1 hour or refrigerate overnight.
4. Preheat the oven to 350°F and put the pine nuts on a baking sheet and toast for about 6 minutes, until golden brown. Transfer the pine nuts to a medium sauce pan. Add the chicken broth and lemon zest and bring to a boil. Simmer over moderately low heat until the pine nuts are soft, about 45 minutes. Discard the lemon zest. Transfer the pine nuts and broth to a blender and puree. Return the sauce to the pan and stir in the lemon juice. Season with salt.
5. Preheat the broiler. In a medium baking dish, toss the coarse sea salt with the bay leaves and lemon zest. Shake the dish so the salt is in an even layer and broil 6 inches from the heat for 3 minutes, until the salt is very hot. Quickly arrange the shrimp on the hot salt and broil for about 2½ minutes per side, until just cooked through.
6. Meanwhile, reheat the pine nut sauce. Arrange the zucchini on plates, drizzle with the sauce, top with the shrimp and serve.

Spinasse
1531 14th Avenue

"If there is anything we are serious about, it is neither religion nor learning, but food."
Lin Yutang

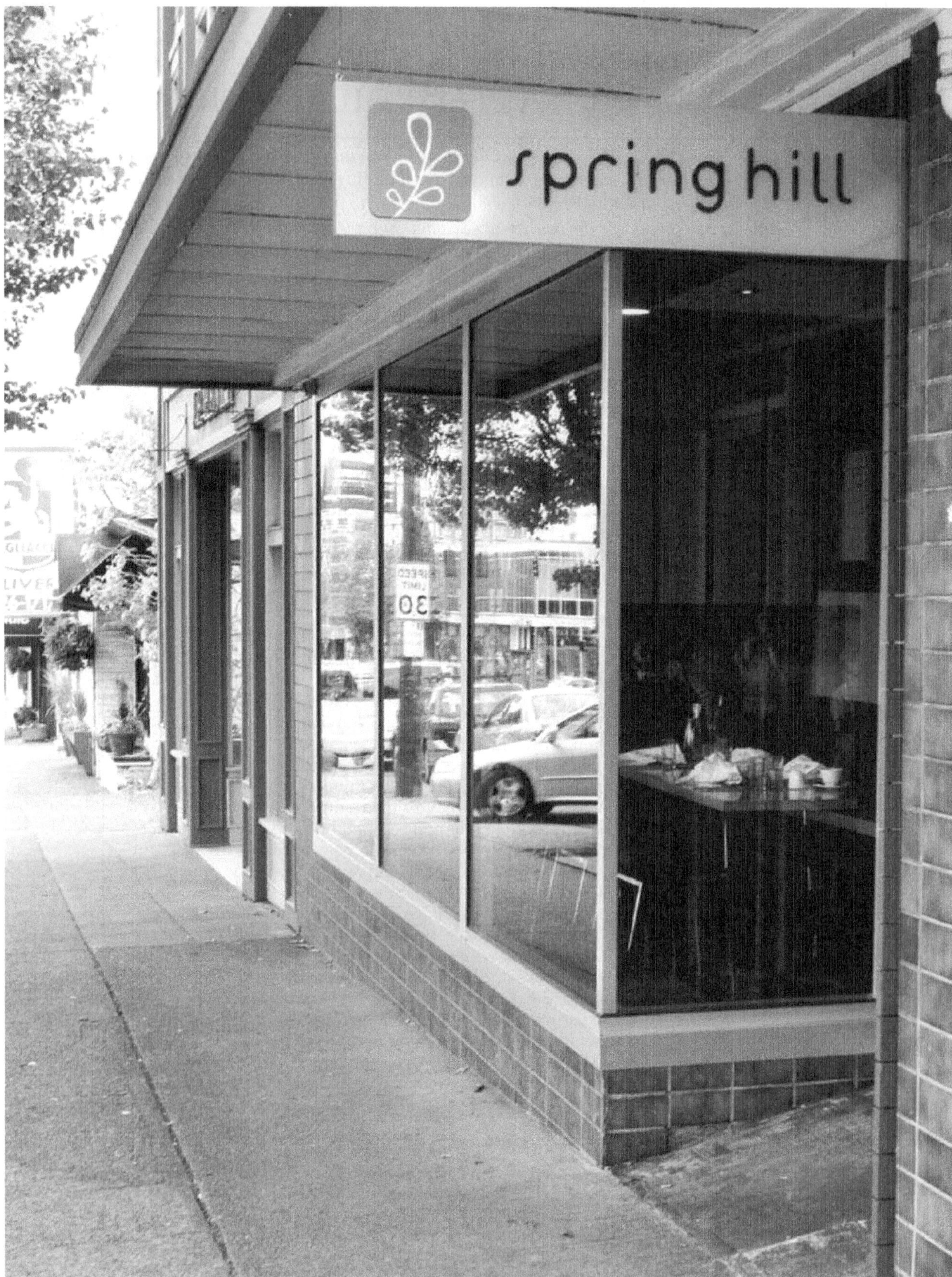
spring hill

Deviled Eggs

Spring Hill brings together the culinary talents of one of the Northwest's emerging chefs with the contemporary design of heliotrope architects. Spring Hill offers innovative regional Northwest foods that are fresh, flavorful, and simple. We are committed to utilizing local ingredients from Northwest farmers and fishermen.

1 dozen large eggs
50 g. egg yolk
10 g. white distilled vinegar
6 g. lemon juice
3 g. Tabasco hot sauce
7 g. Kosher salt
0.5 g. ground black pepper
6 g. sugar
15 g. water
260 g. rice oil or other neutral flavored oil

1. Place the eggs in a high-sided sauce pot and cover with cold tap water 1-inch above the eggs.
2. Place the pot over high heat and set an 8 minute timer. (Depending on how hot your burners are, the pot should be close to boiling.)
3. After 8 minutes, the water should be at a soft boil. Cover the pot with a lid and remove from the heat. Leave the eggs in the covered pot for 12 minutes. Pour off the hot water and jostle the eggs around inside the pot to crack the shells and cover with ice and water. Allow the eggs to chill for 10 minutes.
4. Split the hard cooked eggs down the center lengthwise and separate the whites from the yolk. Reserve the cooked whites in the refrigerator.
5. Push the cooked yolks through the fine mesh sieve and then place in a food processor bowl.
6. Measure the ingredients on a scale, zeroing the scale between ingredients. Measure and reserve the oil separately.
7. Add the scaled ingredients (except the oil) to the food processor with the yolks. While the food processor is running, slowly emulsify with the rice oil. Allow the motor to run until the mixture is very smooth.
8. If you would like to pass the filling through the sieve one final time, it will remove any of the larger granules of ground pepper.
9. Place yolk mixture in a piping bag and fill the hollow whites.

Spring Hill
4437 California Avenue Southwest

"More die in the United States of too much food than of too little."
John Kenneth Galbraith

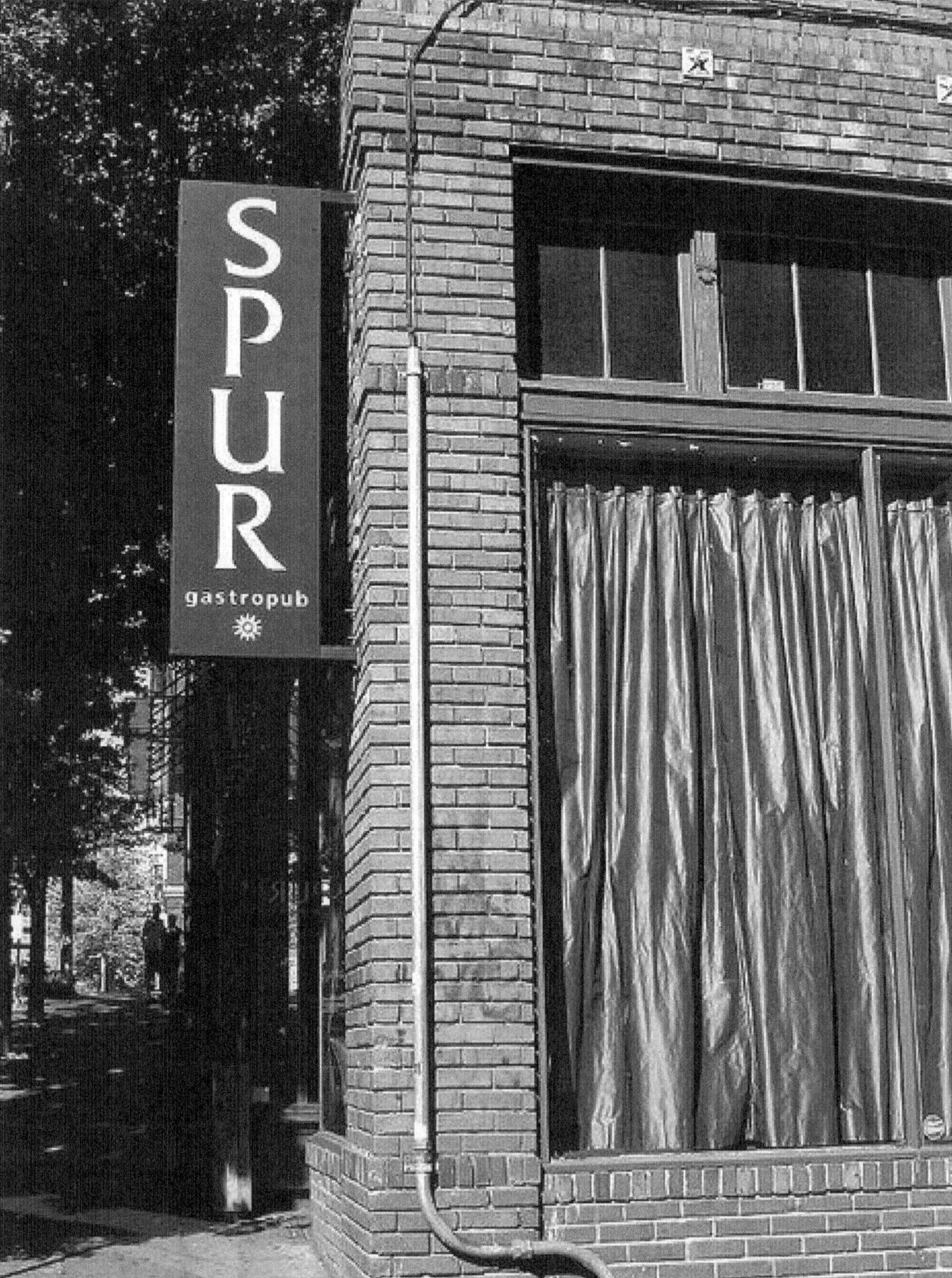
SPUR
gastropub

Beef Carpaccio with Deep-Fried Béarnaise

Housed in a historic Seattle building in Belltown, Spur nods to the area's pioneer, fisherman and occasional outlaw roots. Spur features iconic American imagery in a rotating photo exhibit.

Beef:
2 oz. beef tenderloin
extra virgin olive oil
tarragon vinegar reduction
sea salt and pepper

Béarnaise:
2 egg yolks
1 tbsp warm water
½ lb. butter, melted
1 tbsp calcium lactate
¼ tsp xantham gum
1 tbsp of reduction of tarragon vinegar and shallots
salt and white pepper

Alginate Bath:
1 l. water
6 g. sodium alginate

Fried Béarnaise:
Béarnaise capsules (from above)
all-purpose flour
1 egg, whisked
ground panko bread crumbs
oil (for frying)
salt

Beef:
1. Roll beef in plastic film and continue rolling plastic very tightly until a perfect cylinder is formed. Place in freezer and allow to freeze through.

Béarnaise:
1. Set up a bain marie with boiling water. Combine egg yolk and 1 tbsp. of warm water, place over boiling water and whisk rapidly until yolks coagulate. Continue to whisk, while slowly drizzling in melted butter.
2. Once butter is completely emulsified, add calcium lactate and xantham gum to the mixture.
3. Season with salt, white pepper, and tarragon vinegar-shallot reduction (to taste).
4. Remove bowl from above the boiling water and blend mixture with an immersion blender until smooth and emulsified.

Alginate Bath:
1. Combine water and alginate and blend very well.
2. Place water-alginate mixture (in bowl) in a vacuum packing machine and vacuum until completely clear. This removes all air.

Béarnaise Capsules:
1. Place béarnaise sauce in a squeeze bottle. Using a round measuring tsp., fill tsp. ¾ of the way with béarnaise from the squeeze bottle.
2. Submerge the spoon into the alginate bath and invert to drop the mixture from the spoon; it should form a round ball. Allow the balls to rest in the mixture for about 10 minutes (so that a strong skin forms).
3. Remove the béarnaise balls from the alginate bath and rinse in warm water.

Fried Béarnaise:
1. Heat oil to 375°F. Dust the béarnaise capsules with flour, then dip in whisked egg. Dip in panko, and fry until golden brown (approximately 45 seconds).
2. Remove from fryer, dry on a paper towel, and sprinkle with salt.

To Assemble and Serve:
1. Thinly slice 3-4 slices of beef onto serving plate, and dress with olive oil, tarragon vinegar reduction, sea salt, and pepper. Place one ball of fried béarnaise in the center of each, and garnish with microgreens.
2. Serve, instruct diners to roll one side of the beef round over the ball, to cover, and pop one entire beef-béarnaise portion into their mouth.

Spur
113 Blanchard

"In the state of society in which we now find ourselves, it is difficult to imagine a nation which lived solely on bread and vegetables."
Jean-Anthelme Brillat-Savarin

EXIT
steelhead
diner

Razor Clam Chowder

Our diner is a place of no pretensions where locals hang out, chat with others, watch the kitchen fun and have a great meal. It's the perfect place to bring out-of-town visitors. They'll get a real Seattle experience – great local food in the historic Pike Place Market setting with a view of the Market, Elliott Bay, and the Olympic mountains.

1 qt. whole milk
1 pt. heavy cream
2 medium Yukon gold potatoes, medium dice
Kosher salt and freshly ground pepper
4 tbsp butter
½ lb. thick-sliced applewood-smoked bacon, diced
3 cloves garlic, chopped
2 tbsp chopped fresh thyme
2 bay leaves
2 medium white onions, medium dice
1 medium leek, medium dice
1 bunch celery, medium dice
½ C. all-purpose flour
16 oz. clam juice
1 lb. razor clam meat (cleaned from shell, visceral sac removed), medium dice
Tabasco and Worcestershire sauce, to taste

1. Place milk, heavy cream, potatoes, and one tsp. of salt in a sauce pan and bring to a boil over medium heat, stirring frequently. Reduce heat and simmer.

2. In a large, heavy-gauge soup pot, melt butter over medium heat, then add bacon and cook until crispy. Add garlic and cook until lightly browned.

3. Add thyme and bay leaves and cook, stirring, for 1 minute. Add onions, leeks, and celery, and turn up heat, stirring and cooking for about 5 minutes.

4. When vegetables are tender, reduce heat to medium and add flour, stirring until incorporated. Add clam juice and bring to a boil, stirring constantly. Pour in half of the cream-milk mixture, leaving enough cream with the potatoes to continue cooking them.

5. When potatoes are tender, add mixture to the vegetables. Bring the chowder to a boil, stirring constantly, then reduce heat to low, cover, and simmer for 25 minutes, stirring occasionally.

6. Stir in clams to heat. Add Tabasco, Worcestershire, salt, and pepper to taste.

Steelhead Diner
95 Pine Street

"Happy as a clam, is what my mother says for happy. I am happy as a clam: hard-shelled, firmly closed."
Margaret Atwood

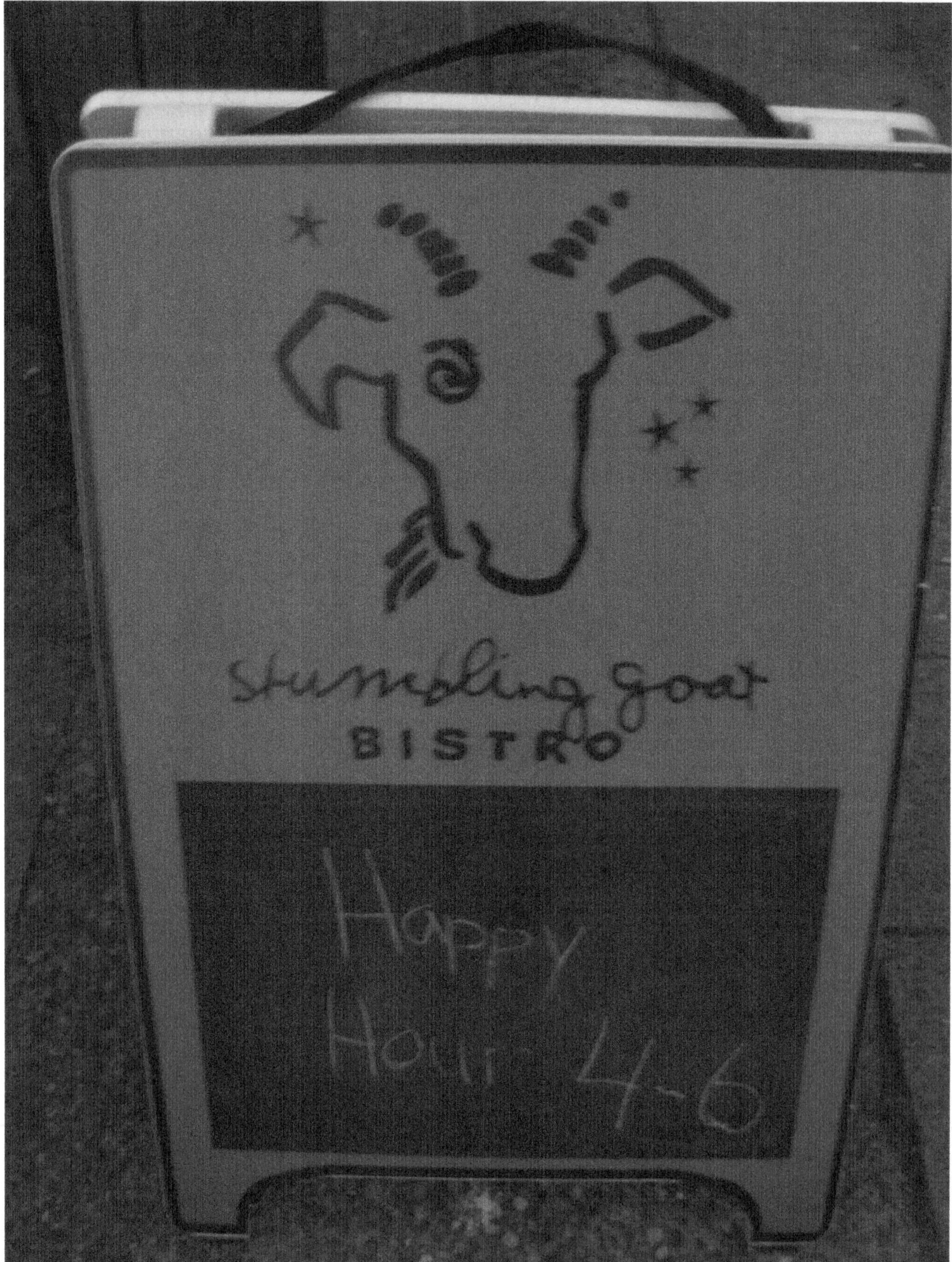
stumbling goat
BISTRO
Happy
Hour 4-6

Honey Crisp Apple and Hazelnut Frangipane Tart with Rosemary Crust

Food is about more than just what you eat, it's about who you share the experience with. At the Stumbling Goat Bistro, we believe that the best experiences come from the knowledge that you are choosing to support your local community.

Tart Shell Dough:
1 egg
½ C. ice water
2½ C. all-purpose flour
16 tbsp chilled, unsalted butter, cubed
1 tbsp sugar
1½ tsp salt
1 tbsp chopped fresh rosemary

Hazelnut Frangipane:
1 C. toasted hazelnuts finely ground
1 C. sugar
4 tbsp unsalted butter (room temperature)
1 egg
1 tbsp Frangelico, Rum, or vanilla extract
pinch of salt

3-4 honey crisp apples, peeled, cored, sliced into ¼-inch slices
raw sugar

Tart Shell Dough:
1. Combine water and egg and set aside.
2. Combine rest of ingredients in a food processor or large mixing bowl until dough is the size of small peas.
3. Add half of the egg and water mixture, pulse a few times, then add the rest and pulse until fully incorporated.
4. Gather dough together into a ball and flatten into a disc, cover with plastic wrap, and chill for a minimum of 2 hours.

Hazelnut Frangipane:
1. Combine all ingredients until mixed fully, cover and refrigerate until needed.

Assembly:
1. Preheat oven to 425°F.
2. Roll chilled tart dough out until it is approximately ⅛-inch in thickness. Cut dough into circles that are ½-inch larger than the tart shells. Line shells with the dough and place 1 tbsp. of the frangipane mixture into shell, spread evenly.
3. Arrange apple slices on top of the frangipane. Sprinkle with raw sugar and chill for 30 minutes before baking.
4. Arrange tart shells on a baking sheet and bake in oven for about 35 minutes, rotating baking sheet halfway through for even baking.
5. Let tarts cool for 30 minutes before unmolding.
6. Serve with ice cream or whipped cream.

Stumbling Goat Bistro
6722 Greenwood Ave N

"Fresh-caught fried fish without hush-puppies are as man without woman, a beautiful woman without kindness, law without policemen."
Marjorie Kinnan Rawlings

Sugar
BAKERY
617-32-SUGAR SUGARBAKERY.NET

Lavender Shortbread

In 2001, we purchased a house with an old overgrown apple tree. The following fall our tree was full of huge apples. We picked, peeled, cored and sliced buckets of apples and made pies and applesauce which we gave to all our friends. Eventually, the caramel apple tartlet was born and we were inspired to start a dessert business. We needed a name so one night my husband and I were out to dinner and looked on the table to find a packet of sugar. It seemed obvious that our bakery should be called "Sugar" because it was simple and sweet, and perfectly expressed our passion for pastry and of course each other.

1 C. granulated sugar, plus 2 tbsp for garnish
2 C. butter
2½ tbsp dried lavender flowers, plus ½ tbsp for garnish
3½ C. all-purpose flour
1 C. white rice flour
½ tbsp salt
parchment paper (optional)

1. Preheat oven to 350°F.

2. In a stand mixer or with a hand-held beater, cream 1 cup of sugar, butter, and lavender until light and fluffy.

3. Add flours and salt and combine until mixture just starts to come together. The dough should be crumbly but stick together when squeezed.

4. Line a 12x16-inch pan with parchment paper. Place dough into the pan and break up any large clumps and spread evenly.

5. Press dough down gently and sprinkle the remaining sugar and lavender flowers on top.

6. With a rolling pin or drinking glass, roll over the dough to smooth the top. Use a little additional sugar if the dough sticks to the rolling pin.

7. With a fork, press indentations into the top of the shortbread to prevent the shortbread from rising unevenly.

8. Bake at 350°F for 20-25 minutes or until shortbread is golden brown.

9. Cut into squares while still warm and remove shortbread from pan when cool.

Sugar Bakery

1014 Madison Street

"Food, like a loving touch or a glimpse of divine power, has that ability to comfort."
Norman Kolpas

Ta.

sushi

MU

kappo

Ra.

Salmon Shioyaki

Using local and seasonal ingredients is the most important element in Japanese cuisine. It also has become the primary principle for the international culinary community. With commitment to that philosophy, Tamura features seasonal ingredients of the Pacific Northwest in authentic Japanese preparation. Tamura is a Kappo style restaurant where food is prepared in an open kitchen and served quickly in a lively environment where staff and guests talk about the food and beyond. Our goal is to become the very best restaurant to our guests by getting to know them and serving them in a personable yet professional manner.

4 sockeye salmon fillets (5- 6 oz.), 1-inch thick, with skin
1½ tsp fine sea salt
1 tbsp vegetable oil
hot cooked sushi rice such as Nishiki or other short-to medium-grain rice
4 sheets nori (about 8-in. square), each cut into 6 pieces
lemon wedges
Furikake (Japanese rice seasoning)

1. Set salmon on a rack in a rimmed pan, sprinkle fillets all over with sea salt and chill, uncovered, at least 2 hours and as long as 5 hours.

2. Heat grill to medium-high (about 450°F). Fold a 12x20-inch sheet of heavy-duty foil in half crosswise. With a knife tip, poke dime-size holes through foil about 2 inches apart. Oil one side of foil. Rub fish all over with oil.

3. Set foil with oiled side up on cooking grate. Set fillets slightly separated, skin side down, on foil. Grill, covered, until fish is barely cooked through, 7-12 minutes.

4. With a wide spatula, slide fish from skin to a platter and tent with foil. Cook skin on foil until crisp, 2-3 minutes. Remove foil from grill, then gently peel off skin, using fingers or a wide spatula (skin may break into pieces).

5. Serve salmon immediately with crispy skin, rice, nori, lemon, and Furikake.

Sushi Kappo Tamura
2968 Eastlake Avenue

"A soup like this is not the work of one man. It is the result of a constantly refined tradition. There are nearly a thousand years of history in this soup."
Willa Cather

sutra
VEGETARIAN CUISINE

Forbidden Black Rice and Yellow Beet Rolls with Grilled Eggplant Mousse and Kaiware Sprouts

We are earnestly trying to keep our carbon footprint as light as possible. Some of the ways we're doing this include using eco-friendly paint inside and out of the restaurant, using beach wood for our bar, using a recycled bar top, organic hand-sewn cloth napkins, etc. We are composting all of our food scraps and growing some of our food in our garden. Our coffee (from Pangaea Roasters) is walked over to us in glass containers, eliminating all transportation waste.

Eggplant Mousse:
2 large eggplants, halved lengthwise
salt
4 cloves garlic
olive oil
½ tsp freshly squeezed lemon juice

Rice:
1½ C. black rice
salt
2 dried ancho chilies
2 dried New Mexico chilies
grapeseed oil
½ C. coconut milk
1 tbsp freshly squeezed lemon juice

Yellow Beets:
2 large yellow beets
oil, as needed

Hijiki:
1 (1-inch piece) ginger, sliced
1 tbsp agave nectar
¾ C. tamari
¼ C. mirin
½ C. hijiki

Rolls:
24 shiso leaves
olive oil

kaiware sprouts

Eggplant Mousse:
1. Score the eggplants with ½-inch slits and cover generously with salt. Set aside for 40 minutes and up to 5 hours. After sweating, wipe eggplant with a paper towel.
2. Preheat oven to 375°F. Insert 1 clove of garlic in the center of each eggplant half. Brush the eggplant with oil and grill, cut side down, until well marked. Flip the eggplants over, drizzle with more oil, and cover with aluminum foil and place on a sheet pan. Bake until the center is very soft. Scoop out the center with a spoon and discard the skin. Puree with lemon juice and salt.

Rice:
1. Bring 2¾ cups of water to boil. Add the rice and a pinch of salt. Reduce the heat to low and cook, covered, for 30 to 40 minutes.
2. Meanwhile, deseed the chilies and fry in hot grapeseed oil, until crispy, about 20 to 30 seconds.
3. Place fried chilies in a bowl and cover with ¼ C. water; let sit for 10 minutes.
4. In a blender, add the coconut milk, chilies and their water, and lemon juice and blend until smooth. Strain through a chinoise.
5. When the rice is finished cooking, add the coconut milk and chili mixture and stir slowly. Set aside to cool.

Yellow Beets:
1. Preheat oven to 375°F. Toss the beets in oil and roast whole until soft, about 1½ hours. Set aside to cool. Once cooled, slice the beets paper thin with a mandoline.

Hijiki:
1. Combine the ginger, agave nectar, tamari, mirin, and ¾ C. water in a sauce pan and bring to simmer.
2. Add the hijiki and cook for 10 to 15 minutes, or until hijiki is tender. Strain the remaining liquid and set the hijiki aside.

Rolls:
1. Preheat oven to 350°F. Place two rows of four shiso leaves on a bamboo roller, smooth side down. Cover ¾ of the shiso with a layer of yellow beets.
2. Cover the beets with one quarter of the black rice. Sprinkle a thin layer of hijiki in the center of the black rice and very gently roll like sushi. Remove the bamboo. Repeat 3 times with remaining ingredients. Place the rolls on a baking sheet, drizzle with oil and bake for 6 minutes. Cut the shiso roll into 1-inch pieces (about 24 total).

To Assemble and Serve:
1. Place dollops of eggplant mousse on a plate. Top each dollop with one piece of shiso roll and garnish with kaiware sprouts.

Sutra
1605 North 45th Street

"Food...can look beautiful, taste exquisite, smell wonderful, make people feel good, bring them together, inspire romantic feelings....At its most basic, it is fuel for a hungry machine...."
Rosamond Richardson

Potato-crusted Salmon

Chef Ludger Szmania and his wife and business partner, Julie, opened Szmania's (pronounced "Smahn-ya's") in September 1990. A 1997 remodel added a beautiful Eocene Period fossil stone fireplace, the curved red bar, 40 additional seats and a lovely new entry. The Exhibition Kitchen Counter, a favorite spot among Szmania's regulars, has 12 entertaining seats next to all the kitchen action. Szmania's underwent a major remodel in 2004, adding the bar and lounge area, leather seats, a community table and beautiful see-through hanging murals designed by Magnolia's Catherine Mayer. In addition to the physical changes in the bar, an extensive menu of hand-crafted cocktails was developed by world-famous mixologist, Ryan Magarian.

4 (6-oz.) salmon fillets, skinned, and deboned
2½ C. potatoes, finely shredded, rinsed and kept in water
1 onion, finely diced
fresh chopped Italian parsley
1 tsp flour
salt and pepper, to taste
olive oil

1. Preheat oven to 350°F.

2. Season salmon fillets with salt and pepper.

3. In a bowl, mix shredded potatoes with onions, parsley, 1 tsp. flour, and salt and pepper, to taste. Form potato into 4 cakes, large enough to hold salmon fillets on top.

4. Heat a large non-stick pan over medium-high heat and add the olive oil. Place potato cakes in pan and place salmon fillets on top of potato cakes. Let potatoes fry to a light golden crisp and flip cakes over carefully with a spatula so the crisp side of the potato faces up. Finish in oven until salmon is cooked through, an additional 2-3 minutes. Serve immediately.

Szmania's
3321 West McGraw Street

"Food is part of the spiritual expression of the French and I do not believe that they have ever heard of calories."
Beverley Baxter

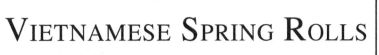

Vietnamese Spring Rolls

One of my favorite Asian restaurants in Seattle is the Tamarind Tree. It is a Vietnamese restaurant located in the international district, tucked away in a little corner. But it is definitely worth visiting if you haven't been. If you are going on the weekends, please do make a reservation there is usually at least a 30 minutes wait during that time at night. At the Tamarind Tree you can sit in the main dinning room, and my preference is right next to the fire, or you can sit outside with the heat lights and waterfall. Either way the place is always busy.

Dipping Sauce:
¼ C. palm sugar or light brown sugar
½ C. boiling water
½ C. rice vinegar
2 tbsp Chinese soy sauce or Maggi sauce
¼ C. Thai red chili sauce
1 tbsp Kosher salt
Thai fish sauce (nam pla), to taste

Spring Rolls:
6 (4½-inch-square) Chinese egg-roll wrappers
oil for frying
2 oz. dried bean-thread noodles
12 large leaves green leaf lettuce,
12 large sprigs fresh basil leaves
12 large sprigs fresh mint
36 sprigs cilantro
4 oz. finely shredded carrot
12 (6-inch round) rice-paper spring-roll wrappers

1. To make the dipping sauce, dissolve the palm sugar in boiling water and stir in the vinegar, soy sauce, chili sauce and salt. Add fish sauce, to taste. Keep at room temperature.
2. To make the spring rolls, cut each of the egg-roll wrappers into 4 long strips. Working with one strip at a time, roll the strips lengthwise into cigarette shapes, sealing the cylinders by brushing the edge of each wrapper with a little water.
3. In a frying pan with about an inch of oil, fry the cylinders, two or three at a time, until they become crisp and golden brown. Drain the fried wrappers on paper towels and hold them at room temperature until you are ready to assemble the spring rolls.
4. Pour just enough hot tap water over the bean-thread noodles to cover them, about 2 cups. When the noodles are clear and pliable, about 15 minutes, drain and keep refrigerated until serving time.
5. Split lettuce leaves in half lengthwise. Keep herbs, lettuce, and carrots cold in separate containers until serving time.
6. Fill a shallow dish or pie pan with hot tap water (about 110°F). Soak the rice-paper spring-roll wrappers, one at a time, in the hot water until just barely soft and pliable, about 30 seconds.
7. Lay a soaked wrapper on a clean work surface and place two pieces of green leaf lettuce end to end in the center of the wrapper with the curly ends hanging out over the edge. Lay a small bundle of the bean-thread noodles and a few shredded carrots on top of the lettuce.
8. Strip the leaves from a sprig of basil and sprig of mint and put the leaves on top of the noodles and carrots. Place two of the fried egg-roll wrappers on top of the pile and roll the spring roll wrapper around the pile, tightening into a neat bundle as you roll.
9. Cut the roll in half. Place the two halves, cut side down on a chilled salad plate. The ends of the lettuce leaves and the fried egg roll wrappers will poke out above the edges of the wrapper.
10. Serve the rolls at once with a small dish of dipping sauce on the plate.

Tamarind Tree
1036 S Jackson St

"Why does man kill? He kills for food. And not only food: frequently there must be a beverage."
Woody Allen

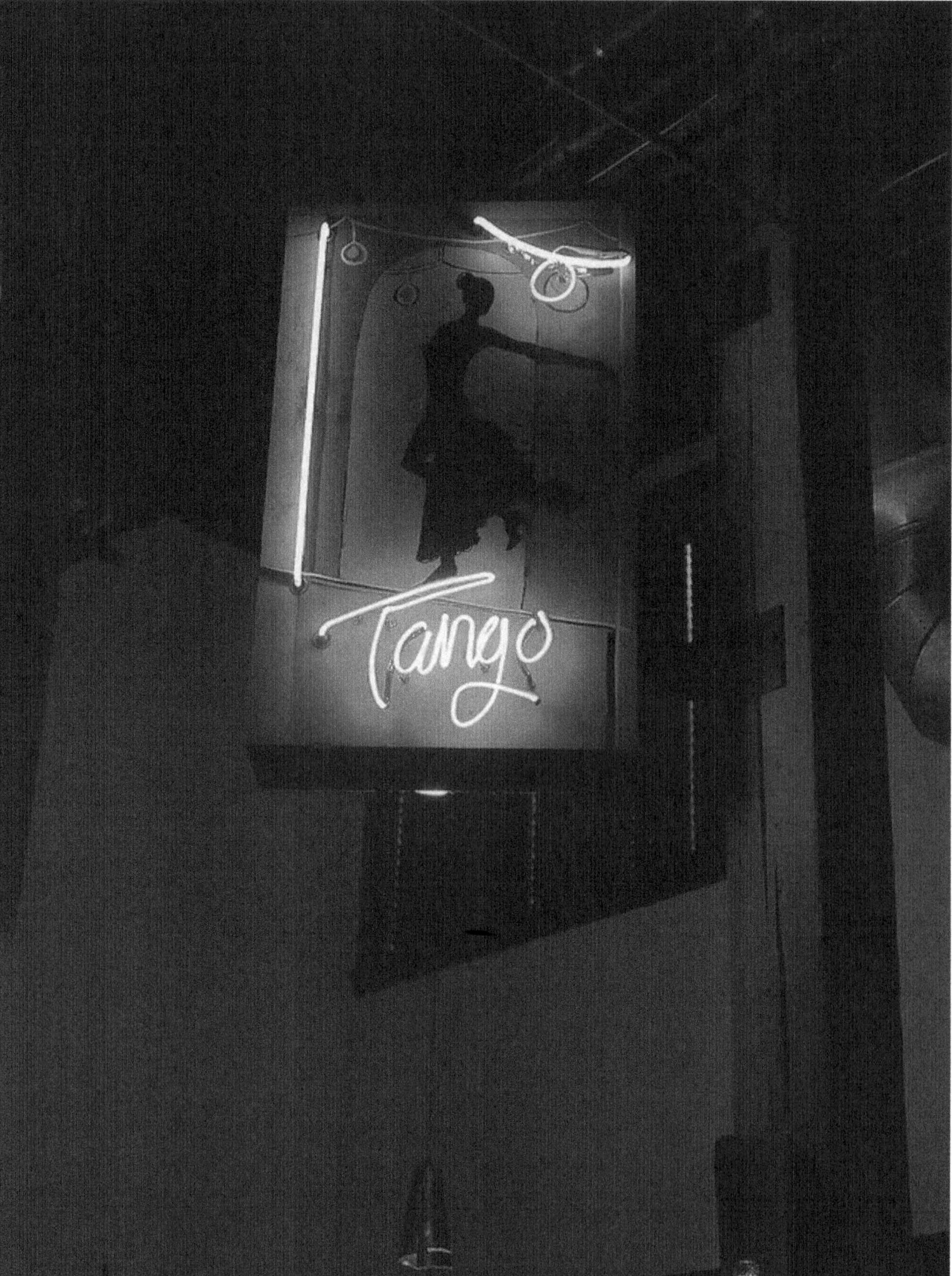
Tango

Espadas de Puerco (Pork Skewers)

Daniel Pérez was immersed in Latin culture and cuisine. He helped open the kitchen of Tango Restaurant in April 2000. After three years he had mastered all of the kitchen stations and moved to San Antonio, Texas, to work under executive chef/owner, Bruce Auden, at Biga on the Bangs. In 2006, Daniel was drawn back to Tango to take over the kitchen and in 2010 was named the Executive Chef. Latin-inspired food has and always will be a passion of Daniel's.

Pork Skewers:
- *2 lb. thinly-sliced pork tenderloin strips*
- *7 oz. achiote paste**
- *¼ C. lime juice*
- *1 tbsp minced garlic*
- *¼ tsp paprika*
- *1 bunch finely chopped cilantro*
- *small wood skewers*

Garnacha Slaw:
- *1 C. olive oil*
- *1 C. lime juice*
- *1 C. orange juice*
- *1 C. garnacha vinegar*
- *1 tbsp of dried oregano*
- *salt and pepper*
- *½ green cabbage, julienned*
- *½ red cabbage, julienned*
- *2 carrots julienned*
- *1 poblano pepper, julienned*
- *1 red bell pepper, julienned*
- *half a pineapple, grilled, chopped*

Pork Skewers:

1. Soak wood skewers in water for 30 minutes.

2. Mix all ingredients together in a bowl, then add pork and marinate for at least one hour.

3. Skewer marinated pork and grill 2-3 minutes each side. Serve on top of garnacha slaw.

Garnacha Slaw:

1. Combine olive oil, lime juice, orange juice, garnacha vinegar, dried oregano, and salt and pepper, to taste, in blender to make dressing (blending helps combine the dried oregano).

2. Combine all vegetables and pineapple with dressing and let sit for at least one hour.

*Achiote paste is made from crushed annatto seed, salt, and garlic, but it can be purchased in a premade paste. It was used long ago by Mayan Indians to color foods and as body paint. It gives the pork a brilliant red color and wonderful flavor.

Tango Restaurant & Lounge
1100 Pike Street

"When I get a little money, I buy books. And if there is any left over, I buy food."
Desiderius Erasmus

TASTE

Heirloom Tomato Gazpacho

TASTE Restaurant, the in house restaurant in the Seattle Art Museum, nourishes its community of guests with great food made from the best local ingredients in an inviting atmosphere while minimizing the impact on our environment. Joining us at TASTE supports your local economy; 89% of all our food purchases are local. TASTE Responsibly.

1 C. chopped red onions
1 jalapeno, seeded
1 C. chopped green bell pepper
1 C. chopped English cucumbers
1 C. Mama Lil's peppers
1 C. chopped and peeled heirloom tomatoes
1½ tsp chopped garlic
1½ tsp Kosher salt
¼ tsp cayenne
¼ C. tomato paste
1 tbsp white wine vinegar
¼ C. + 2 tbsp extra virgin olive oil
1 tbsp fresh lemon juice
3 C. tomato juice
sprig of thyme

Balsamic Glaze:
2 C. balsamic vinegar

Gazpacho:
1. Mix all the ingredients together in a bowl, cover, and let sit in the refrigerator overnight.

2. The next day, remove the thyme sprig and blend all the ingredients in a blender until the gazpacho is smooth, makes about 2 quarts. For a smoother texture, strain the soup to yield about 1 quart. Refrigerate the gazpacho until ready to serve.

3. Ladle the cold soup into chilled bowls and squeeze dots of balsamic glaze over the top.

Balsamic Glaze:
1. Heat 2 cups balsamic vinegar in a heavy sauce pan over medium heat until steam rises from the liquid. Place the sauce pan on a heat diffuser and let the liquid reduce very slowly (it shouldn't simmer) for 2-3 hours, until it has reduced and thickened to a syrupy glaze.

2. You should be left with approximately ½-¾ cup of glaze. Keep the glaze in a squeeze bottle at room temperature for garnishing.

TASTE SAM
1300 1st Avenue

"Cold soup is a very tricky thing and it is the rare hostess who can carry it off. More often than not the dinner guest is left with the impression that had he only come a little earlier he could have gotten it while it was still hot."
Fran Lebowitz

Cauliflower Flan

Welcome to Tilth. We feature New American cuisine prepared with certified-organic or wild ingredients sourced from as many local farmers we are able to support. Our executive chef and owner, Maria Hines, is a James Beard Award winner for Best Chef of the Northwest, as well as one of Food & Wine Magazine's 10 Best New Chefs of 2005. In 2008, the New York Times deemed Tilth one of the best new restaurants in the country. Tilth received its organic certification from Oregon Tilth, an unaffiliated organization that promotes sustainability. Housed (literally) in the renovated first floor of a small Wallingford home, Tilth accommodates only 40 people at a time. This charming intimacy is enhanced by the waitstaff, who offer intelligent advice about the menu.

1 head cauliflower, cut into florets
1½ C. heavy cream
salt and ground white pepper, to taste
2 large eggs, preferably organic, beaten
1 bouquet garni (tie together with butcher string: 2 whole branches fresh parsley, 2 branches fresh thyme, and 1 bay leaf)
1 tbsp butter, softened
hot water, for water bath

1. Preheat oven to 325°F.
2. Heat 1 quart water to a boil. Blanch the cauliflower in boiling water for several minutes until tender. Drain.
3. Puree cauliflower in a blender or food processor until smooth. Add the puree into a sauce pan with the heavy cream and bouquet garni. Let steep over medium-low heat for 30 minutes. Season with salt and ground white pepper to taste. Strain mixture through a fine-meshed sieve.
4. To the beaten eggs, slowly add about ¼ C. of the cauliflower liquid while whisking to temper the eggs and prevent them from curdling. Add the eggs to the cauliflower and whisk to combine. Set aside.
5. Butter 4 (6-oz.) ramekins and set them in a shallow baking pan. Pour the custard into the 4 ramekins. Cover the ramekins with a sheet of parchment paper (one sheet to cover all four is okay). Place baking dish with ramekins in the oven. Add enough of the hot water to the baking sheet to surround the outside of the ramekins (about half way up the sides of the ramekins). This creates a water bath and helps the custard cook more gently.
6. Bake for 25 to 30 minutes or until the flans are set. Remove from oven.
7. To serve, gently slide the blade of a paring knife along the edge of the ramekin to loosen the flan. Tip over onto the center of a dinner plate. This can be served with grilled meat or seafood.

Tilth
1411 North 45th Street

"I prefer my oysters fried; That way I know my oysters died."
Roy Blount, Jr.

Old Fashioned and Chocolate Cochon

Inspired by the mystique of the martini, Tini Bigs lounge has become a Seattle institution when the doors opened on its historic bar and red-lit tin ceiling in 1996. The first is the standard that Michael Cadden, bar artist, uses to determine the expertise of a bartender. The second, by Jamie Boudreau, pushes the boundaries that a Bourbon cocktail can be reinvented as. Regardless, Tini Bigs is "the best martini made exactly the way you like." You have owner Keith Robbins word on it.

Old Fashioned:
1 tsp brown sugar
8 dashes of Angostura bitters
4 dashes of Regan's orange bitters
2 oz. Wild Turkey Rare Breed
2 dashes of cigar tincture (recipe follows)
lemon twist
kirsch-macerated cherries

1. Spoon the brown sugar into the bottom of a double old-fashioned glass. Spread evenly around the bottom.

2. Add the bitters to the sugar.

3. Slowly add the Wild Turkey Rare Breed to the sugar, and stir 42 times.

4. Add 2 dashes of cigar tincture while stirring.

5. Pour over one very large single ice cube, conveniently frozen in a special mold the night before.

6. Garnish with a lemon twist and two skewered kirsh-macerated cherries.

Cigar Tincture:
1. Put about 1 gram of tobacco in 4 oz. of Knob Creek. Let sit for 5 days and filter. Bottle and use sparingly.

Chocolate Cochon
1½ oz. bacon-infused Bourbon
¼ oz. amaro Ramazotti
¼ oz. crème de cacao
¼ oz. kirsch
1 dash of Angostura bitters

Chocolate Cochon:
1. Combine Bourbon, amaro, crème de cacao, kirsch, and bitters in a cocktail shaker filled with ice.

2. Stir and strain into a rocks glass with a large ice cube.

3. Garnish with a flamed orange twist.

"When we decode a cookbook, every one of us is a practicing chemist. Cooking is really the oldest, most basic application of physical and chemical forces to natural materials."
Arthur E. Grosser

TULIO
RISTORANTE

Sweet Potato Gnocchi

An inviting atmosphere and authentically delicious Italian food make Tulio Ristorante a Seattle favorite. Located in the heart of downtown next to Hotel Vintage Park, Tulio bustles with convivial grace. Our comfortably elegant dining room, outstanding service and honest, memorable food keep the critics applauding and guests returning again and again.

2-2½ lb. sweet potatoes
2 oz. fresh grated parmesan
⅛ tsp nutmeg
pepper to taste
1 egg, beaten
2 C. all-purpose flour
1 C. mascarpone cheese, or more, to taste

1. Boil sweet potatoes with skin on for approximately one hour or until soft. Drain the potatoes well and push through a food ricer.

2. Add beaten egg, parmesan, nutmeg, and pepper. Incorporate ingredients until just mixed.

3. Slowly fold sifted flour into mixture. This is imperative in preventing clumps and keeping gnocchi light. After about half of the flour is added, start to feel the mixture for wetness and resistance when pushing in. Keep adding flour until dough is still slightly wet, but coming away from bowl. Allow to rest 10 minutes.

4. Lightly dust a surface with flour, then cut about ⅛ of the dough away and roll into a cylinder shape (about ½-inch wide), and cut into 1-inch pieces. Refrigerate dough for two hours.

5. To cook, drop gnocchi in boiling water for approximately two minutes or until they rise to the top. Cook an additional 30 seconds. Drain well.

6. Heat butter in pan until it foams. Place gnocchi in pan; brown them on each side. Season with cracked black pepper and salt. Place in a bowl and finish with spoonfuls of mascarpone cheese on top of the gnocchi.

Tulio Ristorante
1100 Fifth Ave

"Food is all those substances which, submitted to the action of the stomach, can be assimilated or changed into life by digestion, and can thus repair the losses which the human body suffers through the act of living."
Jean-Antheleme Brillat-Savarin

Pork Shanks

Experience the unique cosmopolitan dining experience at Urbane. One of Seattle's most exciting restaurants, Urbane Restaurant & Bar is delightfully modern, yet approachable and enduring. Our restaurant menus and décor are inspired by the culinary spoils of the Pacific Northwest, and we take great pride in working with our local farmers and producers to ensure quality and dependability. Our lounge has become a neighborhood favorite for happy hour or pre-theater drinks and bites. Our team of mixologists create one-of-a-kind specialty and classic cocktails to pair with our small plate offerings.

Brine the Shanks:
4 pork shanks
4 C. water
1½ C. brown sugar
¾ C. Kosher salt
1 yellow onion, sliced thin
6 garlic cloves, crushed
¼ C. peppercorns (whole)
4 rosemary branches
2 tbsp mustard seed
2 cinnamon stick
5 C. ice

Pork Shanks:
about 8 C. rendered duck fat (lard can also be used)
6 garlic cloves
4 rosemary branches

Maple Sauce:
8 C. chicken stock
1 C. maple syrup
1 yellow onion, rough chopped
2 carrots, peeled, roughly chopped
6 branches fresh thyme

1 C. huckleberries

Brine the Shanks:
1. Heat all ingredients, except ice until sugar and salt dissolve completely. Stir and pull from heat. Add ice to accelerate the cooling time and place in refrigerator until cold.
2. When the brine is cold add the shanks. Refrigerate overnight.

Pork Shanks:
1. Heat oven to 275°F.
2. Heat fat in pot until melted.
3. Remove shanks from brine and pat dry with a kitchen towel.
4. In a large sauté pan, add a bit of the melted fat and sear shanks on all sides until browned.
5. Place shanks in a Dutch oven just big enough to fit all four shanks. Nestle rosemary and garlic among the shanks then carefully pour melted fat to cover. Do not fill pan any further than one inch to the top.
6. Cover Dutch oven and place in oven. Cook for about 3-4 hours. Shanks are done when they are fork tender.
7. Very carefully remove the pot from oven and carefully remove lid. Place entire pot in refrigerator, uncovered, overnight.

Maple Sauce:
1. Place all ingredients in a small pot and reduce liquid by half.
2. Strain and press out as much juice from vegetables as possible.

To Assemble the Dish:
1. Warm fat until it is possible to remove the shanks without tearing them to pieces. Place the shanks into a large sauté pan and ladle maple sauce on top. Heat gently while continuing to turn shanks and baste the tops.
2. Once shanks are warm and starting to glaze, place entire pan in a hot oven. Allow the shanks to finish glazing. Pull pan from oven and add about 1 cup (or more) of huckleberries – the acid will cut the sweetness and fattiness of the dish.
3. Adjust seasoning of the sauce and serve either family style or one pork shank per guest.

Urbane
1639 8th Avenue

"If the soup had been as warm as the wine, if the wine had been as old as the turkey, if the turkey had had a breast like the maid, it would have been a swell dinner."
Duncan Hines

VESSEL

Obama Nation Cocktail

Vessel mixes the old with the new. It's a modern bar in downtown Seattle that serves up expert cocktails in a refined atmosphere. It's located in the historic 1926 Skinner Building, which was originally built to house the 5th Avenue Theatre. Vessel's architectural wonders are the vision of owner Clark C. Neimeyer. Every detail highlights the illuminating staircase that leads to a loft and the patterned ceiling that was once part of the theater next door. When you go, look up at the preserved history that surrounds you.

1 dried fig, sliced in half
Angostura bitters
Stroh over-proof rum
1½ oz. calvados
½ oz. Navan vanilla liqueur
¼ oz. Cynar

1. Place the fig in a mixing glass.

2. Flame with an atomizer filled with 1:1 Angostura bitters and rum.

3. Add the calvados, vanilla liqueur, and Cynar.

4. Shake well with ice and strain twice into a coupé or cocktail glass.

Vessel
1312 5th Ave

"Nearly everyone wants as least one outstanding meal a day."
Duncan Hines

Virginia
INN

Gluten-Free Chicken Gumbo

The Virginia Inn is a casual Seattle bistro in the Pike Place Market Historic District. Our lunch and dinner menus showcase a bounty of Northwest fish and farm presented in a French bistro style. The bar features an excellent wine list, specialty cocktails and one of the best tap selections in the city.

24 chicken legs
3 tbsp paprika
3 tbsp lemon juice

1½ lb. butter
4 C. Bob's gluten-free flour

5 lb. Andouille sausage, chopped into ½-inch slices
4 C. onions, chopped
4 C. celery, chopped
4 C. red bell peppers, chopped

2 gal. chicken stock

4 tbsp file powder
cayenne pepper, to taste

1. De-skin and score the chicken legs then marinate in the lemon and paprika for at least 8 hours.

2. Preheat oven to 350°F and roast the legs until they reach an internal temperature of 160 F°. Once cooled, pull the meat off the bone and reserve in the refrigerator until gumbo base is finished.

3. In a heavy-bottomed pot (large enough to eventually hold the chicken stock) heat the butter over medium heat and gradually add in the flour and cook the roux until it is a deep, dark brown, stirring frequently.

4. In a pot big enough to hold everything, brown the sausage first. Remove from the pan and set aside to drain on paper towels. In the same pot, add the vegetables and brown, then add the sausage back to the pot.

5. After the roux has fully cooked, add the chicken stock and whisk and cook at a simmer for approximately 20 minutes. Pour over the vegetables and sausage and simmer, adding the file powder and cayenne pepper, to taste.

6. Season with salt, add chicken and cook until chicken is warmed through.

Virginia Inn
1937 1st Avenue

"Gumbo, of all other products of the New Orleans cuisine, represents a most distinctive type of the evolution of good cookery under the hands of the famous Creole Cuisinieres of old New Orleans."
The Picayune's Creole Cook Book (1901)

VOLUNTEER PARK CAFE & MARKETPLACE
SEATTLE WA. 98112
EST. 1905
ALWAYS FRESH GOODNESS

Pan-Seared Sockeye Salmon with Zucchini Salad

Volunteer Park Cafe was once considered Seattle's best kept secret, and that was just the way the loyal neighborhood liked it, all to themselves – and then one fateful day, The Stranger dubbed VPC "Heaven on the Hill," and this quintessential neighborhood meeting place quickly became a favorite of many Seattleites – whether dropping by for a morning coffee, lunch with a friend, an afternoon cookie with the kids, or a leisurely dinner with your sweetie, VPC fulfills all the culinary desires of the neighborhood and beyond.

Vinaigrette:
2 tsp minced shallots
2 tsp honey
1 tbsp chopped tarragon
2 tbsp Champagne vinegar
2 tbsp grapeseed oil
1/8 tsp salt and pepper

Zucchini Salad:
2 C. julienne cut zucchini
3/4 C. julienne cut Walla Walla sweet onion
1/3 C. very thinly sliced radishes
1 C. quartered heirloom cherry tomatoes
1/4 C. hand-torn mint leaves
2 tbsp roughly chopped tarragon

Sockeye Salmon:
4 (3-oz.) sockeye salmon fillets, skin on
1/8 tsp salt and pepper
olive or vegetable oil spray
1/8 tsp sea salt

Vinaigrette:
1. Place shallots, honey, and tarragon in bowl of food processor fitted with a steel blade; puree.
2. With motor running, slowly add vinegar, then slowly add oil; puree until vinaigrette is smooth and emulsified; season with salt and pepper. Refrigerate until ready to use.

Zucchini Salad:
1. Place zucchini, onion, radishes, tomatoes, mint and tarragon in a bowl; set aside.

Sockeye Salmon:
1. Preheat oven to 350°F.
2. Season the flesh side of salmon with salt and pepper. Spray a sauté pan with olive oil spray and heat until very hot.
3. Place the salmon fillets, skin side down, in the pan and cook until the skin is golden brown, about 3-4 minutes.
4. Remove the fillets from the pan, being careful not to tear the skin and put on a baking sheet, skin side up. Bake until when you press a finger on the thickest part of the salmon, it springs back and salmon is cooked through, about 6 minutes. Do not over cook.

Assembly:
1. Toss the salad with the vinaigrette and mound it in the center of four plates. Place a salmon fillet, skin side up, on top of each salad, and serve.

Volunteer Park Café
1501 17th Avenue East

"Public and private food in America has become eatable, here and there extremely good. Only the fried potatoes go unchanged, as deadly as before."
Luigi Barzini

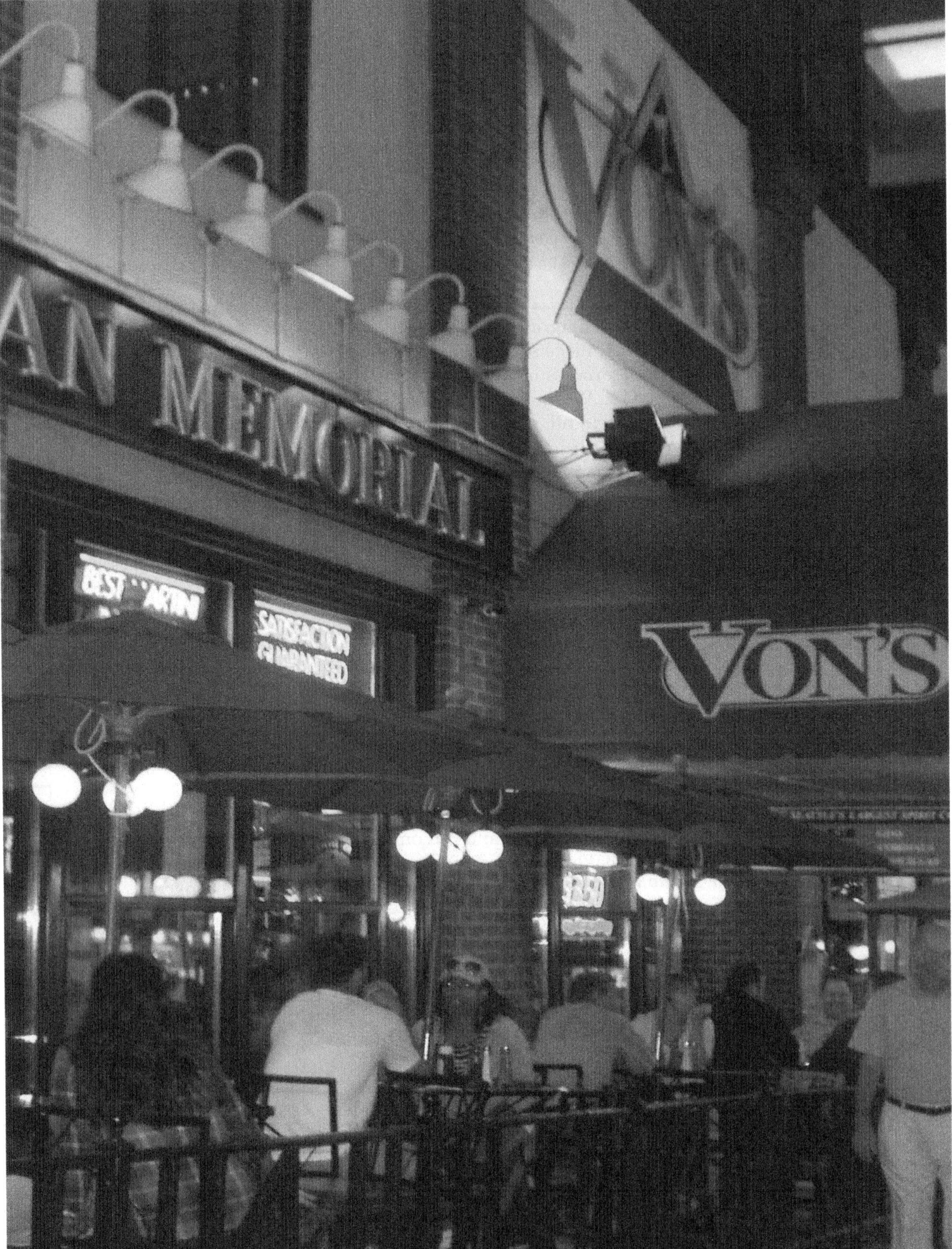

VON'S
AN MEMORIAL
BEST ARTINI
SATISFACTION
GUARANTEED
VON'S
$3.50

Two Day Herb Chicken

Von's opened in 1904 as Rippes on Pike Street. In 1923 the café moved to Fourth Avenue, the center of Seattle's business section. In 1940, theater magnate John von Herberg and chef Anthony Meyers bought it, reopening it as Von's Café. It was crowded at noon and dinner with business people who knew it would be good. It became a great place for the theater crowd or anyone en route home from a festive evening.

(1) fresh chicken, 3-4 lb.
juice of 1 lemon
¼ C. olive oil
8 cloves fresh garlic
2 tsp whole basil
2 tsp whole thyme
1 tsp Kosher salt
1 tsp brown sugar
⅛ tsp fresh ground pepper
rind of 1 lemon
1 produce bag from the grocery store, or a plastic resealable bag

Smoking Ingredients:
½ C. fruitwood chips
1 tsp each garlic and onion powder
1 C. water

Day One:
1. Mix all smoking ingredients together, cover and set aside.

2. In a blender, combine lemon juice, olive oil, garlic, basil, thyme, brown sugar, salt, and pepper and blend until smooth.

3. Brush the chicken liberally with this mix, including the cavity. Put the lemon rind in the cavity, and refrigerate in the produce bag or plastic bag.

Day Two:
1. Heat a charcoal grill until coals are well lit.

2. Drain fruitwood chips and add to the coals.

3. Rebrush the chicken with any remaining marinade.

4. Roast the chicken at 350°F to 400°F on a closed-lid grill for 1 to 1½ hours, or until the hip joint reaches 165°F.

5. Remove chicken from the grill, and allow to rest, 10 minutes.

6. Carve and enjoy with a delicious brew!

Von's Roasthouse
619 Pine Street

"I've run more risk eating my way across the country than in all my driving."
Duncan Hines

WILD
GINGER
& satay bar

Seven Flavor Beef

Over 20 years ago Rick and Ann Yoder embarked on a trip throughout Southeast Asia, they returned to Seattle inspired to create a restaurant modeled after their experiences with the incredible food and culture of the Eastern world. In 1989 they created the Wild Ginger and the result was a tremendous success. This pillar of Asian dining quickly became one of the most popular restaurants in the Northwest and a true Seattle original.

Marinade:
8 oz. sliced flank steak
1 tbsp minced lemongrass
½ tsp peeled and minced fresh ginger
½ tsp minced garlic
½ tsp fish sauce
½ tsp sesame oil
½ tsp honey
1 tsp dried red chili flakes
1 tsp Chinese five-spice powder
1 tsp Kosher salt

2 tbsp vegetable oil
¼ C. thinly sliced red onion
½ bunch thinly sliced green onion
1 C. bean sprouts
2 tbsp hoisin sauce
1 tbsp ground peanuts
20 Thai basil leaves

1. Combine all marinade ingredients in a non-reactive baking dish and marinate flank steak for 1 hour.

2. Heat oil in a wok over high heat. When oil is hot, add red onion, green onion, and bean sprouts and sear for 1 minute, stirring. Set aside on serving platter.

3. Add beef to very hot wok and sear until rare.

4. Add hoisin sauce and toss until coated. Add ground peanuts and basil and cook until meat is medium rare.

5. Serve meat over onions and bean sprouts.

Wild Ginger
1401 3rd Avenue

"The quality of food is in inverse proportion to the altitude of the dining room, with airplanes the extreme example."
Bryan Miller

the
WALRUS
and the
CARPENTER

Potato-Celery Salad with Smoked Trout

The Walrus and the Carpenter blends the elegance of France with the casual comfort of a local fishing pub. The idea is to serve the highest quality food and drink in a space that is stripped of pretense and feels like home.

6 fingerling potatoes, halved lengthwise
⅓ C. water
⅓ C. white wine vinegar
⅓ C. golden raisins
⅛ tsp red pepper flakes
6 celery ribs, thinly sliced on the bias, leaves reserved
1 C. loosely packed flat-leaf parsley
3 tbsp extra virgin olive oil
1 tbsp + 1½ tsp fresh lemon juice
salt and freshly ground black pepper
½ lb. skinless smoked trout, broken into small pieces

1. Place the potatoes in a sauce pan, cover with water and bring to a boil. Simmer over medium-high heat until the potatoes are tender when pierced with a knife, about 12 minutes. Drain and refrigerate the potatoes until you're ready to assemble the salad.

2. In a small sauce pan, bring the water and vinegar to a boil. Remove from the heat and add the raisins and red pepper flakes. Cover and let the raisins plump for 10 minutes. Drain the raisins.

3. In a large bowl, toss the celery with the celery leaves, potatoes, raisins, and parsley. Add the olive oil and lemon juice, season with salt and pepper and toss well.

4. Divide the salad among 4 plates or serve family-style on a large platter. Scatter the pieces of trout over the salad and serve immediately.

The Walrus and the Carpenter
4743 Ballard Avenue Northwest

"He who receives his friends and gives no personal attention to the meal which is being prepared for them, is not worthy of having friends."
Jean-Anthelme Brillat-Savarin

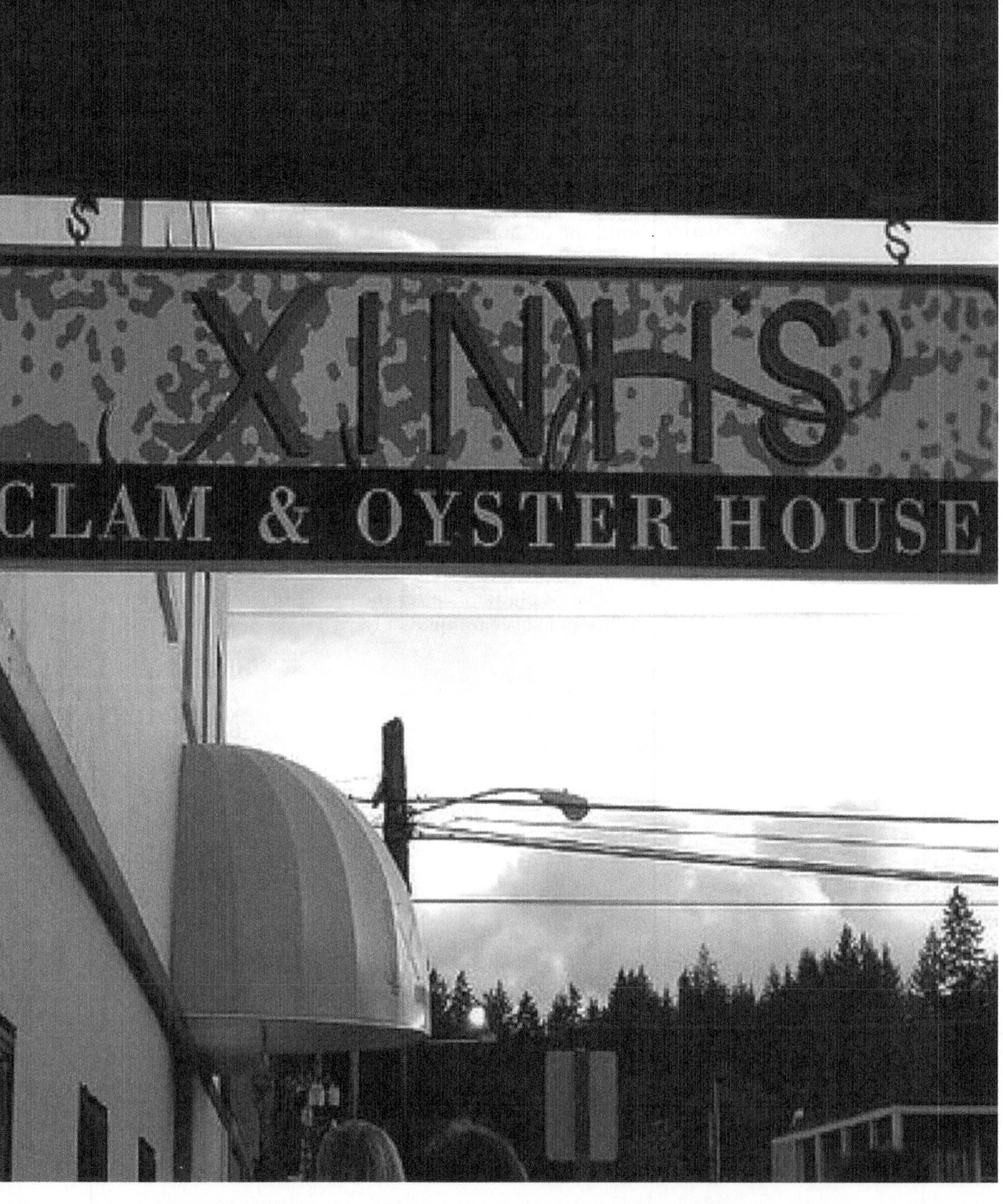
XINH'S
CLAM & OYSTER HOUSE

Asian Seafood Bisque

Chef Xinh Dwelley came to this country in 1970 from Vietnam and settled in the Shelton area. She first began selling her egg rolls at the Olympia Farmers' Market, and then became an oyster shucker for the Taylor Shellfish Farms. She persevered through a great deal of pain to become a very fast oyster shucker indeed; winning the West Coast Oyster Shucking Championship 5 times and retiring unbeaten in 1992. In 1996, she opened Xinh's Clam & Oyster House with a menu that brought together the fresh shellfish of Puget Sound imbued with the flavors of her homeland. The sauces are complex, the spicing well balanced. Her Oyster Stew has no comparison, those famous Curried Mussels won the Seattle Times "Best Bite of 2005," and her prowess with geoduck dishes have been shown recently on the Food Network Channel's "Will Work for Food."

2 tbsp canola oil
1 tbsp minced garlic
1 tbsp finely chopped lemongrass
1 C. water
1 C. pineapple juice
1 C. crushed pineapple
1 tbsp cayenne pepper flakes
1 (14-oz.) can coconut milk
1 package Knorr tamarind soup base (available at Uwajimaya's and other Asian markets)
1 lb. clams
1 lb. mussels
8 oz. raw chicken breast cut into strips
8 oz. large raw shelled and deveined prawns
1 C. chopped green cabbage
1 C. chopped Napa cabbage
1 C. thinly sliced celery
½ C. chopped onion
1 tbsp fish sauce
1 tbsp chili powder
Roux: 3 tbsp water and 2 tbsp flour mixed together in a small bowl
1 tbsp finely chopped fresh basil
1 tbsp finely chopped cilantro
1 tbsp chopped green onion

1. In a large frying pan over medium heat, sauté the lemongrass and garlic in the canola oil.

2. Add water, pineapple juice, crushed pineapple, cayenne pepper, coconut milk, and the tamarind soup base. Bring to a boil.

3. Add clams, mussels, and chicken. Cover and cook until shellfish open. Add vegetables, shrimp, fish sauce and chili powder, stirring to mix. Cover and cook until shrimp are just done and crisp to the bite.

4. Mix in the roux to thicken the bisque.

5. Add cilantro, green onion and basil, stirring to combine thoroughly. Serve immediately in soup bowls.

Xinh's Clam & Oyster House

221 W Railroad Avenue

"Food for thought is no substitute for the real thing."
Walt Kelly

ZIGZAG

Sayonara...a Cocktail

The Zig Zag Café is a classic cocktail bar and restaurant located on the Pike Street Hill Climb behind Seattle's venerable Pike Place Market and on the way to the Seattle Aquarium. We offer three rotating taps featuring Maritime lagers and ales and a small selection of premium bottled beers. Our wine list includes both Old and New World reds and whites and some excellent champagnes. And don't miss our fortified wines. The Zig Zag Café is an unpretentious place with an eclectic crowd of old and young whose common desire is good food, good drink, and good company shared.

¾ oz. habanero-infused vodka
¾ oz. apricot brandy
¾ oz. Calvados
¾ oz. lime juice
⅛ oz. agave nectar

1. Fill two martini glasses with ice and water to chill.

2. In a cocktail shaker filled with ice, combine the infused vodka, apricot brandy, Calvados, lime juice, and agave nectar. Shake vigorously.

3. Empty the icy water from the martini glasses and strain the Sayonara into the two chilled glasses.

Zig Zag Café
1501 Western Avenue

"It is a true saying that a man must eat a peck of salt with his friend before he knows him."
Miguel de Cervantes

Milky Way
I·LAN 6753 KM
RAPUNZEL 1.5 BLKS
LENIN 2 BLKS
BERMUDA TRIANGLE 37,55.3 MI.
UVRE 9757 KM
MACHU PICCHU
FOUNDRY 2.5 BLKS
TU 10,021K M
ATLANTIS 663FATHOMS
CENT

Index O' Recipes

"I should have no objection to go over the same life from its beginning to the end: requesting only the advantage authors have, of correcting in a second edition the faults of the first."

Benjamin Franklin

Steven W. Siler is a firefighter-cum-chef serving in Bellingham, Washington. Long marinated in the epicurean heritage of the Deep South, Steven has spent over 20 years (dear God has it been that long?!) in the much-vaulted restaurant industry from BOH to FOH to chef. In addition, he has served as an editor and contributing writer for several food publications. When not trying to shove food down his fellow firefighters' gullets, he enjoys sailing and sampling the finest of scotches and wines, and has an irrational love affair with opera. He swears one day he will relive the above picture on the Gulf Coast with a good Will.

The Signature Tastes series of cookbooks is the one of the first of a series of culinary celebrations from Smoke Alarm Media, based in the Pacific Northwest. Smoke Alarm Media is named for another series of unfortunate culinary accidents at an unnamed fire department, also in the Pacific Northwest. One of the founders was an active firefighter. Having been trained as a chef, he found himself in the position of cooking frequently at the fire station. Alas, his culinary skills were somewhat lacking in using the broiler and smoke would soon fill the kitchen and station. The incidents became so frequent that the 911 dispatch would call the station and ask if "Chef Smoke Alarm" would kindly refrain from cooking on his shift. Thus Smoke Alarm Media was born.

Smoke Alarm Media series

Signature Tastes

Hidden Eats

Table Facts

Bygone Eras

Art of Culinary Diplomacy

VARSITY

Sublime Nectar

www.SignatureTastes.com